DEMCO

THE MESSAGE IN THE BOTTLE

ALSO BY WALKER PERCY

NOVELS

THE MOVIEGOER (1961)

THE LAST GENTLEMAN (1966)

LOVE IN THE RUINS (1971)

LANCELOT (1977)

THE SECOND COMING (1980)

THE THANATOS SYNDROME (1987)

NONFICTION

LOST IN THE COSMOS (1983)

SIGNPOSTS IN A STRANGE LAND (1991)

THE MESSAGE IN THE BOTTLE

HOW QUEER MAN IS, HOW QUEER LANGUAGE IS,

AND WHAT ONE HAS TO DO WITH THE OTHER

WALKER
PERCY

PICADOR USA

FARRAR, STRAUS AND GIROUX
NEW YORK

PICADOR® IS A U.S. REGISTERED TRADEMARK AND IS USED BY FARRAR, STRAUS AND GIROUX UNDER LICENSE FROM PAN BOOKS LIMITED.

FOR INFORMATION ON PICADOR USA READING GROUP GUIDES, AS WELL AS ORDERING, PLEASE CONTACT THE TRADE MARKETING DEPARTMENT AT ST. MARTIN'S PRESS.
PHONE: 1-800-221-7945 EXTENSION 763
FAX: 212-677-7456
E-MAIL: TRADEMARKETING@STMARTINS.COM

LIBRARY OF CONGRESS CATALOGING-IN-PUBLICATION DATA

PERCY, WALKER.
    THE MESSAGE IN THE BOTTLE: HOW QUEER MAN IS, HOW QUEER LANGUAGE IS, AND WHAT ONE HAS TO DO WITH THE OTHER / WALKER PERCY.
        P.   CM.
    ISBN 0-312-25401-6
    1. LANGUAGE AND CULTURE.   I. TITLE.

PS3566.E6912M4   2000
401—DC21   99-089027
                                                                CIP

FIRST PUBLISHED IN THE UNITED STATES BY FARRAR, STRAUS AND GIROUX

FIRST PICADOR USA EDITION: APRIL 2000

10   9   8   7   6   5   4   3   2   1

For MARY PRATT *and* ANN

AUTHOR'S NOTE

This book was twenty years in the writing. All chapters except the last appeared as articles in journals. One chapter was published in 1954, another in 1975. Since my recurring interest over the years has been the nature of human communication and, in particular, the consequences of man's unique discovery of the symbol, a certain repetitiveness in the articles is inevitable. Some of the repetition has been preserved here, for example, the "Helen Keller phenomenon," if for no other reason as evidence at least of the longevity of my curiosity and my inability to get rid of it. This particular bone, I thought, needed worrying.

Grateful acknowledgment is made to the editors of the following journals for their permission to reprint the articles: *The Southern Review,* University of Houston *Forum, Sewanee Review, Partisan Review, Katallagete, Thought, Psychiatry, The New Scholasticism, The Modern Schoolman, The Journal of Philosophy, Philosophy and Phenomenological Research.*

CONTENTS

THE MESSAGE IN THE BOTTLE

1

THE DELTA FACTOR

*How I Discovered the Delta Factor Sitting
at My Desk One Summer Day in Louisiana in the
1950's Thinking about an Event in the
Life of Helen Keller on Another Summer Day
in Alabama in 1887*

In the beginning was Alpha and the end is Omega, but somewhere between occurred Delta, which was nothing less than the arrival of man
himself and his breakthrough into the daylight of language and consciousness and knowing, of happiness and sadness, of being with and
being alone, of being right and being wrong, of being himself and being
not himself, and of being at home and being a stranger.

WHY DOES MAN feel so sad in the twentieth century?

Why does man feel so bad in the very age when, more than in
any other age, he has succeeded in satisfying his needs and making
over the world for his own use?

Why has man entered on an orgy of war, murder, torture, and
self-destruction unparalleled in history and in the very century
when he had hoped to see the dawn of universal peace and
brotherhood?

Why do people often feel bad in good environments and good in
bad environments?

Why do people often feel so bad in good environments that they
prefer bad environments?

Why does a man often feel better in a bad environment?

Why is a man apt to feel bad in a good environment, say suburban Short Hills, New Jersey, on an ordinary Wednesday afternoon? Why is the same man apt to feel good in a very bad environment, say an old hotel on Key Largo during a hurricane?

Why have more people been killed in the twentieth century than in all other centuries put together?

Why is war man's greatest pleasure?

Why is man the only creature that wages war against its own species?

What would man do if war were outlawed?

Why is it that the only time I ever saw my uncle happy during his entire life was the afternoon of December 7, 1941, when the Japanese bombed Pearl Harbor?

Why did he shortly thereafter become miserable when he learned that he was too old to go to Europe to shoot at Germans and stand a good chance of being shot by Germans?

Why is it that the only time he was happy before was in the Argonne Forest in 1918 when he was shooting at Germans and stood a good chance of being shot by Germans?

Why was he sad from 1918 to 1941 even though he lived in as good an environment as man can devise, indeed had the best of all possible worlds in literature, music, and art?

Why is it that a man riding a good commuter train from Larchmont to New York, whose needs and drives are satisfied, who has a good home, loving wife and family, good job, who enjoys unprecedented "cultural and recreational facilities," often feels bad without knowing why?

Why is it that if such a man suffers a heart attack and, taken off the train at New Rochelle, regains consciousness and finds himself in a strange place, he then comes to himself for the first time in years, perhaps in his life, and begins to gaze at his own hand with a sense of wonder and delight?

What is the difference between such a man, a commuter who feels bad without knowing why, and another commuter who feels bad without knowing why but who begins to read a book about a man who feels bad without knowing why?

Why does it make a man feel better to read a book about a man like himself feeling bad?

Why was it that Jean-Paul Sartre, sitting in a French café and writing *Nausea*, which is about the absurdity of human existence and the nausea of life in the twentieth century—why was he the happiest man in France at the time?

Why was it that when Franz Kafka would read aloud to his friends stories about the sadness and alienation of life in the twentieth century everyone would laugh until tears came?

Why is it harder to study a dogfish on a dissecting board in a zoological laboratory in college where one has proper instruments and a proper light than it would be if one were marooned on an island and, having come upon a dogfish on the beach and having no better instrument than a pocketknife or bobby pin, one began to explore the dogfish?

Why is it all but impossible to read Shakespeare in school now but will not be fifty years from now when the Western world has fallen into ruins and a survivor sitting among the vines of the Forty-second Street library spies a moldering book and opens it to *The Tempest?*

Why is it difficult to see a painting in a museum but not if someone should take you by the hand and say, "I have something to show you in my house," and lead you through a passageway and upstairs into the attic and there show the painting to you?

Why are Americans intrigued by the idea of floating down the Mississippi River on a raft but not down the Hudson?

Why do more people commit suicide in San Francisco, the most beautiful city in America, than in any other city?

Why is the metaphor *Flesh is grass*, which is not only wrong (flesh is not grass) but inappropriate (flesh is not even like grass), better and truer than the sentence *Flesh is mortal*, which is quite accurate and logical?

What would you do if a stranger came up to you on a New York street and, before disappearing into the crowd, gave you a note which read: "I know your predicament; it is such and such. Be at the southeast corner of Lindell Boulevard and Kingshighway in St. Louis at 9 a.m., April 16—I have news of the greatest importance"?

Where are the Hittites?

Why does no one find it remarkable that in most world cities today there are Jews but not one single Hittite, even though the Hittites had a great flourishing civilization while the Jews nearby were a weak and obscure people?

When one meets a Jew in New York or New Orleans or Paris or Melbourne, it is remarkable that no one considers the event remarkable. What are they doing here? But it is even more remarkable to wonder, if there are Jews here, why are there not Hittites here?

Where are the Hittites? Show me one Hittite in New York City.

Given two men living in Short Hills, New Jersey, each having satisfied his needs, working at rewarding jobs, participating in meaningful relationships with other people, etc., etc.: one feels good, the other feels bad; one feels at home, the other feels homeless. Which one is sick? Which is better off?

Why do people driving around on beautiful Sunday afternoons like to see bloody automobile wrecks?

Why did the young French couple driving through the countryside with their baby, having heard the news of a crash nearby of an airliner killing three hundred people and littering the forest with bits of flesh, speed frantically toward the scene, stop the car, and, carrying the baby, rush toward the dead, running through thickets to avoid police barricades? Did they have relatives on the plane?

Why did French and German veterans of Verdun, a catastrophic battle in which one million men were killed, keep returning to Verdun for years after the war, sit quietly in a café at Lemmes on the Sacred Way, speaking softly of those terrible times, and even camp out for a week in the shell hole or trench where they spent the worst days of their lives?

Why is the good life which men have achieved in the twentieth century so bad that only news of world catastrophes, assassinations, plane crashes, mass murders, can divert one from the sadness of ordinary mornings?

Why do young people look so sad, the very young who, seeing how sad their elders are, have sought a new life of joy and freedom with each other and in the green fields and forests, but who instead of finding joy look even sadder than their elders?

2

What does a man do when he finds himself living after an age has ended and he can no longer understand himself because the theories of man of the former age no longer work and the theories of the new age are not yet known, for not even the name of the new age is known, and so everything is upside down, people feeling bad when they should feel good, good when they should feel bad?

What a man does is start afresh as if he were newly come into a new world, which in fact it is; start with what he knows for sure, look at the birds and beasts, and like a visitor from Mars newly landed on earth notice what is different about man.

If beasts can be understood as organisms living in environments which are good or bad and to which the beast responds accordingly as it has evolved to respond, how is man to be understood if he feels bad in the best environment?

Where does one start with a theory of man if the theory of man as an organism in an environment doesn't work and all the attributes of man which were accepted in the old modern age are now called into question: his soul, mind, freedom, will, Godlikeness?

There is only one place to start: the place where man's singularity is there for all to see and cannot be called into question, even in a new age in which everything else is in dispute.

That singularity is language.

Why is it that men speak and animals don't?

What does it entail to be a speaking creature, that is, a creature who names things and utters sentences about things which other similar creatures understand and misunderstand?

Why is it that every normal man on earth speaks, that is, can utter an unlimited number of sentences in a complex language, and that not one single beast has ever uttered a word?

Why are there not some "higher" animals which have acquired a primitive language?

Why are there not some "lower" men who speak a crude, primitive language?

Why is there no such thing as a primitive language?

Why is there such a gap between nonspeaking animals and speaking man, when there is no other such gap in nature?

How can a child learn to speak a language in three years without anyone taking trouble about it, that is, utter and understand an unlimited number of sentences, while a great deal of time and trouble is required to teach a chimpanzee a few hand signals?

Why is it that scientists, who know a great deal about the world, know less about language than about the back side of the moon, even though language is the one observable behavior which most clearly sets man apart from the beasts and the one activity in which all men, scientists included, engage more than in any other?

Why is it that scientists know a good deal about what it is to be an organism in an environment but very little about what it is to be a creature who names things and utters and understands sentences about things?

Why is it that scientists have a theory about everything under the sun but do not have a theory of man?

Is it possible that a theory of man is nothing more nor less than a theory of the speaking creature?

Is it possible that the questions about man's peculiar upside-down and perverse behavior, which he doesn't understand, have something to do with his strange gift of speech, which he also doesn't understand?

Is it possible that man's peculiar predicament, his unhappiness in the twentieth century, his upside-down behavior, disliking things which according to his theory he ought to like, liking things which according to his theory he ought not to like, has come to pass because the old modern age has ended and man has not the beginning of an understanding of himself in the new age because the old theories don't work any more, because they showed man as monster, as centaur organism-plus-soul, as one not different from beasts yet somehow nevertheless possessing "freedom" and "dignity" and "individuality" and "mind" and such—and that such theories, monstrous as they are, worked for a while in the old modern age because there was still enough left of belief in Judeo-Christianity to make such talk of "sacredness of the individual" sound good even while such individuals were being slaughtered by the millions, and because science was still young and exuberant and no one noticed or cared about the contradiction in scientists' understanding other men as organisms-beasts and putting them into the world of things to understand and so putting themselves above the world and other men?

But time ran out and the old modern world ended and the old monster theory no longer works. Man knows he is something more than an organism in an environment, because for one thing he acts like anything but an organism in an environment. Yet he no longer has the means of understanding the traditional Judeo-Christian teaching that the "something more" is a soul somehow locked in the organism like a ghost in a machine. What is he then? He has not the faintest idea. Entered as he is into a new age, he is like a child who sees everything in his new world, names everything, knows everything except himself.

When man doesn't know whether he is an organism or a soul or both, and if both how he can be both, it is good to start with what he does know.

This book is about two things, man's strange behavior and man's strange gift of language, and about how understanding the latter might help in understanding the former.

I have made the assumption that the proper study of man is man and that there does not presently exist a theory of man. Accordingly, the book is an attempt to sketch the beginnings of a theory of man for a new age, the sort of crude guess a visitor from Mars might make if he landed on earth and spent a year observing man and the beasts.

It is the meager fruit of twenty years' off-and-on thinking about the subject, of coming at it from one direction, followed by failure and depression and giving up, followed by making up novels to raise my spirits, followed by a new try from a different direction or from an old direction but at a different level, followed by failure, followed by making up another novel, and so on.

As it stands, it is nothing more than a few trails blazed through a dark wood, most dead-ended. I should consider it worthwhile even if it established no more than that there is such a wood—for not even that much is known now—and that it is very dark indeed.

Most readers will not want to read all chapters. It is hard, for example, to imagine anyone at all at the present time who would want to read the last. Only after writing it did it occur to me that it had, for the moment at least, no readership whatever. Nobody will be interested in it except psycholinguists and transformational grammarians, and the latter won't like it. The only comfort I can take is that this particular excursion into what many readers will take to be the esoteries of language is no ordinary blind alley. Unless I am very much mistaken, it lies across the impasse which must be broken through before the new man in the new age can begin to understand himself.

I make no apologies for being an amateur in such matters, since the one thing that has been clear to me from the beginning is that language is too important to be left to linguisticians. Indeed everything is too important to be left to the specialist of that thing, and the layman is already too deprived by the surrendering of such sovereignty.

If justification is needed, I plead the justification of the visitor from Mars: it is necessary in this case to be to a degree an outsider in order to see these particular woods for the trees.

One must be a Martian or a survivor poking among the ruins to see how extremely odd the people were who lived there.

3

I don't even know what to call it, the object of this mild twenty-year obsession. If I say "language," that would be both accurate and misleading—misleading because it makes you think of words and different human languages rather than the people who utter them and the actual event in which language is uttered. So the book is not about language but about the creatures who use it and what happens when they do. Since no other creature but man uses language, it is really an anthropology, a study of man doing the uniquely human thing.

The proper study of man is man, said Pope. But that's a large order, especially nowadays, when there is no such thing as a study of man but two hundred specialties which study this or that aspect of man. Ethnologists and anthropologists study man's culture and evolution. Linguists study languages. Psychologists study stimuli and responses. Ethologists study those drives and instincts man shares with other creatures. Theologians study God and man's relation to God. But only a Martian can see man as he is, because man is too close to himself and his vision too fragmented. As a nonpsychologist, a nonanthropologist, a nontheologian, a nonethologist—as in fact nothing more than a novelist—I qualify through my ignorance as a terrestial Martian. Since I am only a novelist, a somewhat estranged and detached person whose business it is to see things and people as if he had never seen them before, it is possible for me not only to observe people as data but to observe scientists observing people as data—in short to take a Martian view.

Imagine how it must appear to the Martian making his first visit to earth. Let us suppose that he too is an intelligent being, whose intelligence has, however, evolved without the mediation of language but rather, say, through the development of ESP. So he is something like the angels who, according to Saint Thomas, can see things directly in their essences and communicate thought without language. What is the first thing he notices about earthlings? That they are forever making mouthy little sounds, clicks, hisses, howls, hoots, explosions, squeaks, some of which *name* things in the world and are uttered in short sequences that *say* something about these things and events in the world.

This behavior seems a good deal stranger to the Martian than it does to us. This is the case because language is the very mirror by which we see and know the world and it is very difficult to see the mirror itself, to see how curiously wrought it is.

In order to see the mirror of language, it is necessary to turn it around so that it no longer reflects, distorts, transforms. Say the word *glass*. It is almost impossible to hear the sounds for themselves because they have already been transformed: they sound like glass. The word *glass* sounds brittle, shiny, transparent.

Now try this. Repeat the word aloud fifty times. What happens? Somewhere along the way the word loses its magic transformation and, like Cinderella's other slipper at midnight, becomes the ugly little vocable it really is: a small explosion of the back of the tongue against the palate, the rush of air around the sides of the tongue, a bleat ending in the hissing of breath between the teeth and tip of tongue.

A very odd business.

The Martian is surprised by what he sees and hears. In order to prepare himself for the journey to earth, he has read many scientific books and journals brought to Mars by astronauts. These works, in biology, psychology, physiology, have led him to believe that man is not much different from other earth creatures, certainly not qualitatively different. He has the same kind of anatomical equipment—nerve, bone, and blood—exhibits the same chemical reactions, the same transactions across his bodily membranes, the same capacity to respond to stimuli, adapt to environments, and so on. Imagine the Martian's astonishment after landing when he observes that earthlings *talk all the time* or otherwise traffic in symbols: gossip, tell jokes, argue, make reports, deliver lectures, listen to lectures, take notes, write books, read books, paint pictures, look at pictures, stage plays, attend plays, tell stories, listen to stories, cover blackboards with math symbols—and even at night dream dreams that are a very tissue of symbols.

Earthlings in short seem to spend most of their time trafficking in one kind of symbol or another, while the other creatures of earth— more than two million species—*say not a word.*

When he asks his hosts (in ESP) about this strange behavior, he gets a curious answer from earth scientists. Mostly they seem anxious to convince him how much they are like other creatures rather than different. "Ever since Darwin," say the scientists, "we have known that man is not qualitatively different from other animals. In fact the whole burden of earth science is to discover similarities, not differences, to establish continuities, not gaps."

"Yes," replies the Martian, "but you *talk* all the time; you're talking now."

The earth scientists insist that man is an animal like other animals, that in fact the government is spending millions of dollars investigating the behavior of monkeys and apes in order to learn more about man, that ethologists, trying to account for man's madness, spend much of their time investigating aggressive and territory-protecting behavior among other animals, even a small fish such as the stickleback.

"Yes, but you're still talking," says the Martian. "Why don't you investigate that?"

They refer him to linguists and psychologists, who tell him a great deal about the structure of languages, grammar, phonemes, and morphemes; about the relation of one language to another, the historical changes in a language, the acoustics of language, the physics and physiology of speech; about the rules by which one sentence can be transformed into another; about information theory; about stimulus-response theory; about learning theory, according to which a person learns a language in a way not really different from the way a rat learns to thread a maze or a pigeon learns to do a figure eight.

"But wait," says the Martian. "What about the actual event of language? The central phenomenon? What happens when people talk, when one person names something or says a sentence about something and another person understands him?"

At this point he is apt to encounter a certain evasiveness, even an irritability. From the theoretical linguist he may get (as, in fact, I did) this sort of answer: "Well, I'm not interested in that. What interests me is the formal structure of language—for example, the rules by which new sentences are generated."

The psychologist might reply, "Well, our knowledge of the brain is not sufficient to outline the exact neural pathways, but of course we believe that language behavior is not qualitatively different from the learned responses of other animals. Read Skinner's *Verbal Behavior*."

"Excuse me," says the Martian, "but I am not asking you to identify all the neural pathways and brain structures involved. I want to know only what sort of thing happens. Could you draw me a picture or describe a crude explanatory model—something like what your famous Dr. Harvey did when he speculated that perhaps the heart is like a unidirectional pump that sends the blood around in a circle?"

I used to have a professor in medical school who, when a student gave a particularly murky answer, would hand him a piece of chalk, escort him to the blackboard, and say, "Draw me a picture of it."

The point is that the picture the psychologist draws, showing stimuli and responses, big S's and R's outside the brain, little s's and r's inside the brain, with arrows showing the course of nerve impulses along nerves and across synapses, no matter how complicated it is, will not show what happens when a child understands that the sound *ball* is the name of a class of round objects, or when I say *The center is not holding* and you understand me.

When the Martian says as much to the psychologist, the latter shrugs. "Well, if you're interested in such matters, go see a linguist or a semanticist or a transformationalist."

The Martian is astounded by the runaround. On the one hand he is referred to entire libraries of books about learning theory and stimulus-response theory, factual behavioral science which treats the behavior of both men and beasts. This is what he is looking for—behavior, why men act as they do—but he discovers that these books leave out those very features of language that set it apart from other behavior: for example, that unlike other animals, which learn a very limited repertoire of responses, a four-year-old child can utter and understand an unlimited number of new sentences in his language.

When he mentions this remarkable accomplishment of children, the Martian is referred to linguists who treat the formal and structural features of a body of language.

As for the central phenomenon itself, earthlings seem to know less and, what is more, care less than they do about the back side of the moon.

Could the Martian be mistaken or is it not a fact that earthlings for all their encyclopedic knowledge about the formal and factual aspects of language have managed to straddle the phenomenon itself and *miss* it?

It is as if neither Dr. Harvey nor anyone else had ever discovered that the heart is a pump and that the blood circulates but in the past three hundred years scientists had amassed huge quantities of data about the chemical reaction of heart muscle, and the composition of blood, had described the distribution of the elements of blood, had made comparisons of the blood systems of thousands of mammals, and, finally, had developed a sophisticated computerized method for calculating the velocity and pressure of the blood in any given artery.

Some scientists, I hasten to add, are more honest. The famous theoretician Noam Chomsky is frank to admit our nearly total ignorance on the subject. He does draw a picture. He indicates the central phenomenon of language by a black box, contents unknown, labeled LAD, the "language acquisition device," which receives the random input of language a child hears and somehow converts it into the child's capacity to utter any number of sentences in the language. So certain indeed is Chomsky that what happens inside that box cannot be explained by the S's and R's of psychologists that at one time he saw fit to resurrect the old idea of Descartes that only a mind, a mental substance, can account for the extraordinary phenomenon of language. The black box was full of mind stuff, according to Chomsky. Later he said it probably contained computerlike elements.

What is in the black box then, a ghost or a piece of machinery?

How extraordinary, thinks the Martian, that these earthlings who know so much about the back side of the moon know so little about the one observable thing which even Darwin agreed sets them apart from the beasts!

4

If such a gap in our knowledge of language exists, it should undoubtedly be a matter of concern to those interested in that sort of matter—linguists, psychologists, anthropologists, and the like. But if that were all there were to it, the following essays would not have been written, because I have neither the desire nor the competence to venture into theoretical linguistics. It is true that in the end I propose a crude working model, something like Harvey's notion that perhaps the heart is like a pump, or Malpighi's hunch that the kidney may be a sort of filter, but only on the grounds that such is the prerogative of the amateur in an area shunned by professionals. Something is better than nothing.

No, what has rather concerned me and fueled my mild obsession over the years has been first the inkling, then the growing conviction, that more is at stake than a theory of language.

It turned out that the quest for a theory of language—that human, uniquely human, all too human behavior—ran head on into the larger question of man himself. If Chomsky, the foremost linguistic theorist of our time, talks one minute about explaining the linguistic capacity as a structure of computerlike components and the next about the mind stuff of Descartes, we can't escape the conclusion that the newest and most celebrated theory, the transformational linguistics of Chomsky, has landed us in the midst of the oldest and most vexed question of all, the nature of man.

It was no coincidence then when the Martian discovered that earthlings, who have a theory about everything else, do not have a theory about language and do not have a theory about man.

What interested me was the Martian method of taking man as he found him and looking at him as if he were the strangest of fauna, which he is. That is to say, instead of coming at man from the traditional approaches, this or that theological assumption or scientific assumption about the nature of man—and, believe me, when it comes to settling man's status before the fact, so to speak, scientific theory in the twentieth century can be quite as dogmatic as theological theory in the thirteenth, and perhaps with less sanction—why not come at man like the Martian? Instead of marking him down at the outset as besouled creature or responding organism, why not look at him as he appears, not even as *Homo sapiens*, because attributing sapience already begs the question, but as *Homo loquens*, man the talker, or *Homo symbolificus*, man the symbol-monger? Instead of starting out with such large vexed subjects as soul, mind, ideas, consciousness, why not begin with language, which no one denies, and see how far it takes us toward the rest? Instead of having behaviorists trying to explain language by stimulus-response theory, why not try to account for behaviorists by a larger theory of language (for after all the behavior of behaviorists is notable in that it is not encompassed by behavioral theory: behaviorists not only study responses; they write articles and deliver lectures setting forth what they take to be the truth about responses, and would be offended if anyone suggested that their writings and lectures were nothing more than responses and therefore no more true or false than a dog's salivation)?

Accordingly, the assumption will be made that current theory of language is incoherent, that the formal-descriptive disciplines of linguistics deal with the products, the corpora, of the language phenomenon, that the factual science of psychology deals with the stimuli and responses of organisms, and that between them lies the terra incognita of the phenomenon itself.

A second assumption is that current theories of man, or rather, I should say, notions, are equally incoherent and that one incoherence has something to do with the other, so much so indeed that one suspects that the latter can only be gotten at through the former. If you know why this creature talks, thinks the Martian, you might also know why he behaves so oddly.

Start with God and man's immortal soul and you've lost every reader except those who believe in God and man's immortal soul.

Start with B. F. Skinner and man decreed as organism who learns everything he does by operant conditioning and you've lost every reader who knows there is more to it than that and that Skinner has explained nothing. Skinner explains everything about man except what makes him human, for example, language and his refusal to behave like an organism in an environment.

I take it as going without saying that current theories of man are incoherent. There does not presently exist, that is to say, a consensus view of man such as existed, for instance, in thirteenth-century Europe or seventeenth-century New England, or even in some rural communities in Georgia today. Prescinding from whether such a view is true or false, we are able to say that it was a viable belief in the sense that it animated the culture and gave life its meaning. It was something men lived by, even when they fell short of it and saw themselves as sinners. It was the belief that man was created in the image of God with an immortal soul, that he occupied a place in nature somewhere between the beasts and the angels, that he suffered an aboriginal catastrophe, the Fall, in consequence of which he lost his way and, unlike the beasts, became capable of sin and thereafter became a pilgrim or seeker of his own salvation, and that the clue and sign of his salvation was to be found not in science or philosophy but in news of an actual historical event involving a people, a person, and an institution.

I am not suggesting that there are not believing Christians today for whom this view of man or some variant of it is still viable. What I do suggest is that if one attempts to state a kind of consensus view of man in the present age, the conventional wisdom of the great majority of the denizens of a democratic technological society in the late twentieth century, this Judeo-Christian credo is no longer a significant component.

What has survived and is significant in the culture are certain less precise legacies of this credo: the "sacredness of the individual," "God is love," the "Prince of Peace," "the truth shall make you free," etc. Almost everyone is in favor of love, truth, peace, freedom, and the sacredness of the individual, since, for one thing, these prescriptions are open to almost any reading.

What does exist is a kind of mishmash view of man, a slap-up model put together of disparate bits and pieces. The other major component of the conventional wisdom, along with the ethical legacy of Christianity, is what the layman takes to be the consensus of science—whose credentials after all are far more impressive than those of Judeo-Christianity—that, myths aside and however admirable ethics may be, man is an organism among other organisms.

One sign that the world has ended, the world we knew, the world by which we understood ourselves, an age which began some three hundred years ago with the scientific revolution, is the dawn of the discovery that its world view no longer works and we find ourselves without the means of understanding ourselves.

There is a lag between the end of an age and the discovery of the end. The denizens of such a time are like the cartoon cat that runs off a cliff and for a while is suspended, still running, in mid-air but sooner or later looks down and sees there is nothing under him.

My growing conviction over the years has been that man's theory about himself doesn't work any more, not because one or another component is not true, but because its parts are incoherent and go off in different directions like Dr. Doolittle's pushmi-pullyu.

Those who don't take this matter seriously forfeit the means of understanding themselves. Many people in fact are quite content to live out their lives as the organisms and consumer units their scientists understand them to be; to satisfy their needs, even "higher" needs, according to the prescription of those who profess to understand such things.

Those who do take it seriously find themselves involved in certain characteristic dilemmas and predicaments all too familiar to the denizens of the late twentieth century. One tires of the good life and the best of all possible worlds one has designed for oneself.

One feels anxious without knowing why. One is at home yet feels homeless. One loves bad news and secretly longs for still another of the catastrophes for which the century has become notorious.

It is an inevitable consequence of an incoherent theory that its adherents in one sense profess it—what else can they profess?—yet in another sense feel themselves curiously suspended, footing lost and having no purchase for taking action. Attempts to move issue in paradoxical countermovements. As time goes on, one's professed view has less and less to do with what one feels, how one acts and understands oneself.

If asked to define the conventional wisdom of the twentieth century, that is to say, a kind of low common denominator of belief held more or less unconsciously by most denizens of the century, I would think it not unreasonable to state it in two propositions which represent its two major components, the one deriving from the profound impact of the scientific revolution, the other representing a kind of attenuated legacy of Christianity.

(1) Man can be understood as an organism in an environment, a sociological unit, an encultured creature, a psychological dynamism endowed genetically like other organisms with needs and drives, who through evolution has developed strategies for learning and surviving by means of certain adaptive transactions with the environment.

(2) Man is also understood to be somehow endowed with certain other unique properties which he does not share with other organisms—with certain inalienable rights, reason, freedom, and an intrinsic dignity—and as a consequence the highest value to which a democratic society can be committed is the respect of the sacredness and worth of the individual.

I make the assumption that most educated denizens of the Western world would subscribe in some sense or other to both propositions.

I make the second assumption that the conventional wisdom expressed by these two propositions, taken together, is radically incoherent and cannot be seriously professed without even more serious consequences.

How does a man go about living his life if he takes both propositions seriously? He sees himself as an organism highly evolved enough to have developed certain "values." But what he doesn't realize is that as soon as he looks upon his own individuality and freedom as "values," a certain devaluation sets in.

5

There is an astronomer who works at night on Mount Palomar, observing, recording, hypothesizing, writing equations, predicting, searching the skies, confirming, writing papers for other astronomers. During the day he comes down into town to satisfy his needs as organism and culture member, eats, sleeps, enjoys his wife and family and home, plays golf, and participates in other cultural and recreational activities.

He is one of the more fortunate denizens of the age because he functions well as both angel (scientist-knower) and beast (culture organism). But the question is, what manner of creature is he? Draw me a picture of Dr. Jekyll and a benign Mr. Hyde inhabiting the same skin.

Yet he is one of the lucky ones. It is his century and he is one of its princes. His is the best of both worlds: He theorizes and satisfies his needs. He is like one of the old gods who lived above the earth but took their pleasure from the maids of the earth.

But what about the villagers? What happens to a man when he has to live his life in the twentieth century deprived of the sovereignty and lordship of science and art? What is it like to be a layman and a consumer? Does this consumer, the richest in history, suffer a kind of deprivation?

What are the symptoms of the deprivation?

6

When the scientific component of the popular wisdom is dressed up in the attic finery of a Judeo-Christianity in which fewer and fewer people believe, and men try to understand themselves as organisms somehow endowed with mind and self and freedom and worth, one consequence is that these words are taken less and less seriously as the century wears on, and no one is even surprised at mid-century when more than fifty million people have been killed in Europe alone. In fact there is more talk than ever of the dignity of the individual.

Do not imagine that what has occurred is a victory of science over religion. In the end science suffers too. As the pure research of the first half century, the revolutionary physics of Planck and Einstein, devolved into the technology of the second half, more and more youths turned their backs on both, the new science and the old God, and sought instead the fragile utopias of the right place and the right person and the right emotion at the right time.

What happens when these utopias don't work?

7

There is a secret about the scientific method which every scientist knows and takes as a matter of course, but which the layman does not know. The layman's ignorance would not matter if it were not the case that the spirit of the age had been informed by the triumphant spirit of science. As it is, the layman's ignorance can be fatal, not for the scientist but for the layman.

The secret is this: Science cannot utter a single word about an individual molecule, thing, or creature in so far as it is an individual but only in so far as it is like other individuals. The layman thinks that only science can utter the true word about anything, individuals included. But the layman is an individual. So science cannot say a single word to him or about him except as he resembles others. It comes to pass then that the denizen of a scientific-technological society finds himself in the strangest of predicaments: he lives in a cocoon of dead silence, in which no one can speak to him nor can he reply.

8

At the end of an age, the denizens of the age still profess to believe that they can understand themselves by the theory of the age, yet they behave as if they did not believe it. The surest sign that an age is coming to an end is the paradoxical movement of the most sensitive souls of the age, the artists and writers first, then the youth, in a direction exactly opposite to the direction laid down by the theory of the age.

It was not an accident that in the nineteenth and the early twentieth century, the high-water mark of the old modern age, when the world had been transformed by Western man and the scientific revolution to his own use and people lived peacefully in the ethical twilight of Christianity, man should begin to feel most homeless in the same world where he had expected to feel most at home.

How can the Harvard behaviorist, living in the best of all scientific worlds, begin to understand the behavior of the Harvard undergraduate who comes from the best of all lay worlds, the affluent, informed, democratic, and ethical East (let the professor specify this world, make it as good as he chooses), who nevertheless turns his back on both worlds and prefers to live like Dostoevsky's underground man?

How can the Unitarian minister, good man that he is, who believes in all the good things of the old modern age, the ethics, the democratic values, the tolerance, the individual freedom, and all the rest—how can he begin to understand his son, who wants nothing so much as *out*, out from under this good man and good home and the good things professed there? It is of no moment what the son chooses instead—Hare Krishna, Process, revolution, or Zen; to him anything, *anything*, is better than this fagged-out ethical deadweight of five thousand years of Judeo-Christianity.

9

A theory of man must account for the alienation of man. A theory of organisms in environments cannot account for it, for in fact organisms in environments are not alienated.

Judeo-Christianity did of course give an account of alienation, not as a peculiar evil of the twentieth century, but as the enduring symptom of man's estrangement from God. Any cogent anthropology must address itself to both, to the possibility of the perennial estrangement of man as part of the human condition and to the undeniable fact of the cultural estrangement of Western man in the twentieth century.

By the very cogent anthropology of Judeo-Christianity, whether or not one agreed with it, human existence was by no means to be understood as the transaction of a higher organism satisfying this or that need from its environment, by being "creative" or enjoying "meaningful relationships," but as the journey of a wayfarer along life's way. The experience of alienation was thus not a symptom of maladaptation (psychology) nor evidence of the absurdity of life (existentialism) nor an inevitable consequence of capitalism (Marx) nor the necessary dehumanization of technology (Ellul). Though the exacerbating influence of these forces was not denied, it was not to be forgotten that human alienation was first and last the homelessness of a man who is not in fact at home.

The Judeo-Christian anthropology was cogent enough and flexible enough, too, to accommodate the several topical alienations of the twentieth century. The difficulty was that in order to accept this anthropology of alienation one had also to accept the notion of an aboriginal catastrophe or Fall, a stumbling block which to both the scientist and the humanist seems even more bizarre than a theology of God, the Jews, Christ, and the Church.

So the scientists and humanists got rid of the Fall and re-entered Eden, where scientists know like the angels, and laymen prosper in good environments, and ethical democracies progress through education. But in so doing they somehow deprived themselves of the means of understanding and averting the dread catastrophies which were to overtake Eden and of dealing with those perverse and ungrateful beneficiaries of science and ethics who preferred to eat lotus like the Laodiceans or roam the dark and violent world like Ishmael and Cain.

Then Eden turned into the twentieth century.

10

The modern age began to come to an end when men discovered that they could no longer understand themselves by the theory professed by the age.

After the end of the modern age, its anthropology was still professed for a while and the denizens of the age still believed that they believed it, but they felt otherwise and they could not understand their feelings. They were like men who live by reason during the day and at night dream bad dreams.

The scientists and humanists were saying one thing, but the artists and poets were saying something else.

The scientists were saying that by science man was learning more and more about himself as an organism and more and more about the world as an environment and that accordingly the environment could be changed and man made to feel more and more at home.

The humanists were saying that through education and the application of the ethical principles of Christianity, man's lot was certain to improve.

But poets and artists and novelists were saying something else: that at a time when, according to the theory of the age, men should feel most at home they felt most homeless.

Someone was wrong.

In the very age when communication theory and technique reached its peak, poets and artists were saying that men were in fact isolated and no longer communicated with each other.

In the very age when the largest number of people lived together in the cities, poets and artists were saying there was no longer a community.

In the very age when men lived longest and were most secure in their lives, poets and artists were saying that men were most afraid.

In the very age when crowds were largest and people flocked closest together, poets and artists were saying that men were lonely.

Why were poets and artists saying these things?

Was it because they were out of tune with the spirit of the modern age and so were complaining because the denizens of the age paid no attention to them?

Or was it that they were uttering the true feelings of the age, feelings however which could not be understood by the spirit of the age?

Nobody wants to hear about his unspeakable feelings. It is only when the feelings become speakable, that is, understandable by a new anthropology, that people can bear hearing about them.

It was easy not to take poets and artists seriously because they often behaved badly, seemed to enjoy their suffering and, though they made fun of the spirit of the age, science, and technology, were as willing as the next man to enjoy its benefits. Has anyone ever heard of a poet who refused penicillin when he got a streptococcus?

But most of all, the poets and artists who attacked the spirit of the age had nothing to offer in its stead. If the modern theory of man didn't work, and they said it didn't, what theory did?

11

The end of the age came when it dawned on man that he could not understand himself by the spirit of the age, which was informed by the spirit of abstraction, and that accordingly the spirit of the age could not address one single word to him as an individual self but could address him only as he resembled other selves.

Man did not lose his self in the modern age but rather became incommunicado, being able neither to speak for himself nor to be spoken to.

A man is after all himself and no other, and not merely an example of a class of similar selves. If such a man is deprived of the means of being a self in a world made over by science for his use and enjoyment, he is like a ghost at a feast. He becomes invisible. That is why people in the modern age took photographs by the million: to prove despite their deepest suspicions to the contrary that they were not invisible.

12

At the end of an age the theorists of the age will go to any length to stretch their theory to fit the events of the age in the name of science, even if it means that theory is stretched out of shape and is no longer scientific.

What theorists of the old modern age had to confront were the altogether unexpected disasters of the twentieth century: that after three hundred years of the scientific revolution and in the emergence of rational ethics in European Christendom, Western man in the twentieth century elected instead of an era of peace and freedom an orgy of wars, tortures, genocide, suicide, murder, and rapine unparalleled in history.

The old modern age ended in 1914. In 1916 one million Frenchmen and Germans were killed in a single battle.

Future ages will look back on the attempts to account for man's perverse behavior in the twentieth century by the theory of the old modern age as one of the curiosities of the history of science.

First, given the consensus wisdom of the time, it was to be expected of man, understood as an organism in an environment with a roster of "needs," that as the scientific revolution succeeded in transforming the environment for man's use and increasing man's knowledge and as culture evolved according to rational democratic and ethical principles, man should himself progress toward peace and happiness.

Next, when that did not happen, when men in fact seemed to prefer bad environments to good, a hurricane on Key Largo to an ordinary Wednesday afternoon in Short Hills, and even war to peace—war, the worst of all possible environments—the theorists of the age had only one recourse: to search for explanations either within the "organism" or within the "environment." Accordingly, it did not strike anyone as peculiar when scientists sought an explanation for man's perversity and upsidedownness in this or that atavism from man's evolutionary past. Man blamed the beasts for his madness.

Next, it seemed natural to look for the source of man's "aggressive" behavior in the aggression and "territoriality" of more primitive species, for example, the male stickleback, or in this or that putative ancestor of man, even though no stickleback or any other creature but man has been observed to wage war against itself (suicide) or against its own kind (war).

To the Martian, it seemed curious. If it was the case, as it appeared to be to him, that man exhibited two observable traits wherein he differed most clearly from the beasts, (1) that he had crossed the language barrier and spent most of his time symbol-mongering and (2) that man, alone among creatures, had a perverse penchant for upside-down feelings and behavior, feeling bad when he had expected to feel good, preferring war to peace, and in general being miserable at the time and in the place which he had every reason to expect to be the best of all possible worlds, it seemed to the Martian that earth scientists might do well to search for the explanation of trait 2 in trait 1, or at least to explore the connection between the two.

Instead he discovered that earth scientists were studying sticklebacks and male dominance in baboons and even hypothesizing a putative killer-ape, which perhaps had roamed the African prairies killing for pleasure and whose perverse behavior had somehow persisted in man.

The United States government, he discovered, spent millions funding the study of chimpanzees and other primates, crowding them into cage ghettos or isolating them in cage hermitages in the full expectation of shedding light on man's hatefulness and man's loneliness. Hundreds of papers were written on such subjects as "Sibling Rivalry in a Gibbon Colony" or "Electrically Induced Anxiety in the Macaque."

Very good, said the Martian, the more knowledge the better. But why doesn't the government spend a single dollar or you scientists write a single paper on such subjects as:

"Suicide in San Francisco, or the End of the Frontier: Correlations between Point of Origin, Level of Education, Time of Arrival, and Number of Rotations between New York and San Francisco of 150 Suicides Who Jumped off the Golden Gate Bridge," or "Sadness in Suburbia: Psychiatric Profiles of Twenty-five Housewives before and after Reading Betty Friedan,"

or "Scientific Transcendence and Sexual Imminence, or the Relationship of Lust to the Spirit of Abstraction: The Sexual Behavior of Twelve Scientists at Los Alamos in 1942–45, the Zenith of Transcendence of Twentieth-Century Physics Interrupted by Periodic Re-entry into the Organismic and Cultural Imminence of Santa Fe, Los Angeles, and New York; Sexual Intercourse as Prototype of Re-entry,"

or "The Aesthetic Reversal of Depression on Commuter Trains: Before-and-After Muscle-Tension Studies on Ten Depressed Commuters Reading a Book about Depressed Commuters on a Train,"

or "How Bad Is Bad News? A Survey of the Selective Predeliction of 250 New York City Subway Riders for News Stories Headlined 'War,' 'Plane Crash,' 'Assassination,' 'Rape,' 'Murder,' 'Kidnapping,' "

or "Catastrophe as Catalyst in the Ontology of Joy, or Hurricane Parties on the Gulf Coast during Hurricane Camille: An In-depth Study of Eleven Victims Who Elected to Stay Compared with Eleven Random Control Subjects Who Elected to Leave"?

When the Martian made inquiries about such possible connections between man's peculiar symbol-mongering and his even more peculiar behavior, he was given a copy of *The Naked Ape*.

13

The truth is that man's capacity for symbol-mongering in general and language in particular is so intimately part and parcel of his being human, of his perceiving and knowing, of his very consciousness itself, that it is all but impossible for him to focus on the magic prism through which he sees everything else.

In order to see it, one must be either a Martian, or, if an earthling, sufficiently detached, marooned, bemused, wounded, crazy, one-eyed, and lucky enough to become a Martian for a second and catch a glimpse of it.

14

The day I was thinking about Helen Keller and became a Martian for five seconds, making a breakthrough like Helen's, the difference being that her breakthrough was something she did and my breakthrough was a sudden understanding of what she did.

One ordinary summer day I was sitting at my desk in Louisiana and thinking about a day in the life of Helen Keller in Tuscumbia, Alabama, in 1887. I had been trying to figure out what happens when a child hears a word, a sound uttered by someone else, and understands that it is the name of something he sees. Toward this end I had filled a page with diagrams showing little arrows leaving the speaker's mouth, entering the ear of the hearer, coursing along neurons and synapses; other arrows showing light waves coming from the tree or ball the child was looking at; the two trains of arrows meeting one way or another in the brain.

For a long time the conviction had been growing upon me that three short paragraphs in Helen Keller's *The Story of My Life* veiled a mystery, a profound secret, and that, if one could fathom it, one could also understand a great deal of what it meant to be *Homo loquens, Homo symbolificus*, man the speaking animal, man the symbol-monger.

The literature on the subject was by and large unsatisfactory. It still is. If the Martian wanted to go to the library and look it up or enroll in the university and take a course in it, he'd be out of luck. I too discovered that if you tried to look up *language*, you could find out everything under the sun about it except—the phenomenon itself. What I found was two kinds of thinking on the subject with a narrow but impenetrable terra incognita in between.

There were the behaviorists, who seemed anxious above all to explain language as a stimulus-response event, drawing arrows in and out and around dogs' brains and human brains. A man receiving a symbol could not, it seemed, be altogether different from a pigeon "understanding" a green light which "meant" food-pellet-over-there. The classic case, of course, was Pavlov's dog learning to respond to a buzzer by salivating. Other kinds of animal re-

sponses may be a little different—Skinner's pigeons, for example—
but the model was the same. The same arrows worked for both.

The explanatory model of the behaviorists was all a model
should be; it was simple, elegant, and fruitful. It stood, moreover,
in a direct line of continuity with chemistry and physics. The happenings in a speaker's mouth, in the air, in the ear of the listener,
along the nerves, could all be understood, at least in principle, as
chemical and physical transactions occurring between molecules or
electrons. You could draw a picture of it, showing things and
spaces and arrows flying between them.

It was a valuable model. Beautiful and simple as it was, one did
not abandon it lightly—especially not for fuzzy philosophical notions like "thoughts" and "minds" and "ideas."

The behaviorists knew what they were talking about. The picture
they drew of an organism responding to a learned signal had all the
virtues of a good explanatory model. It explained, satisfied, and
stimulated.

One wanted very much to apply the model, or a variant of it, to
human behavior. And indeed one could—if one picked the right
kind of behavior. The anthropologist Malinowski, who also liked
the model, picked a good example. A party of Trobriand Islanders
are out fishing. One man sights a school and calls out, "Mackerel
here!" The other fishermen converge on the spot and ready their
spears.

The model works in this case. Fisherman B responds to the cry
of fisherman A, as he has learned by past experience and past
rewards to respond: he paddles over and readies his spear. Perhaps
if the cry had been "Shark here!" the response would have been to
paddle in the opposite direction.

Yes, Trobriand fishing fitted the model. But I couldn't help wondering at the time what Malinowski and the behaviorists would
make of the behavior of the fishermen after they returned to the
island, when they had a feast and later sat around the fire and told
stories. Try to draw a picture with arrows of a storyteller spinning a
long tale about long-past or imaginary events and forty islanders listening to him and taking it all in.

Something was wrong. Something in fact usually went wrong with the behaviorist S-R model whenever it was applied to a characteristically symbolic transaction, telling a story and listening to a story, looking at a painting and understanding it, a father pointing at a ball and naming it for his child, a poet hitting on a superb metaphor and the reader "getting" it with that old authentic thrill Barfield speaks of. In order to be fitted to such events, the S-R model had to be distorted, yanked, stretched, added onto, and in general rendered unrecognizable. The behaviorists in fact seemed more anxious to fit the model to the phenomenon than to take a good look at the phenomenon.

When a model ceases to illumine and order or even to fit the case, and when the time comes that you're spending more time tinkering with the model to make it work than taking a good hard look at the happening, it's time to look for another model.

Clearly something is wrong with the behaviorist model when it is applied to symbolic phenomena. To be blunt about it, it doesn't work. No matter how much it is tinkered with, no matter how many little s's and r's, "intervening variables," are added, it still doesn't work. Not only does it fail to account for a particular symbolic transaction, it has been conspicuous by its uselessness in the face of those very features of language that set it apart from animal behavior: (1) the productivity of language, the fact that a child, after two or three years' exposure to a language and without anyone taking much trouble about it, can utter and understand an unlimited number of new sentences in the language; (2) an explanation of names; (3) an account of sentences.

The other great tradition by which man has sought to understand his own peculiar traffic in words and symbols runs from Plato through Kant to Ernst Cassirer. Here the starting point is not the "real" objective world out there with its sticks and stones, plants and bugs, amoebae shrinking, dogs salivating, Trobriand Islanders fishing—all these items and many more out there, and out there too perhaps the oddest lot of all, a group of scientists looking at these happenings and trying to explain them to each other. No, the emphasis is rather on the mind, the idea, the word, the self-generated symbol, the interior picture, the transcendental form which we make and by which we not only understand the world but construe it, even constitute it. To make a long story much too short, and so to make as quick as possible an end to the longest and most boring argument in philosophy, it is not really the world which is known but the idea or symbol which becomes the all-construing form, while that which it symbolizes, the great wide world, gradually vanishes into Kant's unknowable noumenon.

At any rate Cassirer did indeed give the symbol the full weight and primacy I thought it deserved, but in so doing he seemed to have fallen victim to the old interior itch of German philosophers and let the world slip away.

How to account in this tradition for the unending sweat and toil and mistakes and wrong guesses and quarrels and finally triumphs of scientists who go to so much trouble to get at the truth, or at least the hows and whys, of what is going on out there?

American behaviorists kept solid hold on the world of things and creatures, yet couldn't fit the symbol into it.

German idealists kept the word as internal form, logos, and let the world get away. From Kant to Cassirer, man became ever more securely locked up inside his own head. Even outside happenings seemed to be ordered by the interior forms of the mind. All questions could be given inside answers—except the kind of awkward questions children ask: Yes, but how does it happen that you can talk and I can understand you? Or, how does it happen that you can write a book and I can read it? Or, if the world is really unknowable, why do scientists act as if there were something out there to be known and as if they could even get at the truth of the way things are?

Accordingly, I was sitting at my desk in Louisiana on a summer day in the 1950's wondering whether this split in human knowing was not in the very nature of things and whether, also, that peculiar and most human of all phenomenon, language, did not fall between the two, and was not somehow unapproachable from either, a forbidden island, a terra incognita.

My instincts, I confess, were on the side of the scientists in general and in particular on the side of the hardheaded empiricism of American behavioral scientists. The entire spectacular history of modern science seemed to bear out their unspoken assumption that there was indeed something to be known out there and it was worth the effort to try to find out what it was.

Yet the natural scientists, with all their understanding of interactions, energy exchanges, stimuli, and responses, could not seem to utter a single word about what men did and what they themselves were doing: observing and recording, telling and listening, uttering sentences and hearing sentences, writing papers and reading papers, delivering lectures, listening to the six o'clock news, writing a letter to one's daughter in college.

Was it possible, I wondered, to preserve the objective stance of the psychologist, which always seemed so right and valuable to me, which assumes there are real things and events happening, and to make some sense out of what happens when people talk and other people listen and understand or misunderstand? Maybe it wasn't possible, to judge from the spectacular default of the behaviorists when confronted by language as behavior. Not since Noam Chomsky wrote his famous review of Skinner's *Verbal Behavior* has it been possible to take seriously the application to language of the old stimulus-response theory, however refined and modified it might be.

Sitting there in Louisiana, I was thinking about these things. Then I began thinking about what happened between Helen Keller and Miss Sullivan in Tuscumbia, Alabama, on another summer morning in 1887. You recall the story. The heart of it is in three short paragraphs. Earlier, Helen had learned to respond like any other good animal: When she wanted a piece of cake, she spelled the word in Miss Sullivan's hand and Miss Sullivan fetched her the cake (like the chimp Washoe, who gives hand signals: tickle, banana, etc.). Then Miss Sullivan took her for a walk.

> We walked down the path to the well-house, attracted by the fragrance of the honeysuckle with which it was covered. Someone was drawing water and my teacher placed my hand under the spout. As the cool stream gushed over one hand, she spelled into the other the word

water, first slowly then rapidly. I stood still, my whole attention fixed
upon the motion of her fingers. Suddenly I felt a misty consciousness as
of something forgotten—a thrill of returning thought; and somehow the
mystery of language was revealed to me. I knew then that "w-a-t-e-r"
meant the wonderful cool something that was flowing over my hand.
That living word awakened my soul, gave it light, hope, joy, set it free!
There were barriers still, it is true, but barriers that could in time be
swept away.

I left the well-house eager to learn. Everything had a name, and each
name gave birth to a new thought. As we returned to the house every
object which I touched seemed to quiver with life. That was because I
saw everything with the strange, new sight that had come to me. On
entering the door I remembered the doll I had broken. [She had earlier
destroyed the doll in a fit of temper.] I felt my way to the hearth and
picked up the pieces. I tried vainly to put them together. Then my eyes
filled with tears; for I realized what I had done, and for the first time I
felt repentance and sorrow.

I learned a great many new words that day. I do not remember what
they all were; but I do know that *mother, father, sister, teacher* were
among them—words that were to make the world blossom for me, "like
Aaron's rod with flowers." It would have been difficult to find a happier
child than I was as I lay in my crib at the close of that eventful day and
lived over the joys it had brought me, and for the first time longed for a
new day to come.

If there was a bifurcation in our knowledge of ourselves and our
peculiar and most characteristically human activity, with a terra incognita in between concealing the mystery, surely I was straddling
it and looking straight down at it. Here in the well-house in Tuscumbia in a small space and a short time, something extremely important and mysterious had happened. Eight-year-old Helen made
her breakthrough from the good responding animal which behaviorists study so successfully to the strange name-giving and sen-
tence-uttering creature who begins by naming shoes and ships and
sealing wax, and later tells jokes, curses, reads the paper, writes *La
sua volontade e nostra pace*, or becomes a Hegel and composes an
entire system of philosophy.

For a long time I had believed and I still believe that if one had
an inkling of what happened in the well-house in Alabama in the
space of a few minutes, one would know more about the *phenome-*

non of language and about man himself than is contained in all the
works of behaviorists, linguists, and German philosophers.

What did happen?

Once again, as I had done many times before and as my hardheaded professor had taught me, I began drawing diagrams, behaviorist models, showing the usual arrows. After all the arrows *were*
there: Miss Sullivan traced certain sensory patterns in Helen's
hand, which were then coded by the touch receptors in the skin
and transmitted by afferent nerves to the sensory cortex, the gray
matter of the brain. And, at least in the incident with the cake,
once Helen received a "word" which she had learned to associate
with a certain pleasant consequence, other arrows could be drawn
showing that Helen's attention and behavior were directed to the
fetching and eating of the cake. Then did something of the sort
happen in the well-house? Begin then with this diagram:

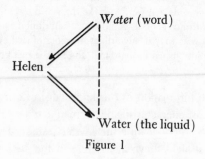

Figure 1

Now I had something very close to Ogden and Richards's triangle. The arrows showed "real causal" relations between the word
water spelled in Helen's hand and Helen's brain, and between the
brain event which issues in Helen's attention being directed toward
the "referent," the water flowing over her other hand.

What about the relation between the word *water* and the water
itself? There is no "real causal" relation but only the relation of
naming which Miss Sullivan teaches Helen to "impute" between
the two. So, if we want to follow Ogden and Richards, we can draw

a dotted line between the word *water* and the water and call it an "unreal imputed relation."

But wait. Something was very wrong. For one thing, I felt like handing a piece of chalk to Professors Ogden and Richards, inviting them to the blackboard, and making a polite request: Would you mind drawing me a picture of an "unreal imputed relation"? What does the dotted line mean?

For another thing, it wasn't the case that Helen had received the word *water*, which had then directed her attention or behavior toward the water. That wasn't what happened. What happened was that she received *both*, both the sensory message from the hand Miss Sullivan was spelling in and that from the other hand, which the water was flowing over. The direction of one arrow should be reversed, as in Figure 2.

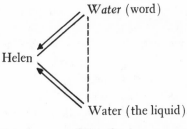

Figure 2

Then what happened inside Helen's head? Clearly, even if I were a neuroanatomist I would hardly be in a position to say, because for one thing not even a neuroanatomist can look. But I was asking myself, rather, what sort of thing happened? The old model had broken down. I needed a new one, however crude. After all, modern medicine began with Harvey making the crudest sort of guess about the heart and the blood: Maybe the latter works like a unidirectional pump and the blood goes round and round.

Accordingly, I kept thinking about Helen's breakthrough and drew dozens of diagrams, triangles, arrows, dotted lines, nerve nets linking portions of the sensory cortex.

Unquestionably Helen's breakthrough was critical and went to the very heart of the terra incognita. Before, Helen had behaved like a good responding organism. Afterward, she acted like a rejoicing symbol-mongering human. Before, she was little more than an animal. Afterward, she became wholly human. Within the few minutes of the breakthrough and the several hours of exploiting it Helen had concentrated the months of the naming phase that most children go through somewhere around their second birthday.

It was like holding a test tube of pure uranium which had been smelted from thousands of tons of ore-bearing rock. I was looking straight at it, but what to make of it?

Not only that, not only did Helen's experience distill the essence of the two-year-old's language learning, but also—and this was enough to quicken your pulse and keep you drawing diagrams by the hour—if the biologist's motto were true and ontogeny does recapitulate phylogeny, then Helen's breakthrough must bear some relation to the breakthrough of the species itself, at that faraway time when our ancestor, having harnessed fire, for the first time found himself seated by the flickering embers, looking into the eyes of his comrades and thinking (not really thinking, of course) about the vivid events of the day's hunt and "knowing" that the others must be "thinking" about the same thing: One of them tries to recapture it, to savor it, and so repeats the crude hunting cry meaning *Bison here!*; another, hearing it, knows somehow that the one doesn't mean *get up and hunt now* or do this or do anything, but means something else, means *Remember him, remember the bison*, and as the other waits and sees it, sees the bison, savors the seeing it, something happens, a spark jumps . . .

What happened?

The arrows tell part of the story but not the breakthrough. What seems to have lain at the heart of the breakthrough, what in fact *was* the breakthrough, was the fact that somehow the old arrow route, the six-billion-year-old chain of causal relations, the energy exchanges which had held good from the earliest collision of hydrogen atoms to the responses of amoeba and dogs and chimps, that ancient circuit of causes, my troop of arrows, had been short-circuited.

Then it was that I made my own Helen Keller breakthrough, a "discovery" which I was later to learn that Charles Peirce had hit on a hundred years earlier and from a different direction and to which no one had paid much attention, not even Peirce's greatest admirers. Peirce's "triad" or "thirdness" was rather part and parcel of a heavy metaphysic and so could hardly be seen as something that happened among persons, words, and things.

What dawned on me was that what happened between Helen and Miss Sullivan and water and the word was "real" enough all right, no matter what Ogden and Richards said, as real as any S-R sequence, as real as H_2SO_4 reacting to $NaOH$, but that *what happened could not be drawn with arrows.*

In short, it could not be set forth as a series of energy exchanges or causal relations.

It was something new under the sun, evolutionarily speaking.

It was a natural phenomenon but a nonlinear and nonenergic one.*

15

A NONLINEAR NONENERGIC
NATURAL PHENOMENON
(that is to say, a natural
phenomenon in which energy exchanges
account for some but not all
of what happens)

If the event which occurred in the well-house in Tuscumbia in 1887 was not primarily a linear energy exchange, what was it?

I stopped drawing arrows and saw that I had a triangle (Figure 3).

---

* I am aware of course that other phenomena can be described in a sense as nonlinear, e.g., action of a force field, gestalt perception, transactions in a neural net, etc. Yet these events lend themselves to formulation by equation and to explanatory models which discern this or that causal or statistical relationship within a structure.

The utterance or understanding of a sentence does not so lend itself.

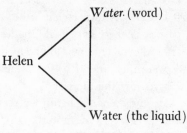

Figure 3

Undoubtedly there were three elements somehow involved in the event—Helen, the water, and the word *water*. But how? What was the base of the triangle? What is the nature of the mysterious event in which one perceives that *this* (stuff) "is" *water*? What is the natural phenomenon signified by the simplest yet most opaque of all symbols, the little copula "is"?

My breakthrough was the sudden inkling that the triangle was absolutely irreducible. Here indeed was nothing less, I suspected, than the ultimate and elemental unit not only of language but of the very condition of the awakening of human intelligence and consciousness.

What to call it? "Triad"? "Triangle"? "Thirdness"? Perhaps "Delta phenomenon," the Greek letter Δ signifying irreducibility.

Alpha was the beginning, omega will be the end, but somewhere in between, some five billion years after alpha, and x years before omega, there first occurred delta, Δ.

The Delta phenomenon lies at the heart of every event that has ever occurred in which a sentence is uttered or understood, a name is given or received, a painting painted and viewed.

What Helen had discovered, broken through to, was the Delta phenomenon.

I sat there looking at this queer triangle, drawing it over and over again (Figure 4). Even though I did not have the words to name it or think about it, I suspected that Delta Δ might somehow prove to be the key, not perhaps for unlocking the mysteries of language and the human condition, but at least for opening a new way of thinking about them.

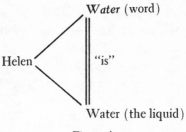

Figure 4

Using the concept of the Delta phenomenon, mightn't one set out to understand man as the languaged animal? Mightn't one even begin to understand the manifold woes, predicaments, and estrangements of man—and the delights and savorings and home-comings—as nothing more nor less than the variables of the Delta phenomenon, just as responses, reinforcements, rewards, and such are the variables of stimulus-response phenomena?

Mightn't one even speak of such a thing as the Helen Keller phenomenon, which everyone experiences at the oddest and most unlikely times? Prince Andrei lying wounded on the field of Borodino and discovering clouds for the first time. Or the Larchmont commuter whose heart attack allows him to see his own hand for the first time.

Or the reverse Helen Keller phenomenon: the couple who build the perfect house with the perfect view in the perfect neighborhood and who after living in the house five years can't stand the house or the view or each other.

Accordingly, I was wondering in Louisiana in the 1950's: Is it possible that Delta Δ might provide the key to understanding not only what happened to Helen in the well-house but also how Americans who have everything are bored and French existentialists who write about boredom and despair are happy?

What did I have to lose? The conventional wisdom was a mishmash: man set forth as "organism in an environment" but man also and somehow, though God alone knew how, set forth as repository of democratic and Judeo-Christian "values."

Delta Δ might be the new key, but it itself was a mystery. It described a kind of event, a natural phenomenon, yet something new under the sun. And recent. Life has existed on the earth for perhaps three billion years, yet Delta Δ could not be more than a million years old, no older certainly than *Homo erectus* and perhaps a good deal more recent, as late as the time of *Homo neanderthalensis*, when man underwent an astonishing evolutionary explosion which in the scale of earth time was as sudden as biblical creation. Was not in fact the sudden 54 per cent increase in brain size not the cause but the consequence of the true urphenomenon, the jumped circuit by which Delta Δ first appeared? The spark jumped, language was born, the brain flowered with words, and man became man.

At any rate the Alabama well-house was the place to set out from.

If one could ever fathom what happened when Helen knew that water "was" *water*, one might begin to understand a great many other things, perhaps even why people get bored in Short Hills and move to the Gulf Coast to enjoy hurricanes.

The Strangeness of Delta

The longer one thought about the irreducible triangle and its elements and relations, the queerer they got.

Compare Delta Δ phenomenon with the pseudo triangle of Ogden and Richards: buzzer → dog → food. The latter is a pseudo triangle because one needn't think of it as a triangle at all but can conceive the event quite easily as a series of energy exchanges beginning with buzzer and ending in the dog's salivation and approaching food.

But consider the Delta phenomenon in its simplest form. A boy has just come into the naming stage of language acquisition and one day points to a balloon and looks questioningly at his father. The father says, "That's a balloon," or perhaps just, "Balloon."

Here the Delta phenomenon is as simple as Helen's breakthrough in the well-house, the main difference being that the boy is stretching out over months what Helen took by storm in a few hours.

But consider.

Unlike the buzzer-dog-salivation sequence, one runs immediately into difficulty when one tries to locate and specify the Delta elements—balloon (thing), *balloon* (word), boy (organism).

In a word, my next discovery was bad news. It was the discovery of three mystifying negatives. In the Delta phenomenon it seems: The balloon is not the balloon out there. The word *balloon* is not the sound in the air. The boy is not the organism boy.

For example: Where, what is the word *balloon?* Show me the word *balloon* as I can show you the sound of the buzzer. Unlike the dog "understanding" the sound of the buzzer to "mean" food, the boy does not understand the particular sound *balloon*—which his father makes and which enters his ear—to mean the balloon. For it is precisely the nature of the boy's breakthrough that he understands his father's utterance as a particular instance of the word *balloon.* Where is the word itself? Is it the little marks in the dictionary which you point to when I ask you to show me the word *balloon?*

Charles Peirce said the word *balloon* is not a concrete thing at all but a general one, a law.

What about the balloon itself? Cannot one at least say that what the boy is pointing to and "means" is that particular round red rubbery inflated object?

No.

It is precisely the nature of the boy's breakthrough that the object he points to is understood by him as a member of a class of inflated objects. A few minutes later he might well point to a blue sausage-shaped inflated object and say, "Balloon."

What about the boy himself? Can he not be understood, as the dog is understood, as the organism within whose neurons and molecules certain interactions occur which lead to his uttering and understanding the name?

No.

For it is not the case of the boy being the site where certain interactions and energy exchanges take place, arrows flying along neurons and jumping synapses. Something else happens. However many arrows fly along the boy's neurons (and they do), he does something else. He couples *balloon* with balloon. But who, what couples? Who, what is the coupler? Do you mean some part of his brain does the coupling? I could not say whether it is his brain which couples, his "mind," his "self," his "I." All one can say for certain is that if two things which are otherwise unconnected are coupled, there must be a coupler.

Then what can one say for sure about the three elements of the Delta phenomenon?

Only this: The boy in Delta is not the organism boy. The balloon in Delta is not the balloon in the world. The *balloon* in Delta is not the sound *balloon*.

An unpromising beginning.

Indeed there was not much to be said for my own Helen-Keller breakthrough (was this the nature of the beast too, that it couldn't be said?) and very little to be sure of. Only this: the Delta phenomenon yielded a new world and maybe a new way of getting at it. It was not the world of organisms and environments but just as real and twice as human.

Would it be possible, I was wondering then in Louisiana, to use the new key to open a new door and see in a new way? See man not the less mysterious but of a piece, maybe even whole, a whole creature put together again after the three-hundred-year-old Cartesian split that sundered man from himself in the old modern age, when man was seen as a "mind" somehow inhabiting a "body," neither knowing what one had to do with the other, a lonesome ghost in an abused machine?

Perhaps it was not a case of exorcising the ghost, as the scientists wanted to do, but of discovering a creature who was neither ghost nor machine.

These hopes have not of course been realized.

What follows here is only a very tentative exploration of the terra incognita, an edging into it from its opposite sides.

From one side, the far side, set out with man's breakthrough—with Helen Keller or with species man perhaps in the cave in the Neander valley a hundred thousand years ago or with any man two years old.

What does it mean for a good organism to break through into the daylight of language?

Set out from the other side, this side, the near side, with the full-blown woes, estrangements, and peculiar upside-down delights and miseries of the late twentieth century.

Two unique happenings: man learning to speak and man behaving as he does now.

Does one have anything to do with the other?

Is the organism who breaks into Delta daylight and learns to speak also and for this very reason the same creature who feels bad in Short Hills when he should feel good and feels good in hurricanes when he should feel bad?

Is there any other way to understand why people feel so bad in the twentieth century and writers feel so good writing about people feeling bad than in terms of the peculiar parameters, the joys and sorrows of symbol-mongering?

There is a difference between the way things are and saying the way things are.

Here, in what follows, only a few trails will be blazed into this dark forest, my only tool the Delta Δ blade of the symbolic breakthrough, Helen's magic Excalibur which she found in Alabama water.

In the beginning was alpha, the end is omega, but somewhere in between came Delta, man himself. Man became man by breaking into the daylight of language—whether by good fortune or bad fortune, whether by pure chance, the spark jumping the gap because the gap was narrow enough, or by the touch of God, it is not for me to say here.

But it happened, and to this day man knows less about what happened than he knows about the back side of the moon.

2

THE LOSS

OF THE CREATURE

EVERY EXPLORER NAMES his island Formosa, beautiful. To him it is beautiful because, being first, he has access to it and can see it for what it is. But to no one else is it ever as beautiful—except the rare man who manages to recover it, who knows that it has to be recovered.

García López de Cárdenas discovered the Grand Canyon and was amazed at the sight. It can be imagined: One crosses miles of desert, breaks through the mesquite, and there it is at one's feet. Later the government set the place aside as a national park, hoping to pass along to millions the experience of Cárdenas. Does not one see the same sight from the Bright Angel Lodge that Cárdenas saw?

The assumption is that the Grand Canyon is a remarkably interesting and beautiful place and that if it had a certain value P for Cárdenas, the same value P may be transmitted to any number of sightseers—just as Banting's discovery of insulin can be transmitted to any number of diabetics. A counterinfluence is at work, however, and it would be nearer the truth to say that if the place is seen by a million sightseers, a single sightseer does not receive value P but a millionth part of value P.

It is assumed that since the Grand Canyon has the fixed interest value P, tours can be organized for any number of people. A man in Boston decides to spend his vacation at the Grand Canyon. He visits his travel bureau, looks at the folder, signs up for a two-week tour. He and his family take the tour, see the Grand Canyon, and return to Boston. May we say that this man has seen the Grand Canyon? Possibly he has. But it is more likely that what he has done is the one sure way not to see the canyon.

Why is it almost impossible to gaze directly at the Grand Canyon under these circumstances and see it for what it is—as one picks up a strange object from one's back yard and gazes directly at it? It is almost impossible because the Grand Canyon, the thing as it is, has been appropriated by the symbolic complex which has already been formed in the sightseer's mind. Seeing the canyon under approved circumstances is seeing the symbolic complex head on. The thing is no longer the thing as it confronted the Spaniard; it is rather that which has already been formulated—by picture postcard, geography book, tourist folders, and the words *Grand Canyon*. As a result of this preformulation, the source of the sightseer's pleasure undergoes a shift. Where the wonder and delight of the Spaniard arose from his penetration of the thing itself, from a progressive discovery of depths, patterns, colors, shadows, etc., now the sightseer measures his satisfaction *by the degree to which the canyon conforms to the preformed complex.* If it does so, if it looks just like the postcard, he is pleased; he might even say, "Why it is every bit as beautiful as a picture postcard!" He feels he has not been cheated. But if it does not conform, if the colors are somber, he will not be able to see it directly; he will only be conscious of the disparity between what it is and what it is supposed to be. He will say later that he was unlucky in not being there at the right time. The highest point, the term of the sightseer's satisfaction, is not the sovereign discovery of the thing before him; it is rather the measuring up of the thing to the criterion of the preformed symbolic complex.

Seeing the canyon is made even more difficult by what the sightseer does when the moment arrives, when sovereign knower confronts the thing to be known. Instead of looking at it, he photographs it. There is no confrontation at all. At the end of forty years of preformulation and with the Grand Canyon yawning at his feet, what does he do? He waives his right of seeing and knowing and records symbols for the next forty years. For him there is no present; there is only the past of what has been formulated and seen and the future of what has been formulated and not seen. The present is surrendered to the past and the future.

The sightseer may be aware that something is wrong. He may simply be bored; or he may be conscious of the difficulty: that the great thing yawning at his feet somehow eludes him. The harder he looks at it, the less he can see. It eludes everybody. The tourist cannot see it; the bellboy at the Bright Angel Lodge cannot see it: for him it is only one side of the space he lives in, like one wall of a room; to the ranger it is a tissue of everyday signs relevant to his own prospects—the blue haze down there means that he will probably get rained on during the donkey ride.

How can the sightseer recover the Grand Canyon? He can recover it in any number of ways, all sharing in common the stratagem of avoiding the approved confrontation of the tour and the Park Service.

It may be recovered by leaving the beaten track. The tourist leaves the tour, camps in the back country. He arises before dawn and approaches the South Rim through a wild terrain where there are no trails and no railed-in lookout points. In other words, he sees the canyon by avoiding all the facilities for seeing the canyon. If the benevolent Park Service hears about this fellow and thinks he has a good idea and places the following notice in the Bright Angel Lodge: *Consult ranger for information on getting off the beaten track*—the end result will only be the closing of another access to the canyon.

It may be recovered by a dialectical movement which brings one back to the beaten track but at a level above it. For example, after a lifetime of avoiding the beaten track and guided tours, a man may deliberately seek out the most beaten track of all, the most commonplace tour imaginable: he may visit the canyon by a Greyhound tour in the company of a party from Terre Haute—just as a man who has lived in New York all his life may visit the Statue of Liberty. (Such dialectical savorings of the familiar as the familiar are, of course, a favorite stratagem of *The New Yorker* magazine.) The thing is recovered from familiarity by means of an exercise in familiarity. Our complex friend stands behind his fellow tourists at the Bright Angel Lodge and sees the canyon through them and their predicament, their picture taking and busy disregard. In a sense, he exploits his fellow tourists; he stands on their shoulders to see the canyon.

Such a man is far more advanced in the dialectic than the sightseer who is trying to get off the beaten track—getting up at dawn and approaching the canyon through the mesquite. This stratagem is, in fact, for our complex man the weariest, most beaten track of all.

It may be recovered as a consequence of a breakdown of the symbolic machinery by which the experts present the experience to the consumer. A family visits the canyon in the usual way. But shortly after their arrival, the park is closed by an outbreak of typhus in the south. They have the canyon to themselves. What do they mean when they tell the home folks of their good luck: "We had the whole place to ourselves"? How does one see the thing better when the others are absent? Is looking like sucking: the more lookers, the less there is to see? They could hardly answer, but by saying this they testify to a state of affairs which is considerably more complex than the simple statement of the schoolbook about the Spaniard and the millions who followed him. It is a state in which there is a complex distribution of sovereignty, of zoning.

It may be recovered in a time of national disaster. The Bright Angel Lodge is converted into a rest home, a function that has nothing to do with the canyon a few yards away. A wounded man is brought in. He regains consciousness; there outside his window is the canyon.

The most extreme case of access by privilege conferred by disaster is the Huxleyan novel of the adventures of the surviving remnant after the great wars of the twentieth century. An expedition from Australia lands in Southern California and heads east. They stumble across the Bright Angel Lodge, now fallen into ruins. The trails are grown over, the guard rails fallen away, the dime telescope at Battleship Point rusted. But there is the canyon, exposed at last. Exposed by what? By the decay of those facilities which were designed to help the sightseer.

This dialectic of sightseeing cannot be taken into account by planners, for the object of the dialectic is nothing other than the subversion of the efforts of the planners.

The dialectic is not known to objective theorists, psychologists, and the like. Yet it is quite well known in the fantasy-consciousness of the popular arts. The devices by which the museum exhibit, the Grand Canyon, the ordinary thing, is recovered have long since been stumbled upon. A movie shows a man visiting the Grand Canyon. But the moviemaker knows something the planner does not know. He knows that one cannot take the sight frontally. The canyon must be approached by the stratagems we have mentioned: the Inside Track, the Familiar Revisited, the Accidental Encounter. Who is the stranger at the Bright Angel Lodge? Is he the ordinary tourist from Terre Haute that he makes himself out to be? He is not. He has another objective in mind, to revenge his wronged brother, counterespionage, etc. By virtue of the fact that he has other fish to fry, he may take a stroll along the rim after supper and then we can see the canyon through him. The movie accomplishes its purpose by concealing it. Overtly the characters (the American family marooned by typhus) and we the onlookers experience pity for the sufferers, and the family experience anxiety for themselves; covertly and in truth they are the happiest of people and we are happy through them, for we have the canyon to ourselves. The movie cashes in on the recovery of sovereignty through disaster. Not only is the canyon now accessible to the remnant; the members of the remnant are now accessible to each other; a whole new ensemble of relations becomes possible—friendship, love, hatred, clandestine sexual adventures. In a movie when a man sits next to a woman on a bus, it is necessary either that the bus break down or that the woman lose her memory. (The question occurs to one: Do you imagine there are sightseers who see sights just as they are supposed to? a family who live in Terre Haute, who decide to take the canyon tour, who go there, see it, enjoy it immensely, and go home content? a family who are entirely innocent of all the barriers, zones, losses of sovereignty I have been talking about? Wouldn't most people be sorry if Battleship Point fell into the canyon, carrying all one's fellow passengers to their death, leaving one alone on the South Rim? I cannot answer this. Perhaps there are such people. Certainly a great many American families would swear they had no such problems, that they came, saw, and went away happy. Yet it is just these families who would be happiest if they had gotten the Inside Track and been among the surviving remnant.)

It is now apparent that as between the many measures which may be taken to overcome the opacity, the boredom, of the direct confrontation of the thing or creature in its citadel of symbolic investiture, some are less authentic than others. That is to say, some stratagems obviously serve other purposes than that of providing access to being—for example, various unconscious motivations which it is not necessary to go into here.

Let us take an example in which the recovery of being is ambiguous, where it may under the same circumstances contain both authentic and unauthentic components. An American couple, we will say, drives down into Mexico. They see the usual sights and have a fair time of it. Yet they are never without the sense of missing something. Although Taxco and Cuernavaca are interesting and picturesque as advertised, they fall short of "it." What do the couple have in mind by "it"? What do they really hope for? What sort of experience could they have in Mexico so that upon their return, they would feel that "it" had happened? We have a clue: Their hope has something to do with their own role as tourists in a foreign country and the way in which they conceive this role. It has something to do with other American tourists. Certainly they feel that they are very far from "it" when, after traveling five thousand miles, they arrive at the plaza in Guanajuato only to find themselves surrounded by a dozen other couples from the Midwest.

Already we may distinguish authentic and unauthentic elements. First, we see the problem the couple faces and we understand their efforts to surmount it. The problem is to find an "unspoiled" place. "Unspoiled" does not mean only that a place is left physically intact; it means also that it is not encrusted by renown and by the familiar (as is Taxco), that it has not been discovered by others. We understand that the couple really want to get at the place and enjoy it. Yet at the same time we wonder if there is not something wrong in their dislike of their compatriots. Does access to the place require the exclusion of others?

Let us see what happens.

The couple decide to drive from Guanajuato to Mexico City. On the way they get lost. After hours on a rocky mountain road, they find themselves in a tiny valley not even marked on the map. There they discover an Indian village. Some sort of religious festival is going on. It is apparently a corn dance in supplication of the rain god.

The couple know at once that this is "it." They are entranced. They spend several days in the village, observing the Indians and being themselves observed with friendly curiosity.

Now may we not say that the sightseers have at last come face to face with an authentic sight, a sight which is charming, quaint, picturesque, unspoiled, and that they see the sight and come away rewarded? Possibly this may occur. Yet it is more likely that what happens is a far cry indeed from an immediate encounter with being, that the experience, while masquerading as such, is in truth a rather desperate impersonation. I use the word *desperate* advisedly to signify an actual loss of hope.

The clue to the spuriousness of their enjoyment of the village and the festival is a certain restiveness in the sightseers themselves. It is given expression by their repeated exclamations that "this is too good to be true," and by their anxiety that it may not prove to be so perfect, and finally by their downright relief at leaving the valley and having the experience in the bag, so to speak—that is, safely embalmed in memory and movie film.

What is the source of their anxiety during the visit? Does it not mean that the couple are looking at the place with a certain standard of performance in mind? Are they like Fabre, who gazed at the world about him with wonder, letting it be what it is; or are they not like the overanxious mother who sees her child as one performing, now doing badly, now doing well? The village is their child and their love for it is an anxious love because they are afraid that at any moment it might fail them.

We have another clue in their subsequent remark to an ethnologist friend. "How we wished you had been there with us! What a
perfect goldmine of folkways! Every minute we would say to each
other, if only you were here! You must return with us." This surely
testifies to a generosity of spirit, a willingness to share their experience with others, not at all like their feelings toward their fellow
Iowans on the plaza at Guanajuato!

I am afraid this is not the case at all. It is true that they longed
for their ethnologist friend, but it was for an entirely different reason. They wanted him, not to share their experience, but to certify
their experience as genuine.

"This is it" and "Now we are really living" do not necessarily
refer to the sovereign encounter of the person with the sight that
enlivens the mind and gladdens the heart. It means that now at last
we are having the acceptable experience. The present experience is
always measured by a prototype, the "it" of their dreams. "Now I
am really living" means that now I am filling the role of sightseer
and the sight is living up to the prototype of sights. This quaint and
picturesque village is measured by a Platonic ideal of the Quaint
and the Picturesque.

Hence their anxiety during the encounter. For at any minute
something could go wrong. A fellow Iowan might emerge from a
'dobe hut; the chief might show them his Sears catalogue. (If the
failures are "wrong" enough, as these are, they might still be turned
to account as rueful conversation pieces: "There we were expecting
the chief to bring us a churinga and he shows up with a Sears catalogue!") They have snatched victory from disaster, but their experience always runs the danger of failure.

They need the ethnologist to certify their experience as genuine.
This is borne out by their behavior when the three of them return
for the next corn dance. During the dance, the couple do not
watch the goings-on; instead they watch the ethnologist! Their
highest hope is that their friend should find the dance interesting.
And if he should show signs of true absorption, an interest in the
goings-on so powerful that he becomes oblivious of his friends—
then their cup is full. "Didn't we tell you?" they say at last. What

they want from him is not ethnological explanations; all they want is his approval.

What has taken place is a radical loss of sovereignty over that which is as much theirs as it is the ethnologist's. The fault does not lie with the ethnologist. He has no wish to stake a claim to the village; in fact, he desires the opposite: he will bore his friends to death by telling them about the village and the meaning of the folkways. A degree of sovereignty has been surrendered by the couple. It is the nature of the loss, moreover, that they are not aware of the loss, beyond a certain uneasiness. (Even if they read this and admitted it, it would be very difficult for them to bridge the gap in their confrontation of the world. Their consciousness of the corn dance cannot escape their consciousness of their consciousness, so that with the onset of the first direct enjoyment, their higher consciousness pounces and certifies: "Now you are doing it! Now you are really living!" and, in certifying the experience, sets it at nought.)

Their basic placement in the world is such that they recognize a priority of title of the expert over his particular department of being. The whole horizon of being is staked out by "them," the experts. The highest satisfaction of the sightseer (not merely the tourist but any layman seer of sights) is that his sight should be certified as genuine. The worst of this impoverishment is that there is no sense of impoverishment. The surrender of title is so complete that it never even occurs to one to reassert title. A poor man may envy the rich man, but the sightseer does not envy the expert. When a caste system becomes absolute, envy disappears. Yet the caste of layman-expert is not the fault of the expert. It is due altogether to the eager surrender of sovereignty by the layman so that he may take up the role not of the person but of the consumer.

I do not refer only to the special relation of layman to theorist. I refer to the general situation in which sovereignty is surrendered to a class of privileged knowers, whether these be theorists or artists. A reader may surrender sovereignty over that which has been written about, just as a consumer may surrender sovereignty over a thing which has been theorized about. The consumer is content to receive an experience just as it has been presented to him by theorists and planners. The reader may also be content to judge life by whether it has or has not been formulated by those who know and write about life. A young man goes to France. He too has a fair time of it, sees the sights, enjoys the food. On his last day, in fact as he sits in a restaurant in Le Havre waiting for his boat, something happens. A group of French students in the restaurant get into an impassioned argument over a recent play. A riot takes place. Madame la concierge joins in, swinging her mop at the rioters. Our young American is transported. This is "it." And he had almost left France without seeing "it"!

But the young man's delight is ambiguous. On the one hand, it is a pleasure for him to encounter the same Gallic temperament he had heard about from Puccini and Rolland. But on the other hand, the source of his pleasure testifies to a certain alienation. For the young man is actually barred from a direct encounter with anything French excepting only that which has been set forth, authenticated by Puccini and Rolland—those who know. If he had encountered the restaurant scene without reading Hemingway, without knowing that the performance was so typically, charmingly French, he would not have been delighted. He would only have been anxious at seeing things get so out of hand. The source of his delight is the sanction of those who know.

This loss of sovereignty is not a marginal process, as might appear from my example of estranged sightseers. It is a generalized surrender of the horizon to those experts within whose competence a particular segment of the horizon is thought to lie. Kwakiutls are surrendered to Franz Boas; decaying Southern mansions are surrendered to Faulkner and Tennessee Williams. So that, although it is by no means the intention of the expert to expropriate sovereignty—in fact he would not even know what sovereignty meant in this context—the danger of theory and consumption is a seduction and deprivation of the consumer.

In the New Mexican desert, natives occasionally come across strange-looking artifacts which have fallen from the skies and which are stenciled: *Return to U.S. Experimental Project, Alamogordo.*

Reward. The finder returns the object and is rewarded. He knows nothing of the nature of the object he has found and does not care to know. The sole role of the native, the highest role he can play, is that of finder and returner of the mysterious equipment.

The same is true of the layman's relation to *natural* objects in a modern technical society. No matter what the object or event is, whether it is a star, a swallow, a Kwakiutl, a "psychological phenomenon," the layman who confronts it does not confront it as a sovereign person, as Crusoe confronts a seashell he finds on the beach. The highest role he can conceive himself as playing is to be able to recognize the title of the object, to return it to the appropriate expert and have it certified as a genuine find. He does not even permit himself to see the thing—as Gerard Hopkins could see a rock or a cloud or a field. If anyone asks him why he doesn't look, he may reply that he didn't take that subject in college (or he hasn't read Faulkner).

This loss of sovereignty extends even to oneself. There is the neurotic who asks nothing more of his doctor than that his symptom should prove interesting. When all else fails, the poor fellow has nothing to offer but his own neurosis. But even this is sufficient if only the doctor will show interest when he says, "Last night I had a curious sort of dream; perhaps it will be significant to one who knows about such things. It seems I was standing in a sort of alley—" (I have nothing else to offer you but my own unhappiness. Please say that it, at least, measures up, that it is a *proper* sort of unhappiness.)

2

A young Falkland Islander walking along a beach and spying a dead dogfish and going to work on it with his jackknife has, in a fashion wholly unprovided in modern educational theory, a great advantage over the Scarsdale high-school pupil who finds the dogfish on his laboratory desk. Similarly the citizen of Huxley's *Brave New World* who stumbles across a volume of Shakespeare in some vine-grown ruins and squats on a potsherd to read it is in a fairer way of getting at a sonnet than the Harvard sophomore taking English Poetry II.

The educator whose business it is to teach students biology or poetry is unaware of a whole ensemble of relations which exist between the student and the dogfish and between the student and the
Shakespeare sonnet. To put it bluntly: A student who has the desire
to get at a dogfish or a Shakespeare sonnet may have the greatest
difficulty in salvaging the creature itself from the educational package in which it is presented. The great difficulty is that he is not
aware that there is a difficulty; surely, he thinks, in such a fine
classroom, with such a fine textbook, the sonnet must come across!
What's wrong with me?

The sonnet and the dogfish are obscured by two different processes. The sonnet is obscured by the symbolic package which is
formulated not by the sonnet itself but by the *media* through which
the sonnet is transmitted, the media which the educators believe for
some reason to be transparent. The new textbook, the type, the
smell of the page, the classroom, the aluminum windows and the
winter sky, the personality of Miss Hawkins—these media which
are supposed to transmit the sonnet may only succeed in transmitting themselves. It is only the hardiest and cleverest of students who
can salvage the sonnet from this many-tissued package. It is only
the rarest student who knows that the sonnet must be salvaged from
the package. (The educator is well aware that something is wrong,
that there is a fatal gap between the student's learning and the
student's life: The student reads the poem, appears to understand it,
and gives all the answers. But what does he recall if he should happen to read a Shakespeare sonnet twenty years later? Does he recall
the poem or does he recall the smell of the page and the smell of
Miss Hawkins?)

One might object, pointing out that Huxley's citizen reading his
sonnet in the ruins and the Falkland Islander looking at his dogfish
on the beach also receive them in a certain package. Yes, but the
difference lies in the fundamental placement of the student in the
world, a placement which makes it possible to extract the thing
from the package. The pupil at Scarsdale High sees himself placed
as a consumer receiving an experience-package; but the Falkland
Islander exploring his dogfish is a person exercising the sovereign

right of a person in his lordship and mastery of creation. He too could use an instructor and a book and a technique, but he would use them as his subordinates, just as he uses his jackknife. The biology student does not use his scalpel as an instrument; he uses it as a magic wand! Since it is a "scientific instrument," it should do "scientific things."

The dogfish is concealed in the same symbolic package as the sonnet. But the dogfish suffers an additional loss. As a consequence of this double deprivation, the Sarah Lawrence student who scores A in zoology is apt to know very little about a dogfish. She is twice removed from the dogfish, once by the symbolic complex by which the dogfish is concealed, once again by the spoliation of the dogfish by theory which renders it invisible. Through no fault of zoology instructors, it is nevertheless a fact that the zoology laboratory at Sarah Lawrence College is one of the few places in the world where it is all but impossible to see a dogfish.

The dogfish, the tree, the seashell, the American Negro, the dream, are rendered invisible by a shift of reality from concrete thing to theory which Whitehead has called the fallacy of misplaced concreteness. It is the mistaking of an idea, a principle, an abstraction, for the real. As a consequence of the shift, the "specimen" is seen as less real than the theory of the specimen. As Kierkegaard said, once a person is seen as a specimen of a race or a species, at that very moment he ceases to be an individual. Then there are no more individuals but only specimens.

To illustrate: A student enters a laboratory which, in the pragmatic view, offers the student the optimum conditions under which an educational experience may be had. In the existential view, however—that view of the student in which he is regarded not as a receptacle of experience but as a knowing being whose peculiar property it is to see himself as being in a certain situation—the modern laboratory could not have been more effectively designed to conceal the dogfish forever.

The student comes to his desk. On it, neatly arranged by his instructor, he finds his laboratory manual, a dissecting board, instruments, and a mimeographed list:

Exercise 22

Materials: 1 dissecting board
            1 scalpel
            1 forceps
            1 probe
            1 bottle india ink and syringe
            1 specimen of *Squalus acanthias*

The clue to the situation in which the student finds himself is to be found in the last item: 1 specimen of *Squalus acanthias*.

The phrase *specimen of* expresses in the most succinct way imaginable the radical character of the loss of being which has occurred under his very nose. To refer to the dogfish, the unique concrete existent before him, as a "specimen of *Squalus acanthias*" reveals by its grammar the spoliation of the dogfish by the theoretical method. This phrase, *specimen of*, example of, instance of, indicates the ontological status of the individual creature in the eyes of the theorist. The dogfish itself is seen as a rather shabby expression of an ideal reality, the species *Squalus acanthias*. The result is the radical devaluation of the individual dogfish. (The *reductio ad absurdum* of Whitehead's shift is Toynbee's employment of it in his historical method. If a gram of NaCl is referred to by the chemist as a "sample of" NaCl, one may think of it as such and not much is missed by the oversight of the act of being of this particular pinch of salt, but when the Jews and the Jewish religion are understood as—in Toynbee's favorite phrase—a "classical example of" such and such a kind of *Voelkerwanderung*, we begin to suspect that something is being left out.)

If we look into the ways in which the student can recover the dogfish (or the sonnet), we will see that they have in common the stratagem of avoiding the educator's direct presentation of the object as a lesson to be learned and restoring access to sonnet and dogfish as beings to be known, reasserting the sovereignty of knower over known.

In truth, the biography of scientists and poets is usually the story of the discovery of the indirect approach, the circumvention of the educator's presentation—the young man who was sent to the *Tech-*

nikum and on his way fell into the habit of loitering in book stores and reading poetry; or the young man dutifully attending law school who on the way became curious about the comings and goings of ants. One remembers the scene in *The Heart Is a Lonely Hunter* where the girl hides in the bushes to hear the Capehart in the big house play Beethoven. Perhaps she was the lucky one after all. Think of the unhappy souls inside, who see the record, worry about scratches, and most of all worry about whether they are *getting it*, whether they are bona fide music lovers. What is the best way to hear Beethoven: sitting in a proper silence around the Capehart or eavesdropping from an azalea bush?

However it may come about, we notice two traits of the second situation: (1) an openness of the thing before one—instead of being an exercise to be learned according to an approved mode, it is a garden of delights which beckons to one; (2) a sovereignty of the knower—instead of being a consumer of a prepared experience, I am a sovereign wayfarer, a wanderer in the neighborhood of being who stumbles into the garden.

One can think of two sorts of circumstances through which the thing may be restored to the person. (There is always, of course, the direct recovery: A student may simply be strong enough, brave enough, clever enough to take the dogfish and the sonnet by storm, to wrest control of it from the educators and the educational package.) First by ordeal: The Bomb falls; when the young man recovers consciousness in the shambles of the biology laboratory, there not ten inches from his nose lies the dogfish. Now all at once he can see it, directly and without let, just as the exile or the prisoner or the sick man sees the sparrow at his window in all its inexhaustibility; just as the commuter who has had a heart attack sees his own hand for the first time. In these cases, the simulacrum of everydayness and of consumption has been destroyed by disaster; in the case of the bomb, literally destroyed. Secondly, by apprenticeship to a great man: One day a great biologist walks into the laboratory; he stops in front of our student's desk; he leans over, picks up the dogfish, and, ignoring instruments and procedure, probes with a broken fingernail into the little carcass. "Now here is a curious business," he says, ignoring also the proper jargon of the specialty. "Look here how this little duct reverses its direction and drops into the pelvis. Now if you would look into a coelacanth, you would see that it—" And all at once the student can see. The technician and the sophomore who loves his textbook are always offended by the genuine research man because the latter is usually a little vague and always humble before the thing; he doesn't have much use for the equipment or the jargon. Whereas the technician is never vague and never humble before the thing; he holds the thing disposed of by the principle, the formula, the textbook outline; and he thinks a great deal of equipment and jargon.

But since neither of these methods of recovering the dogfish is pedagogically feasible—perhaps the great man even less so than the Bomb—I wish to propose the following educational technique which should prove equally effective for Harvard and Shreveport High School. I propose that English poetry and biology should be taught as usual, but that at irregular intervals, poetry students should find dogfishes on their desks and biology students should find Shakespeare sonnets on their dissecting boards. I am serious in declaring that a Sarah Lawrence English major who began poking about in a dogfish with a bobby pin would learn more in thirty minutes than a biology major in a whole semester; and that the latter upon reading on her dissecting board

> That time of year Thou may'st in me behold
> When yellow leaves, or none, or few, do hang
> Upon those boughs which shake against the cold—
> Bare ruin'd choirs where late the sweet birds sang.

might catch fire at the beauty of it.

The situation of the tourist at the Grand Canyon and the biology student are special cases of a predicament in which everyone finds himself in a modern technical society—a society, that is, in which there is a division between expert and layman, planner and consumer, in which experts and planners take special measures to teach and edify the consumer. The measures taken are measures appropriate to the consumer: The expert and the planner *know* and *plan*, but the consumer *needs* and *experiences*.

There is a double deprivation. First, the thing is lost through its

packaging. The very means by which the thing is presented for consumption, the very techniques by which the thing is made available
as an item of need-satisfaction, these very means operate to remove
the thing from the sovereignty of the knower. A loss of title occurs.
The measures which the museum curator takes to present the thing
to the public are self-liquidating. The upshot of the curator's efforts
are not that everyone can see the exhibit but that no one can see it.
The curator protests: Why are they so indifferent? Why do they
even deface the exhibits? Don't they know it is theirs? But it is not
theirs. It is his, the curator's. By the most exclusive sort of zoning,
the museum exhibit, the park oak tree, is part of an ensemble, a
package, which is almost impenetrable to them. The archaeologist
who puts his find in a museum so that everyone can see it accomplishes the reverse of his expectations. The result of his action
is that no one can see it now but the archaeologist. He would have
done better to keep it in his pocket and show it now and then to
strangers.

The tourist who carves his initials in a public place, which is
theoretically "his" in the first place, has good reasons for doing so,
reasons which the exhibitor and planner know nothing about. He
does so because in his role of consumer of an experience (a "recreational experience" to satisfy a "recreational need") he knows that
he is disinherited. He is deprived of his title over being. He knows
very well that he is in a very special sort of zone in which his only
rights are the rights of a consumer. He moves like a ghost through
schoolroom, city streets, trains, parks, movies. He carves his initials
as a last desperate measure to escape his ghostly role of consumer.
He is saying in effect: I am not a ghost after all; I am a sovereign
person. And he establishes title the only way remaining to him, by
staking his claim over one square inch of wood or stone.

Does this mean that we should get rid of museums? No, but it
means that the sightseer should be prepared to enter into a struggle
to recover a sight from a museum.

The second loss is the spoliation of the thing, the tree, the rock,
the swallow, by the layman's misunderstanding of scientific theory.
He believes that the thing is *disposed of* by theory, that it stands in

the Platonic relation of being a *specimen of* such and such an underlying principle. In the transmission of scientific theory from theorist to layman, the expectation of the theorist is reversed. Instead of the marvels of the universe being made available to the public, the universe is disposed of by theory. The loss of sovereignty takes this form: As a result of the science of botany, trees are not made available to every man. On the contrary. The tree loses its proper density and mystery as a concrete existent and, as merely another *specimen of* a species, becomes itself nugatory.

Does this mean that there is no use taking biology at Harvard and Shreveport High? No, but it means that the student should know what a fight he has on his hands to rescue the specimen from the educational package. The educator is only partly to blame. For there is nothing the educator can do to provide for this need of the student. Everything the educator does only succeeds in becoming, for the student, part of the educational package. The highest role of the educator is the maieutic role of Socrates: to help the student come to himself not as a consumer of experience but as a sovereign individual.

The thing is twice lost to the consumer. First, sovereignty is lost: It is theirs, not his. Second, it is radically devalued by theory. This is a loss which has been brought about by science but through no fault of the scientist and through no fault of scientific theory. The loss has come about as a consequence of the seduction of the layman by science. The layman will be seduced as long as he regards beings as consumer items to be experienced rather than prizes to be won, and as long as he waives his sovereign rights as a person and accepts his role of consumer as the highest estate to which the layman can aspire.

As Mounier said, the person is not something one can study and provide for; he is something one struggles for. But unless he also struggles for himself, unless he knows that there is a struggle, he is going to be just what the planners think he is.

3

METAPHOR AS MISTAKE

IN MISSISSIPPI, coin record players, which are manufactured by Seeburg, are commonly known to Negroes as seabirds.

During the Korean War, one way of saying that someone had been killed was to say that he had bought the farm.

I remember hunting as a boy in south Alabama with my father and brother and a Negro guide. At the edge of some woods we saw a wonderful bird. He flew as swift and straight as an arrow, then all of a sudden folded his wings and dropped like a stone into the woods. I asked what the bird was. The guide said it was a blue-dollar hawk. Later my father told me the Negroes had got it wrong: It was really a blue darter hawk. I can still remember my disappointment at the correction. What was so impressive about the bird was its dazzling speed and the effect of alternation of its wings, as if it were flying by a kind of oaring motion.

As a small boy of six or seven walking the streets of Cambridge I used often to pass little dead-end streets, each with its signpost which at its top read, say, Trowbridge Place or Irving Terrace, and underneath in letters of a different color and on a separate board, the following mysterious legend: Private Way Dangerous Passing. The legend meant of course merely that the City of Cambridge, since it neither built nor maintained the roadbed of this place or this terrace, would not be responsible for injury to life or property sustained through its use. But to me it meant something else. It meant that there was in passing across its mouth a clear and present danger which might, and especially at dusk, suddenly leap out and overcome me. Thus, to say the least of it, I had the regular experience of that heightened, that excited sense of being which we find in poetry, whenever I passed one of those signs.

Misreadings of poetry, as every reader must have found, often give examples of this plausibility of the opposite term. I had at one time a great admiration for that line of Rupert Brooke's about

> *The keen*
> *Impassioned beauty of a great machine,*

a daring but successful image, it seemed to me, for that contrast between the appearance of effort and the appearance of certainty, between forces greater than human and control divine in its foreknowledge, which is what excites one about engines; they have the calm of *beauty* without its complacence, the strength of *passion* without its disorder. So it was a shock to me when I looked at one of the quotations of the line one is always seeing about, and found that the beauty was *unpassioned*, because machines, as all good nature poets know, have no hearts. I still think that a prosaic and intellectually shoddy adjective, but it is no doubt more intelligible than my emendation, and sketches the same group of feelings.

Four of the five examples given above are mistakes: misnamings, misunderstandings, or misrememberings. But they are mistakes which, in each case, have resulted in an authentic poetic experience—what Blackmur calls "that heightened, that excited sense of being"—an experience, moreover, which was notably absent before the mistake was made. I have included the fifth, the Korean War expression "He bought the farm," not because it is a mistake but because I had made a mistake in including it. The expression had struck me as a most mysterious one, peculiarly potent in its laconic treatment of death as a business transaction. But then a kind Korean veteran told me that it may be laconic all right, but he didn't see anything mysterious about it: The farm the G. I. was talking about was six feet of ground. This is probably obvious enough, but I have preserved this example of my own density as instructive in what follows.

It might be useful to look into the workings of these accidental stumblings into poetic meaning, because they exhibit in a striking fashion that particular feature of metaphor which has most troubled philosophers: that it is "wrong"—it asserts of one thing that it is

something else—and further, that its beauty often seems propor-
tionate to its wrongness or outlandishness. Not that the single
linguistic metaphor represents the highest moment of the poetic
imagination; it probably does not. Dante, as Allen Tate reminds us,
uses very few linguistic metaphors. The "greatest thing by far"
which Aristotle had in mind when he spoke of the mastery of the
metaphor as a sign of genius may very well have been the sort of
prolonged analogy which Dante did use, in which the action takes
place among the common things of concrete experience and yet
yields an analogy—by nothing so crude as an allegorization
wherein one thing is designated as standing for another but by the
very density and thingness of the action. As Tate puts it: "Nature
offers the symbolic poet clearly denotable objects in depth and in
the round, which yield the analogies to the higher syntheses." Yet
the fact remains that the linguistic metaphor is, for better or worse,
more peculiarly accessible to the modern mind—it may indeed be
a distinctive expression of modern sensibility. And it has the added
advantage from my point of view of offering a concentrated field for
investigation—here something very big happens in a very small
place.

Metaphor has scandalized philosophers, including both scholastics and semioticists, because it seems to be wrong: It asserts an
identity between two different things. And it is wrongest when it is
most beautiful. It is those very figures of Shakespeare which eighteenth-century critics undertook to "correct" because they had so
obviously gotten off the track logically and were sometimes even
contradictory—it is just those figures which we now treasure most.

This element of outlandishness has resulted in philosophers
washing their hands of beauty and literary men being glad that they
have, in other words, in a divorce of beauty and ontology, with
unhappy consequences to both. The difficulty has been that inquiries into the nature of metaphor have tended to be either literary or
philosophical with neither side having much use for the other. The
subject is divided into its formal and material aspects, with philosophers trying to arrive at the nature of metaphor by abstracting from
all metaphors, beautiful and commonplace, and with critics paying

attention to the particular devices by which a poet brings off his effects. Beauty, the importance attached to beauty, marks the parting
of the ways. The philosopher attends to the formal structure of metaphor, asking such general questions as, What is the relation between metaphor and myth? Is metaphor an analogy of proper or
improper proportionality? and in considering his thesis is notably
insensitive to its beauties. In fact, the examples he chooses to dis-
sect are almost invariably models of tastelessness, such as smiling
meadow, leg of a table, John is a fox. One can't help wondering,
incidentally, if Aristotle's famous examples of "a cup as the shield
of Ares" and "a cup as the shield of Dionysius" didn't sound like
typical philosophers' metaphors to contemporary poets. Literary
men, on the other hand, once having caught sight of the beauty of
metaphor, once having experienced what Barfield called "that old
authentic thrill which binds a man to his library for life," are constrained to deal with beauty alone, with the particular devices
which evoke the beautiful, and let the rest go. If the theorist is insensitive to the beauty of metaphor, the critic is insensitive to its
ontology. To the question, why is this beautiful? the latter will
usually give a *material* answer, pointing to this or that effect which
the poet has made use of. He is unsympathetic—and under-
standably so—to attempts to get hold of art by some larger schema,
such as a philosophy of being—feeling in his bones that when the
cold hand of theory reaches for beauty, it will succeed in grabbing
everything except the beautiful.

Being neither critic nor philosopher, I feel free to venture into
the no-man's-land between the two and to deal with those very metaphors which scandalize the philosopher because they are "wrong"
and scandalize the critic because they are accidental. Philosophers
don't think much of metaphor to begin with and critics can hardly
have much use for folk metaphors, those cases where one stumbles
into beauty without deserving it or working for it. Is it possible to
get a line on metaphor, to figure out by a kind of lay empiricism
what is going on in those poetic metaphors and folk metaphors
where the wrongness most patently coincides with the beauty?

When the Mississippi Negro calls the Seeburg record player a *seabird*, it is not enough to say that he is making a mistake. It is also not enough to say that he is making a colorful and poetic contribution to language. It is less than useless to say that in calling a machine a bird he is regressing into totemism, etc. And it is not even accurate to say that he knows what the thing is and then gives it a picturesque if farfetched name. In some fashion or other, he conceives the machine under the symbol *seabird*, a fashion, moreover, in regard to which we must be very wary in applying the words *right* or *wrong*, *poetic* or *discursive*, etc. Certainly the machine is not a seabird and no one imagines that it is, whatever the semanticists may say. Yet we may make a long cast and guess that in conceiving it as a *seabird*, the namer conceives it with richer overtones of meaning and, in some sense neither literal nor figurative, even as being more truly what it is than under its barbarous title Seeburg automatic coin record player. There is a danger at this point in my being misunderstood as trying to strike a blow for the poetic against the technical, feeling against science, and on the usual aesthetic grounds. But my intention is quite the reverse. I mean to call attention to the rather remarkable fact that in conceiving the machine under the "wrong" symbol *seabird*, we somehow know it better, conceive it in a more plenary fashion, have more immediate access to it, than under its descriptive title. The sooner we get rid of the old quarrel of artistic versus prosaic as constituting the grounds of our preference, the sooner we shall be able to understand what is going on. Given these old alternatives, I'll take the prosaic any day—but what is going on here is of far greater moment.

The moments and elements of this meaning-situation are more easily grasped in the example of the boy seeing the strange bird in Alabama. The first notable moment occurred when he saw the bird. What struck him at once was the extremely distinctive character of the bird's flight—its very great speed, the effect of alternation of the wings, the sudden plummeting into the woods. This so distinctive and incommunicable something—the word which occurs to one is Hopkins's "inscape"—the boy perceived perfectly. It is this very uniqueness which Hopkins specifies in inscape: "the unspeakable stress of pitch, distinctiveness, selving."

The next moment is, for our purposes, the most remarkable of all, because it can receive no explanation in the conventional sign theory of meaning. The boy, having perfectly perceived the flight of the hawk, now suffers a sort of disability, a tension, even a sense of imminence! He puts the peculiar question, *What is that bird?* and puts it importunately. He is really anxious to know. But to know what? What sort of answer does he hope to hear? What in fact is the meaning of his extraordinary question? Why does he want an answer at all? He has already apprehended the hawk in the vividest, most plenary way—a sight he will never forget as long as he lives. What more will he know by having the bird named? (No more, say the semioticists, and he deceives himself if he imagines that he does.)

We have come already to the heart of the question, and a very large question it is. For the situation of the boy in Alabama is very much the same sort of thing as what Cassirer calls the "mythico-religious Urphenomenon." Cassirer, following Usener and Spieth, emphasized the situation in which the primitive comes face to face with something which is both entirely new to him and strikingly distinctive, so distinctive that it might be said to have a *presence*— an oddly shaped termite mound, a particular body of water, a particular abandoned road. And it is in the two ways in which this tensional encounter is resolved that the Urphenomenon is said to beget metaphor and myth. The Tro or momentary god is born of the sense of unformulated presence of the thing; the metaphor arises from the symbolic act in which the emotional cry of the beholder becomes the vehicle by which the thing is conceived, the name of the thing. "In the vocables of speech and in primitive mythic configurations, the same inner process finds its consummation: they are both resolutions of an inner tension, the representation of subjective impulses and excitations in definite object forms and figures."

One recognizes the situation in one's own experience, that is, the metaphorical part of it. Everyone has a blue-dollar hawk in his childhood, especially if he grew up in the South or West, where place names are so prone to poetic corruption. Chaisson Falls, named properly after its discoverer, becomes Chasin' Falls. Scapegoat Mountain, named after some Indian tale, becomes Scrapegoat Mountain—mythic wheels within wheels. And wonderfully: Purgatoire River becomes Picketwire River. A boy grows up in the shadow of a great purple range called Music Mountain after some forgotten episode—perhaps the pioneers' first hoedown after they came through the pass. But this is not how the boy conceives it. When the late afternoon sun strikes the great pile in a certain light, the ridges turn gold, the crevasses are cast into a thundering blue shadow, then it is that he imagines that the wind comes soughing down the gorges with a deep organ note. The name, mysterious to him, tends to validate some equally mysterious inscape of the mountain.

So far so good. But the question on which everything depends and which is too often assumed to be settled without ever having been asked is this: Given this situation and its two characteristics upon which all agree, the peculiar presence or distinctiveness of the object beheld and the peculiar need of the beholder—is this "need" and its satisfaction instrumental or ontological? That is to say, is it the function of metaphor merely to diminish tension, or is it a discoverer of being? Does it fit into the general scheme of need-satisfactions?—and here it doesn't matter much whether we are talking about the ordinary pragmatic view or Cassirer's symbolic form: both operate in an instrumental mode, one, that of biological adaption; the other, according to the necessities of the mythic consciousness. Neither provides for a real knowing, a truth-saying about what a being is. Or is it of such a nature that at least two sorts of realities must be allowed: one, the distinctive something beheld; two, the beholder (actually *two* beholders, one who gives the symbol and one who receives the symbol as meaningful, the Namer and the Hearer), whose special, if imperfect, gift it is to know and affirm this something for what it actually is? The question can't be bracketed, for the two paths lead in opposite directions, and everything one says henceforth on the subject must be understood from one or the other perspective. In this primitive encounter which is at the basis of man's cognitive orientation in the world, either we are trafficking in psychological satisfactions or we are dealing with that

unique joy which marks man's ordainment to being and the knowing of it.

We come back to the "right" and "wrong" of blue-dollar hawk
and blue darter hawk. Is it proper to ask if the boy's delight at the
"wrong" name is a psychological or an ontological delight? And if
the wrong name is cognitive, how is it cognitive? At any rate, we
know that the hawk is named for the boy and he has what he
wants. His mind, which had really suffered a sort of hunger (an
ontological hunger?), now has something to feast on. The bird is,
he is told, a blue-dollar hawk. Two conditions, it will be noticed,
must be met if the naming is to succeed. There must be an authority behind it—if the boy's brother had made up the name on the
spur of the moment, it wouldn't have worked. Naming is more
than a matter of a semantic "rule." But apparently there must also
be—and here is the scandal—an element of obscurity about the
name. The boy can't help but be disappointed by the logical modifier, blue darter hawk—he feels that although he has asked what
the bird *is*, his father has only told him what it *does*. If we will pre-
scind for a moment from premature judgments about the "prelogical" or magic character of the boy's preference, and also forgo the
next question, why is it called a blue-dollar hawk? which the boy
may or may not have put but probably did not because he knew
there was no logical answer the guide could give *—the function of
the answer will become clearer. It is connected with the circumstance that the mysterious name, blue-dollar hawk, is both the
"right" name—for it has been given in good faith by a Namer who
should know and carries an *ipso facto* authority—and a "wrong"
name—for it is not applicable as a logical modifier as blue darter is
immediately and univocally applicable. Blue-dollar is not applicable as a modifier at all, for it refers to a *something else* besides the
bird, a something which occupies the same ontological status as the
bird. Blue darter tells us something about the bird, what it does,
what its color is; blue-dollar tells, or the boy hopes it will tell, what

* Or if the guide did give an answer, it would be its very farfetchedness which
would satisfy: "They calls him that because of the way he balls hisself up and
rolls—"

the bird *is. For this ontological pairing, or, if you prefer, "error" of identification of word and thing, is the only possible way in which the apprehended nature of the bird, its inscape, can be validated as being what it is.* This inscape is, after all, otherwise ineffable. I can describe it, make crude approximations by such words as *darting, oaring, speed, dive,* but none of these will suffice to affirm this so distinctive something which I have seen. This is why, as Marcel has observed, when I ask what something is, I am more satisfied to be given a name even if the name means nothing to me (especially if?), than to be given a scientific classification. Shelley said that poetry pointed out the before unapprehended relations of things. Wouldn't it be closer to the case to say that poetry validates that which has already been privately apprehended but has gone unformulated for both of us?

Without getting over one's head with the larger question of truth, one might still guess that it is extraordinarily rash of the positivist to limit truth to the logical approximation—to say that we cannot know what things are but only how they hang together. The copy theory gives no account of the *what* we are saying *how* about. As to the what: since we are not angels, it is true that we cannot know what it is intuitively and as it is in itself. The modern semioticist is scandalized by the metaphor *Flesh is grass;* but he is also scandalized by the naming sentence *This is flesh.* As Professor Veatch has pointed out, he is confusing an instrument of knowing with what is known. The word *flesh* is not this solid flesh, and this solid flesh is not grass. But unless we name it *flesh* we shall not know it at all, and unless we call flesh grass, we shall not know how it is with flesh. The semioticist leaves unexplained the act of knowing. He imagines naïvely that I know what this is and then give it a label, whereas the truth is, as Cassirer has shown so impressively, that I cannot know anything at all unless I symbolize it. We can only conceive being, sidle up to it by laying something else alongside. We approach the thing not directly but by pairing, by apposing symbol and thing. Is it not premature to say with the mythist that when the primitive calls the lightning serpentine he conceives it as a snake and is logically wrong? Both truth and error may be served here, error in so far as the lightning is held to participate magically in snakeness, truth in so far as the conception of snake may allow the privately apprehended inscape of the lightning to be formulated. I would have a horror of finding myself allied with those who in the name of instrumentality or inner warmth or whatnot would so attenuate and corrupt truth that it meant nothing. But an analysis of the symbol relation reveals aspects of truth which go far beyond the notion of structural similarity which the symbolic logicians speak of. Two other traits of the thing are discovered and affirmed: one, that it *is*; two, that it is *something*.

Everything depends on this distinction between the thing privately apprehended and the thing apprehended and validated for you and me by naming. But is it proper to make such a distinction? Is there any difference, no difference, or the greatest possible difference, between that which I privately apprehend and that which I apprehend and you validate by naming in such a way that I am justified in hoping that you "mean" that very ineffable thing?

For at the basis of the beautiful metaphor—which one begins to see as neither logically "right" nor "wrong" but analogous—at the basis of that heightened sensibility of the poetic experience, there is always the hope that this secret apprehension of my own, which I cannot call knowing because I do not even know that I know it, has a chance of being validated by what you have said.

There must be a space between name and thing, for otherwise the private apprehension is straitened and oppressed. What is required is that the thing be both sanctioned and yet allowed freedom to be what it is. Heidegger said that the essence of truth is freedom. The essence of metaphorical truth and the almost impossible task of the poet is, it seems to me, to name unmistakably and yet to name by such a gentle analogy that the thing beheld by both of us may be truly formulated for what it is.

Blackmur's and Empson's examples are better "mistakes" than mine. The street sign in Cambridge, *Private Way Dangerous Passing*, misunderstood, allowed the exciting possibility that it was one's own secret forebodings about the little dead-end streets that was meant. But for all of Blackmur's unsurpassed analysis of this myste-

rious property of language, I think it unfortunate that he has
chosen to call it "gesture," in view of the semioticist's use of the
word to denote a term in a stimulus-response sequence (i.e.,
Mead's "conversation of gesture")—because this is exactly what it is
not. It is a figurational and symbolic import in that sense which is
farthest removed from gestural intercourse (such as the feint and
parry of Mead's two boxers). It is, in fact, only when the gesture,
word, or thing is endowed with symbolic meaning, that is, united
with a significance other than itself, that it takes on the properties
which Blackmur attributes to it.

In Empson's examples, the beauty of the line depends on an actual misreading of what the poet wrote or on a corruption of the
spelling. In the former case the poetic instincts of the reader are
better than the poet's. What is important is that the reader's "mistake" has rescued the poet's figure from the logical and univocal
similarity which the poet despite his best efforts could not escape
and placed it at a mysterious and efficacious distance. The remem-
bering of Brooke's *unpassioned machine* as *impassioned machine* is
a good example of this. Another is a line of Nash which may or
may not have been a mistake. What matters for our purpose is that
it could have been.

> Beauty is but a flower
> Which wrinkles will devour.
> Brightness falls from the air.

There is a cynical theory, Empson writes, that Nash wrote or
meant *hair*:

> Brightness falls from the hair.

which is appropriate to the context, adequate poetically, but less
beautiful. Why? I refer to Professor Empson's analysis and venture
only one comment. It may be true, as he says, that the very Pre-
Raphaelite vagueness of the line allows the discovery of something
quite definite. In the presence of the lovely but obscure metaphor,
I exist in the mode of hope, hope that the poet may mean such and
such, and joy at any further evidence that he does. What Nash's

line may have stumbled upon (if it is a mistake) is a perfectly definite but fugitive something—an inscape familiar to one and yet an inscape in bondage because I have never formulated it and it has never been formulated for me. Could the poet be referring to that particular time and that particular phenomenon of clear summer evenings when the upper air holds the last trembling light of day: one final moment of a soft diffused brilliance, then everything *falls* into dusk?

But Empson's most entertaining mistake is

> Queenlily June with a rose in her hair
> Moves to her prime with a languorous air.

For what saves the verse from mediocrity is the misreading of queenlily as Queen Lily, where the poet had intended the rather dreary adverb of queenly! Again I defer to Professor Empson's *material* analysis of what gives the misread line its peculiar charm. The question I would raise, in regard to this and many other examples in *Seven Types of Ambiguity*, has to do with Empson's main thesis. This thesis is, of course, that beauty derives from ambiguity—in this particular case, the felt possibility and interaction of the *two* readings of *queenlily*. But I submit that in this and other examples, as I read it and apparently as Empson read it, *the intended adverbial reading is completely overlooked!* The line is read with Queenlily and is charming; it only belatedly occurs to one, if it occurs at all, that the poet meant the adverb—and I feel certain Empson is not maintaining that I was aware of the adverb all along but "unconsciously." What one wonders, in this and in many other of Empson's quotations, is whether it is the ambiguity which is the operative factor, or *whether the beauty does not derive exclusively from the obscure term of the ambiguity*, the logically "wrong" but possibly analogous symbol.

In all those cases where the poet strains at the limits of the logical and the univocal, and when as a result his figure retains a residue of the logical and so has two readings—the univocal and the analogous—is it not in the latter that he has struck gold? We must be careful not to confuse ambiguity, which means equivocity, with true analogy, simply because both are looked upon as more or less vague. It is always possible, of course, to do what Empson does so well with his obscure metaphors, that is, to cast about for all the different interpretations the line will allow. But does the beauty of the line reside in its susceptibility to two or more possible readings or in the possibility of a *single* figurational meaning, which is the less analyzable as it is the more beautiful?

I can't help thinking, incidentally, that this hunt for the striking catachrestic metaphor in a poet of another time, such as Chaucer or Shakespeare, is a very treacherous game. For both the old poet and his modern reader are at the mercy of time's trick of canceling the poet's own hard-won figures and setting up new ones of its own. A word, by the very fact of its having been lost to common usage or by its having undergone a change in meaning, is apt to acquire thereby an unmerited potency.

One is aware of skirting the abyss as soon as one begins to repose virtue in the obscure. Once we eliminate the logical approximation, the univocal figure, as unpoetic and uncreative of meaning—is it not then simply an affair of trotting out words and images more or less at random in the hope of arriving at an obscure, hence efficacious, analogy? and the more haphazard the better, since mindfulness, we seem to be saying, is of its very nature self-defeating? Such in fact is the credo of the surrealists: "To compare two objects, as remote from one another in character as possible, or by any other method put them together in a sudden and striking fashion, this remains the highest task to which poetry can aspire." * There is something to this. If, as so many modern poets appear to do, one simply shuffles words together, words plucked from as diversified contexts as possible, one will get some splendid effects. Words are potent agents and the sparks are bound to fly. But it is a losing game. For there is missing that essential element of the meaning situation, the authority and intention of the Namer. Where the Namer means nothing or does not know what

---

* André Breton, quoted by Richards in *The Philosophy of Rhetoric*.

he means or the Hearer does not think he knows what he means, the Hearer can hardly participate in a cointention. Intersubjectivity fails. Once the good faith of the Namer is so much as called into question, the jig is up. There is no celebration or hope of celebration of a thing beheld in common. One is only trafficking in the stored-up energies of words, hard won by meaningful usage. It is a pastime, this rolling out the pretty marbles of word-things to see one catch and reflect the fire of another, a pleasant enough game but one which must eventually go stale.

It is the cognitive dimension of metaphor which is usually overlooked, because cognition is apt to be identified with conceptual and discursive knowing. Likeness and difference are canons of discursive thought, but analogy, the mode of poetic knowing, is also cognitive. Failure to recognize the discovering power of analogy can only eventuate in a noncognitive psychologistic theory of metaphor. There is no knowing, there is no Namer and Hearer, there is no world beheld in common; there is only an interior "transaction of contexts" in which psychological processes interact to the reader's titillation.

The peculiar consequences of judging poetic metaphor by discursive categories are especially evident in Professor Richards's method. Lord Kames had criticized the metaphor "steep'd" in Othello's speech

> Had it pleas'd heaven
> To try me with affliction, had he rain'd
> All kinds of sores, and shames, on my bare head,
> Steep'd me in poverty to the very lips,

by saying that "the resemblance is too faint to be agreeable—Poverty must here be conceived to be a fluid which it resembles not in any manner." Richards goes further: "It is not a case of lack of resemblances but too much diversity, too much sheer oppositeness. For Poverty, the Tenor, is a state of deprivation, of desiccation; but the vehicle—the sea or vat in which Othello is to be steep'd—gives an instance of superfluity . . ." True, disparity as well as resemblance works in metaphor, but Richards says of this instance of disparity: "I do not myself find any defence of the word except this, which seems indeed quite sufficient—as dramatic necessities commonly are—that Othello is himself horribly disordered, that the utterance is part of the 'storm of horrour and outrage.' " Thus, Professor Richards gives "steep'd" a passing mark, but only because Othello is crazy. He may be right: The figure is extravagant, in a sense "wrong," yet to me defensible even without a plea of insanity. The only point I wish to make is that there is another cognitive ground on which it can be judged besides that of logical rightness and wrongness, univocal likeness and unlikeness. Judged accordingly, it must always be found wanting—an eighteenth-century critic would have corrected it. But do the alternatives lie between logical sense and nonsense? Or does such a view overlook a third way, the relation of analogy and its cognitive dimension? In the mode of analogy, "steep'd" is not only acceptable, it is striking; "steep'd" may be wrong univocally but right analogically. True, poverty is, logically speaking, a deprivation; but in its figuration it is a veritable something, very much a milieu with a smell and taste all its own, in which one is all too easily steep'd. Poverty is defined as a lack but is conceived as a something. What is univocally unlike in every detail may exhibit a figurative proportionality which is more generative of meaning than the cleverest simile.

An unvarying element in the situation is a pointing at by context. There must occur a preliminary meeting of minds and a mutually intended subject before anything can be said at all. The context may vary all the way from a literal pointing-by-finger and naming in the aboriginal naming act, to the pointing context of the poem which specifies the area where the metaphor is to be applied. There is a reciprocal relationship between the selectivity of the pointing and the univocity of the metaphor: The clearer the context and the more unmistakable the pointing, the greater latitude allowed the analogy of the metaphor. The aboriginal naming act is, in this sense, the most obscure and the most creative of metaphors; no modern poem was ever as obscure as Miss Sullivan's naming water *water* for Helen Keller. A perfectly definite something is

pointed at and given a name, a sound or a gesture to which it bears
only the most tenuous analogical similarities.*

Given the situation of naming and hearing, there can only be
one of three issues to an act of pointing at and naming. What is
said will either be old, that is, something we already know and
know quite overtly; or something new, and if it is utterly new, I can
only experience bafflement; or new-old, that is, something that I
had privately experienced but which was not available to me because it had never been formulated and rendered intersubjective.
Metaphor is the true maker of language.

The creative relationship of *inscape*, the distinctive reality as it is
apprehended, and the distanced metaphor is illustrated by Hopkins's nature metaphors. His favorite pursuit in the nature journals
is the application of striking (sometimes strained) like-yet-unlike
metaphors to nature inscapes. There are some pleasing effects. A
bolt of lightning is

> a straight stroke, broad like a stroke with chalk and liquid, as if the
> blade of an oar just stripped open a ribbon scar in smooth water and it
> caught the light.

---

* The old debate, started in the *Cratylus*, goes on as lively as ever: what is the
relation between the name and the thing, between the word *green* and the color
green, between *slice* and slice, *tree* and tree? Most linguists would probably say there
is no relation, that the name is purely an arbitrary convention (except in a few cases
like *boom*), that any seeming resemblance is false onomatopoeia (no matter how
much you might imagine that *slice* resembles and hence expresses the act of slicing,
it really does not).

But here again, do likeness and unlikeness exhaust the possibilities?

Apparently not. Curtius remarks that "despite all change, a conservative instinct is
discernible in language. All the peoples of our family from the Ganges to the Atlan-
tic designate the notion of standing by the phonetic group *sta-*; in all of them the
notion of flowing is linked with the group *plu*, with only slight modifications. This
cannot be an accident. Assuredly the same notion has remained associated with the
same sounds through all the millennia, because the peoples felt a certain *inner connection* between the two, i.e., because of an instinct to express this notion by these
particular sounds. The assertion that the oldest words presuppose some relation between sounds and the representations they designate has often been ridiculed. It is
difficult, however, to explain the origin of language without such assumptions."

It is this "inner connection" which concerns us. The sounds *plu* and *sta*, which
could hardly be more different from the acts of flowing and standing, must nevertheless exhibit some mysterious connection which the mind fastens upon, a connection
which, since it is not a kind of univocal likeness, must be a kind of analogy.

We are aware that the effect is achieved by applying the notions of water and scars to lightning, the most unwaterlike or unscarlike thing imaginable. But are these metaphors merely pleasing or shocking or do they discover?—discover an aspect of the thing which had gone unformulated before?

Clouds are called variously bars, rafters, prisms, mealy, scarves, curds, rocky, a river (of dull white cloud), rags, veils, tatters, bosses.

The sea is

> paved with wind . . . bushes of foam
> Chips of foam blew off and gadded about without weight in the air.
> Straps of glassy spray.

In these metaphors both the likeness and unlikeness are striking and easily discernible. One has the impression, moreover, that their discovering power has something to do with their unlikeness, the considerable space between tenor and vehicle. Hard things like rocks, bosses, chips, glass, are notably unlike clouds and water; yet one reads

> Chips of foam blew off and gadded about

with a sure sense of validation.

If we deviate in either direction, toward a more univocal or accustomed likeness or toward a more mysterious unlikeness, we feel at once the effect of what Richards calls the tension of the bow, both the slackening and tightening of it. When one reads fleecy clouds or woolly clouds, the effect is slack indeed. Vehicle and tenor are totally interarticulated: clouds are ordinarily conceived as being fleecy; fleecy is what clouds are (just as checkered is what a career is). You have told me nothing. Fleecy cloud, leg of a table, are tautologies, a regurgitation of something long since digested. But

> A straight river of dull white cloud

is lively. One feels both knowledgeable and pleased. But

> A white shire of cloud

is both more interesting and more obscure. The string of the bow is definitely tightened. The mind is off on its favorite project, a casting about for analogies and connections. Trusting in the good faith of the Namer, I begin to wonder if he means thus and so—this particular sort of cloud. The only "shire" I know is a geographical area and what I more or less visualize is a towering cumulus of an irregular shire-shape.

Two levels of analogy-making can be distinguished here. There is the level of metaphor proper, the saying about one thing that it is something else: one casts about to see *how* a cloud can be a shire, and in hitting on an analogy, one validates an inscape of cloud. But there is the more primitive level of naming, of applying a sound to a thing, and of the certification of some sounds as being analogous to the thing without being like it (as in the mysterious analogy between *plu* and flowing, *sta* and standing). Thus *shire* may be applicable to a certain kind of cloud *purely as a sound* and without a symbolized meaning of its own. For as it happens, concrete nouns beginning with *sh* often refer to objects belonging to a class of segmented or sectioned or roughly oblong flattened objects, a "geographical" class: shape, sheath, shard, sheet, shelf, shield, shire, shoal, shovel, shroud, etc. One speculates that the vocable *sh*—is susceptible of this particular spatial configuration. (I easily imagine that the sound *sh* has a flatness or parallelness about it.) This relation is very close to the psychological phenomenon of synesthesia, the transsensory analogy in which certain sounds, for example, are characteristically related to certain sounds—*blue* to color blue (could blue ever be called *yellow?*).

To summarize: The examples given of an accidental blundering into authentic poetic experience both in folk mistakes and in mistaken readings of poetry are explored for what light they may shed on the function of metaphor in man's fundamental symbolic orientation in the world. This "wrongness" of metaphor is seen to be not a vagary of poets but a special case of that mysterious "error" which is the very condition of our knowing anything at all. This "error," the act of symbolization, is itself the instrument of knowing and is an error only if we do not appreciate its intentional character. If we

do not take note of it, or if we try to exorcise it as a primitive residue, we shall find ourselves on the horns of the same dilemma
which has plagued philosophers since the eighteenth century. The
semanticists, on the one horn, imply that we know as the angels
know, directly and without mediation (although saying in the next
breath that we have no true knowledge of reality); all that remains is
to name what we know and this we do by a semantic "rule"; but
they do not and cannot say how we know. The behaviorists, on the
other, imply that we do not know at all but only respond and that
even art is a mode of sign-response; but they do not say how they
know this. But we do know, not as the angels know and not as dogs
know but as men, who must know one thing through the mirror of
another.

4

THE MAN ON THE TRAIN

THERE IS no such thing, strictly speaking, as a literature of alienation. In the re-presenting of alienation the category is reversed and becomes something entirely different. There is a great deal of difference between an alienated commuter riding a train and this same commuter reading a book about an alienated commuter riding a train. (On the other hand, Huck Finn's drifting down the river is somewhat the same as a reader's reading about Huck Finn drifting down the river.) The nonreading commuter exists in true alienation, which is unspeakable; the reading commuter rejoices in the speakability of his alienation and in the new triple alliance of himself, the alienated character, and the author. His mood is affirmatory and glad: Yes! that is how it is!—which is an aesthetic reversal of alienation. It is related that when Kafka read his work aloud to his friends, they would all roar with laughter until tears came to their eyes. Neither Kafka nor his reader is alienated in the movement of art, for each achieves a reversal through its re-presenting. To picture a truly alienated man, picture a Kafka to whom it had never occurred to write a word. The only literature of alienation is an alienated literature, that is, a bad art, which is no art at all. An Erle Stanley Gardner novel is a true exercise in alienation. A man who finishes his twentieth Perry Mason is that much nearer total despair than when he started.

I hasten to define what I mean by alienation, which has become almost as loose an epithet as existentialism (if you do not agree with me, it is probably because you are alienated). I mean that whereas one commuter may sit on the train and feel himself quite at home, seeing the passing scene as a series of meaningful projects full of signs which he reads without difficulty, another commuter, although he has no empirical reason for being so, although he has satisfied the same empirical needs as commuter A, is alienated. To say the least, he is bored; to say the most, he is in pure anxiety; he is horrified at his surroundings—he might as well be passing through a lunar landscape and the signs he sees are absurd or at least ambiguous. (It will not be necessary at this point to consider the further possibility that commuter A's tranquillity is no guarantee against alienation, that in fact he may be more desperately lost to himself than B in the sense of being anonymous, the "one" of "one says.")

Alienation, in its turn, is itself a reversal of the objective-empirical. This is a purely existential reversal and has nothing to do with art. It is very simply illustrated in the case of the alienated commuter. This man—though he will have met every "need" which can be abstracted by the objective-empirical method—sexual needs, nutritional, emotional, in-group needs, needs for a productive orientation, creativity, community service—this man may nevertheless be alienated. Moreover he is apt to be alienated in proportion to his staking everything on the objective-empirical. By his alienation, the objective-empirical categories are reversed. What causes anxiety in the one is the refuge from anxiety in the other. For example, speaking objectively-empirically, it is often said that it is no wonder people are anxious nowadays, what with the possibility that the Bomb might fall any minute. The Bomb would seem to be sufficient reason for anxiety; yet as it happens the reverse is the truth. The contingency "what if the Bomb should fall?" is not only not a cause of anxiety in the alienated man but is one of his few remaining refuges from it. When everything else fails, we may always turn to our good friend just back from Washington or Moscow, who obliges us with his sober second thoughts—"I can tell you this much, I am profoundly disturbed . . ."—and each of us has what he came for, the old authentic thrill of the Bomb and the Coming of the Last Days. Like Ortega's romantic, the heart's desire of the alienated man is to see vines sprouting through the masonry.

The real anxiety question, the question no one asks because no one wants to, is the reverse: What if the Bomb should *not* fall? What then?

The estrangement of the existing self is not capable of being grasped by the objective-empirical method simply because the former is specified by the latter as its reverse. I would like to avoid a polemical tone here. I do not wish to be understood as attacking the objective-empirical method and contemning its truth and beauty and fruitfulness—which the European existentialists do indiscriminately while at the same time living very well on its fruits— but as stating the fact of the reversal: It does happen that the *Dasein* or existing self characteristically reverses objective-empirical sociological categories and discovers in them not the principle of its health but the root source of its alienation.

To illustrate the specific character of the reversal: it is just when the Method tries to grasp and categorize the existential trait that it is itself reversed and becomes a powerful agent not of progress but of alienation. It is just when the alienated commuter reads books on mental hygiene which abstract immanent goals from existence that he comes closest to despair. One has only to let the mental-health savants set forth their own ideal of sane living, the composite reader who reads their books seriously and devotes every ounce of his strength to the pursuit of the goals erected: emotional maturity, inclusiveness, productivity, creativity, belongingness—there will emerge, far more faithfully than I could portray him, the candidate for suicide. Take these two sentences that I once read in a book on mental hygiene: "The most profound of all human needs, the prime requisite for successful living, is to be emotionally inclusive. Socrates, Jesus, Buddha, St. Francis were emotionally inclusive." These words tremble with anxiety and alienation, even though I would not deny that they are, in their own eerie way, true. The alienated commuter shook like a leaf when he read them.

To go back to the aesthetic reversal of alienation by art: Literature, like a polarizing crystal, makes a qualitative division among existential traits accordingly as it transmits some more or less intact, reverses some, and selectively polarizes others, transmitting certain elements and canceling others. Alienation is reversed: There can no more be a re-presenting of alienation than Kierkegaard's category of trial, for it, like trial, absolutely transcends the objective-empirical; Job's and Abraham's trials are lost in the telling. The categories, rotation and repetition, on the other hand, not being purely existential but aesthetic-existential, are transmitted. Yet they are transmitted with a difference. Rotation is conveyed more or less intact, whereas repetition is accomplished only by a mediate act of identification. Thus, reading about Huck going down the river or Tenente Frederic Henry escaping from the carabinieri in A *Farewell to Arms* is somewhat like going down the river and escaping. It is by virtue of the fact that rotation is the quest for the new as the new, the reposing of all hope in what may lie around the bend, a mode of experience which is much the same in the reading as in the experiencing. But repetition, in order to occur, requires a more radical identification. Thus when Charles Gray in Marquand's *Point of No Return* returns to Clyde, Massachusetts, or when Tom Wolfe's hero returns to the shabby boardinghouse in St. Louis, the reader can experience repetition only if he imagines that he too is a native of Clyde or has lived in St. Louis. (He doesn't have to imagine he is Huck—it is he, the reader, who is drifting down the river.)

The moments of rotation and repetition are of such peculiar interest to the contemporary alienated consciousness because they represent the two obvious alternatives or deliverances from alienation. The man riding a train—or his analogues, Huck on a raft, Philip Marlowe in a coupé—is of an extraordinary interest because this situation realizes in a concrete manner the existential placement of all three modes, alienation, rotation, and repetition. The train rider can, as in the case of the commuter on the eight-fifteen, actually incarnate, as we shall see in a moment, the elements of alienation. On the other hand, the fugitive in the English thriller who catches the next available train from Waterloo station and who finds himself going he knows not where, experiences true rotation; equally, the exile or amnesiac who, thinking himself on a routine journey, suddenly catches sight of a landmark which strikes to the heart and who with every turn of the wheel comes that much closer to the answer to who am I?—this one has stumbled into pure repetition (as when Captain Ryder alighted from his blacked-out train to find himself—back in Brideshead).

To begin with, the alienated commuter riding the eight-fifteen actually finds himself in a situation in which his existential placement in the world, the subject-object split, the *pour soi–en soi*, is physically realized. In an absolute partitioning of reality, he is both in the world he is traveling through and not in it. Beyond all doubt he is in Metuchen, New Jersey, during the few seconds the train stops there, yet in what a strange sense is he there—he passes through without so much as leaving his breath behind. Even if this is the one thousandth time he has stopped there, even if he knows a certain concrete pillar better than anything else in the world, yet he remains as total a stranger to Metuchen as if he had never been there. He passes through, the transient possible I through the static indefeasible It. The landscape through which he passes for the thousandth time has all the traits of the *en soi*; it is dense, sodden, impenetrable, and full of itself; it is exactly what it is, no more, no less, and as such it is boring in the original sense of the word. It is worse than riding a subway through blackness, because the familiar things one sees are not neutral or nugatory; they are aggressively assertive and thrust themselves upon one: they bore. Whereas beyond the subway window there is nothing at all. As is especially noticeable on the subway, the partition exists as well between oneself and one's fellow commuters, a partition which is impenetrable by anything short of disaster. It is only in the event of a disaster, the wreck of the eight-fifteen, that one is *enabled* to discover his fellow commuter as a comrade; thus, the favorite scene of novels of good will in the city: the folks who discover each other and help each other when disaster strikes. (Do we have here a clue to the secret longing for the Bomb and the Last Days? Does the eschatological thrill conceal the inner prescience that it will take a major catastrophe to break the partition?)

Actually the partition is closer than this. It exists as well between me and my own body. One's own hand participates in the everydayness of the *en soi* and is both dense and invisible; it is only on the rarest occasions that one may see his own hand, either by a deliberate effort of seeing, as in the case of Sartre's Roquentin, or through the agency of disaster, as when the commuter on the New York Central had a heart attack and had to be taken off at Fordham station: Upon awakening, he gazed with astonishment at his own hand, turning it this way and that as though he had never seen it before.

To illustrate the zoning of the alienated train ride: Suppose the eight-fifteen breaks down between Mount Vernon and New Rochelle, breaks down beside a yellow cottage with a certain lobular stain on the wall which the commuter knows as well as he knows the face of his wife. Suppose he takes a stroll along the right-of-way while the crew is at work. To his astonishment he hears someone speak to him; it is a man standing on the porch of the yellow house. They talk and the man offers to take him the rest of the way in his car. The commuter steps into the man's back yard and enters the house. This trivial event, which is of no significance objectively-empirically, is of considerable significance aesthetically-existentially. A zone crossing has taken place. It is of extraordinary interest to the commuter that he may step *out* of the New York Central right-of-way and into the yellow house. It is of extraordinary interest to stand in the kitchen and hear from the owner of the house who he is, how he came to build the house, etc. For he, the commuter, has done the impossible: he has stepped through the mirror into the *en soi*.

Zone crossing is of such great moment to the alienated I because the latter is thereby able to explore the It while at the same time retaining his option of noncommitment. The movie *It Happened One Night* stumbled into this fertile field when it showed Clark and Claudette crossing zones without a trace of involvement, from bus to hitchhiking to meadow to motel. It is a triumph of rotation to be able to wander into Farmer Jones's barnyard, strike up an acquaintance, be taken for a human being, then pass on impassible as a ghost. The reason the formula ran into diminishing returns was that this particular zone crossing created its own zone, and its imitators, instead of zone crossing, were following a well-worn track.

A more memorable zone crossing was Hemingway's fisherman leaving the train in the middle of the Minnesota woods and striking out on his own. To leave the fixed right-of-way at a random point and enter the trackless woods is a superb rotation. Swedes know this better than anyone else. Travelers in Sweden report two national traits: boredom and love of the North country—alienation and rotation. This penchant for taking to the woods reverses the objective-empirical: when Swedish planners took note of this particular "recreational need" and provided wooded areas in the vicinity of Stockholm, the Swedes were not interested. And it is no coincidence that when the Swedish government did take measures to set aside the North country for hiking, there occurred a sudden increase of Swedish tourists in quaint out-of-the-way *English* villages.

2

The road is better than the inn, said Cervantes—and by this he meant that rotation is better than the alienation of everydayness. The best part of Huckleberry Finn begins when Huck escapes from his old man's shack and ends when he leaves the river for good at Phelps farm. Mark Twain hit upon an admirable rotation, whether he knew it or not (and probably did not or he would not have written the last hundred pages). A man who sets out adrift down the Mississippi has thrice over insured the integrity of his possibility without the least surrender of access to actualization—there is always that which lies around the bend. He is, to begin with, on water, the mobile element; he is, moreover, adrift, the random on the mobile; but most important, he is on the Mississippi, which, during the entire journey, flows *between* states: he is in neither Illinois nor Missouri but in a privileged zone between the two. To appreciate the nicety of this placement, consider the extremes. A less radical possibility would be his floating down the Hudson River; one sees at once how rotation is hindered here: One remains entirely *within* New York State; there is no zoning; there is no sense of pushing free of land into a privileged zone of the mobile. No one ever had the ambition of floating down the Hudson on a raft. On the other hand, the more radical possibility, his finding himself adrift on the ocean, is too rarified a possibility for rotation. The absolutely new, the exotic landfall, is too foreign to the *pour soi* to exhibit by contrast the freedom of the self. Compare, for example, the fantastic rotation of Tom Sawyer floating in his balloon over the Sahara in his latter-day adventures; compare this with Huck and Jim slipping by Cairo at night. The former is the standard comic-book rotation; the latter is a remarkable coup, the snatching of freedom from under the very nose of the *en soi*. A Cairo businessman sits reading his paper, immured in everydayness, while not two hundred yards away Huck slips by in the darkness. Huck has his cake and eats it: he wins pure possibility without losing access to actualization. The *en soi* is never farther away than the nearest towhead; the sweetest foray into the actual is a landing in the willows and a striking out across the fields to the nearest town. It is noteworthy that the success of his sojourns ashore has as its condition the keeping open of a line of retreat to the beachhead where the raft lies hidden—and in fact the times ashore do most characteristically and happily end disastrously with a headlong flight from some insuperable difficulty and a casting off into the mainstream, leaving the pursuers shaking their fists on the bank. What does happen when the beachhead is lost for good and Huck and Jim are stranded ashore? Rotation and possibility are both lost and in their stead we have dreary Tom and his eternal play-acting.

The role of Jim should not be overlooked. The chance encounter with Jim on Jackson's Island is a prepuberty version of *la solitude à deux*. When the Bomb falls and the commuter picks his way through the rubble of Fifth Avenue to Central Park, there to take up his abode in an abandoned tool shed à la Robert Nathan, everything depends upon his meeting *her* and meeting her accidentally (or, as they say in Hollywood, meeting cute: note here the indispensability of chance as an ingredient of rotation; he may not seek an introduction to her but must become entangled in her wirehaired's leash). To be sure, a certain narrow range of solitary rotation is possible: Huck's life on Jackson's Island before meeting

Jim is very fine, but after catching the fish, eating it, taking a nap, that's about the end of it. He meets Jim none too soon. Crusoe, it is true, achieved a memorable rotation, but it is only on the condition of the abiding possibility of the encounter; at any moment and around the next curve of the beach, he may meet . . .

Rotation may occur by a trafficking in zones, the privileged zone of possibility, which is the river in Huck Finn; the vagrancy zones of Steinbeck: ditches, vacant lots, whorehouses, weed-grown boilers, packing cases; the parabourgeois zone of *You Can't Take It with You* with Jean Arthur and her jolly eccentric family (an exceedingly short-lived rotation: what could be drearier than the madcap adventures of these jolly folks experienced a second time?). Or it may occur simply by getting clean away. Huck's escape is complete because he is thought actually dead. The getting clean away requires a moral as well as a physical freedom. Rotation is eminently attractive to Pepper Young in the soap opera, living out his life with Linda in Elmwood—yet he may not simply walk out one fine day. If, however, on his annual trip to Chicago for Father Young the train should be wrecked and he should develop amnesia—that is another matter. A notable escape is managed by Frederic Henry in his getting clean away from the carabinieri at Caporetto by diving into the river. Later he boards a freight car carrying guns packed in grease. A very fine rotation occurs here: "—it was very fine under the canvas and pleasant with the guns." What is notable about Henry's escape is that it is rotation raised to the third power. First, there is the American in Bohemia, in Paris, in Pamplona: he has gotten clean away from the everydayness of Virginia; next, there is *el inglés* lying on a needle-covered forest floor in the Spanish Civil War, or Tenente Henry in the Italian infantry: he has gotten clean away from the everydayness of Bohemia; next, there is Tenente Henry escaping the everydayness of the Italian army. (And later even to the fourth power: Catherine and the baby die and he gets clean away from them and walks back to the hotel in the rain. This last is a concealed reversal, for although it is offered as an undesired turn of events, a tragedy, it clearly would not have done for Catherine and Henry to have settled down and raised a family. Although Hemingway sets forth the end as tragic, it was also very fine walking away in the rain.)

Hemingway's literature of rotation, escape within escape, approaches asymptotically the term of all rotation: amnesia. Amnesia is the perfect device of rotation and is available to anyone and everyone, in the same way that double suicide is available to any and all tragedians. Whether it is Smitty in *Random Harvest* on his way to Liverpool or Pepper on his way to Chicago, amnesia is the supreme rotation. Who can blame the soap-opera writer if he returns to it again and again, even after he has been kidded about it? Life in Elmwood with Linda and Father and Mother Young achieves a degree of alienation such as was never dreamed of by Joseph K. in Mitteleuropa; the difference between them is nothing less than the difference between the despair that knows itself and the despair that does not know itself. Since Bohemia is despised by Pepper, since also the zone-sanctuaries of the Mississippi, Steinbeck's friendly whorehouse, Nathan's tool shed, and the Bomb are closed to him; and since the obvious alternative to life in Elmwood, suicide, is also unacceptable—only amnesia remains. From the literal everydayness of the soap opera, amnesia is the one, the only, the perfect rotation. Yet medically speaking, amnesia, attractive though it is as a rotative device, is not its final asymptotic term. For, though it is very gratifying for Pepper to come to himself while walking in Grant Park, with no recollection of Linda, and though it is all very well for him to meet *her*, the stranger, to conceal her from the police after she, in an act of desperation, snatches a purse—it is only a question of time before everydayness overtakes them. Whether it is Elmwood or the tool shed in the park, Linda or the fugitive girl, Pepper being Pepper, hardly a week passes before he is again in the full grip of everydayness and once more a candidate for suicide. Perfect rotation could only be achieved by a progressive amnesia in which the forgetting kept pace with time so that every corner turned, every face seen, is a rotation. Every night with Linda is a night with a stranger, the lustful rotative moment of the double plot in which one man is mistaken for another and is called upon to be husband to the beautiful neglected wife of the other. One man's everydayness is another man's rotation.

The modern literature of alienation is in reality the triumphant reversal of alienation through its re-presenting. It is not an existential solution such as Hölderlin's Homecoming or Heidegger's openness to being, but is an aesthetic victory of comradeliness, a recognition of plight in common. Its motto is not "I despair and do not know that I despair" but "At least we know that we are lost to ourselves"—which is very great knowledge indeed. A literature of rotation, however, does not effect the reversal of its category, for it is nothing more nor less than one mode of escape from alienation. Its literary re-presenting does not change its character in the least, for it is, to begin with, the category of the New. Both Kierkegaard and Marcel mention rotation but as an experiential, a travel category, rather than an aesthetic. One tires of one's native land, says Victor Eremita, and moves abroad; or one becomes *Europamüde* and goes to America. Marcel sees it both as a true metaphysical concern to discover the intimate at the heart of the remote and as an absurd optical illusion—"for Hohenschwangau represents to the Munich shopkeeper just what Chambord means to a tripper from Paris." But what is notable about it for our purposes, this quest for the remote, is that it is peculiarly suited to re-presenting; it transmits through art without the loss of a trait. As a mode of deliverance from alienation, experiencing it directly is no different from experiencing it through art.

The Western movie is an exercise in rotation stripped of every irrelevant trait. The stranger dropping off the stagecoach into a ritual adventure before moving on is the Western equivalent of Huck's foray ashore, with the difference that where Huck loses the stranger wins—but win or lose it is all the same: One must in any case be on the move. The shift from East to West accomplishes a rotation from the organic to the inorganic, from the green shade of Huck's willow towhead (or Novalis's leafy bower) to the Southwestern desert. But both the chlorophyll rotation (Hudson's Riolama) and John Ford's desert are themselves rotations from the human nest, the family familiar, Sartre's category of the viscous. The true smell of everydayness is the smell of Sunday dinner in the living room. Rotation from the human organic may occur to the animal organic (Mowgli in the wolf den), to the vegetable organic (Hudson in

Riolama), to the inorganic (John Wayne in the desert), or back again. To the alienated man of the East who has rotated to Santa Fe, the green shade of home becomes a true rotation; to his blood brother in Provence, it is the mesa and the cobalt sky. The I-It dichotomy is translated intact in the Western movie. Who is he, this Gary Cooper person who manages so well to betray nothing of himself whatsoever, who is he but I myself, the locus of pure possibility? He is qualitatively different from everyone else in the movie. Whereas they are what they are—the loyal but inept friend, the town comic, the greedy rancher, the craven barber—the stranger exists as pure possibility in the axis of nought-infinity. He is either nothing, that is, the unrisked possibility who walks through the town as a stranger and keeps his own counsel—above all he is silent—or he is perfectly realized actuality, the conscious *en soi*, that is to say, the Godhead, who, when at last he does act, acts with a ritual and gestural perfection. Let it be noted that it is all or nothing: Everything depends on his gestural perfection—an aesthetic standard which is appropriated by the moviegoer at a terrific cost in anxiety. In the stately dance of rotation, Destry when challenged borrows a gun and shoots all the knobs off the saloon sign. *But what if he did not? What if he missed?* The stranger in the movie walks the tightrope over the abyss of anxiety and he will not fail. But what of the moviegoer? The stranger removes his hat in the ritual rhythm and wipes his brow with his sleeve, but the moviegoer's brow is dry when he emerges and he has a headache, and if he tried the same gesture he might bump into his nose. Both Gary Cooper and the moviegoer walk the tightrope of anxiety, but Gary Cooper only seems to: his rope is only a foot above the ground. The moviegoer is over the abyss. The young man in a Robert Nathan novel or in a Huxleyan novel of the Days after the Bomb may rest assured that if he lies under his bush in Central Park, sooner or later *she* will trip over him. But what of the reader? He falls prey to his desperately unauthentic art by transposing the perfect aesthetic rotation to the existential: He will lie in his green shade until doomsday and no fugitive Pier Angeli will ever trip over him. He must seek an introduction; his speech will be halting, his

gestures will not come off, and having once committed himself to
the ritual criterion of his art and falling short of it, he can only
be—nothing. In no event can he become a person; not even Cooper can do that, for the choice lies between the perfected actual and
nothing at all. His alienated art of rotation instead of healing him
catches him up in a spiral of despair whose only term is suicide or
total self-loss.

3

A man riding a train may incarnate alienation (the commuter) or
rotation (i.e., the English variety: "I was taking a long-delayed holi-
day. In the same compartment and directly opposite me, I noticed
a young woman who seemed to be in some sort of distress. To my
astonishment she beckoned to me. I had planned to get off at North
Ealing, but having nothing better to do, I decided to stay on to
render what assistance I could . . .") But he is also admirably
placed to encounter the Return or repetition. Tom Wolfe, lying in
his berth while the train passes by night through lonely little Mid-
western towns, is alienation re-presented and so reversed. He may
be lost and by the wind grieved but he is withal triumphant. But
George Webber going home again and Charles Gray going back to
Clyde are transmitted intact—once the reader, who has never been
to Clyde or Asheville, has made the shift. But this is not rotation,
for it is a deliberate quest for the very thing rotation set out at any
cost to avoid; the rider has turned his back upon the new and the
remote and zone crossing, and now voyages into his own past in the
search for himself. It is thus in the nature of a conversion. Unlike
rotation, it is of two kinds, the aesthetic and the existential, which
literature accordingly polarizes. The aesthetic repetition captures
the savor of repetition without surrendering the self as a locus of experience and possibility. When Proust tastes the piece of cake or
Captain Ryder finds himself in Brideshead, the incident may serve
as an occasion for either kind: an excursion into the interesting, a
savoring of the past as experience; or two, the passionate quest in
which the incident serves as a thread in the labyrinth to be followed

at any cost. This latter, however, no matter how serious, cannot fail to be polarized by art, transmitting as the interesting. The question what does it mean to stand before the house of one's childhood? is thus received in two different ways—one as an occasion for the connoisseur sampling of a rare emotion, the other literally and seriously: what does it really mean?

Repetition is the conversion of rotation. In rotation, Shane cannot stay. In repetition, Shane neither moves on nor stays, but turns back to carry the search into his own past (we need not consider here Kierkegaard's distinction that true religious repetition has nothing to do with travel but is "consciousness raised to the second power"—which I take to be equivalent to Marcel's secondary reflection). In *East of Eden* Steinbeck leaves the wheel of rotation, the wayward bus, and with a great flourish turns back to Salinas and the past. In a less cluttered repetition, *In Sicily*, Vittorini's "I," on the occasion of a letter from his father, leaves his life of everydayness in Milan, where he is besieged by "abstract furies," and makes the pilgrimage back to Sicily. It is a very good repetition, or as Hemingway says in a somewhat purple introduction, it has rain in it. Like rotation, repetition offers itself as a deliverance from everydayness, yet it is, in a sense, the reverse of rotation. It is also a reversal of the objective-empirical. The latter world view cannot get hold of it without radically perverting it. For example, the dust jacket of Vittorini's book says something, as I recall, about modern man's renewing his vital energies by rediscovering his roots, etc. This remark is no doubt true in a garrulous dust-jacket sense, yet it is the very stuff of the "abstract furies" which drove him from Milan in the first place. It is the objective-empirical counterattack, the attempt to seize and render according to its own modes the existential trait—which it does only by re-reversing and alienating. (Even when a critic tries to stay clear of the abstract furies and writes of *The Adventures of Augie March* that it has the "juices of life in it," if it did have any juices, he is already drying them up.)

To say the least of it, then, whatever the ultimate metaphysical issues may be, the alienated man has in literature, as reader or writer, three alternatives. He may simply affirm alienation for what it is and as the supreme intersubjective achievement of art set forth the truth of it: how it stands with both of us. Such is Joseph K.: Kafka's pointing at and naming alienation has already reversed it, healing the very wound it re-presents. For an intersubjective discovery of alienation is already its opposite. Rotation, on the other hand, is transmitted intact. Repetition is polarized, transmitting as the interesting, canceling as the existential. What is omitted is the serious character of the search. If it should happen that a real Charles Gray came to himself one morning in the full realization of the absurdity of his life in the suburbs and if on the occasion of a chance recollection of Clyde he had the strongest inkling that back there, not ahead, lay the thread in the labyrinth he had lost, and if, like Kierkegaard's young man, he developed a passion for recovering himself beside which his family, his work, science, art, were of no account whatsoever—such a passion would not transmit aesthetically as a passion but only as the interesting. This is to testify not to an artistic deficiency of the writers of repetition but to the validity of Kierkegaard's aesthetic stage—which can in no wise be self-transcending.

Marquand hit the mother lode when he applied the device of the Return to the promising vein of exurbanite alienation. The disenchantment of Charles Gray may never go beyond the genteel limits of irony, of the attractive emotion with which he suffers his wife's conversation ("Aren't you going to wear your ruptured duck today?"); it needn't go beyond this limit; indeed it should not—it is impossible to imagine Charles Gray in the full grip of anxiety, staring at his hand like Roquentin and shaking like a leaf at what he sees. It is altogether inappropriate that he should be. His little excursion into alienation—the pleasant return to Clyde, the mild disenchantment, stoically borne, which follows—is no more nor less than what we bargained for. It would not do at all for Charles Gray to come to despair or to experience a religious conversion.

Whatever may be the ultimate decision—and one is tempted to contrast Marquand's Book-of-the-Month Club disenchantment with Kafka's Mitteleuropa alienation—the fact is that Charles Gray is the suburban counterpart of Joseph K. (and in my opinion, a not unworthy counterpart: the first hundred pages of *Point of No Return* are of a very high order). Charles Gray is a gentle wayfarer who is true to himself in the search for himself, and if he moderately despairs in the end and has recourse to a poetic Stoa, at least he knows and we know how it stands with him.

It is otherwise with the hero of *The Man in the Gray Flannel Suit,* who is said to be plowing the same field but who actually exists one whole spiral beneath Marquand. Tom Rath is interesting as a regression from whatever authenticity Charles Gray achieves in his recognition of alienation and the deliverance therefrom, a regression which masquerades as rotation and is not even that. We come upon Tom Rath in the same promising wasteland as Charles Gray, the everydayness of the Manhattan-to-suburb axis. His way out is not repetition, however, but rotation and a remarkably shoddy variety of rotation. It is a device in which dishonesty is compounded at least twice—once in what the writer intends to do and again in what he does without intending to do—to issue in the standard rotative rhythm of the soap opera. Whatever Marquand's shortcomings, he knows what he can do and he does it very well. He shows a man in an unauthentic situation and he explores one interesting alternative to it. Tom Rath, on the other hand, embarks on a career of bad faith and counterfeit motivation in which righteous alternatives conceal their opposites.

Marquand's formula might be summed up as suburban alienation recognized, plus the way out of the Return, plus a gentle disillusionment stoically borne. And this is in fact what happens. Tom Rath's formula is: alienation recognized, the prevailing marketing orientation rejected, and a becoming one's authentic self by devoting oneself to family and the P.T.A.—an admirable turn of events, but this is not what really happens. Behind this façade an altogether different (and desperately unauthentic) bid for authenticity is made. At least two concealed reverses can be disentangled from this skein of bad faith.

The first reverse: Overtly, the episode with Maria and the begetting of an illegitimate child is offered as a wartime lapse, bringing

on a serious crisis in Rath's life which must be faced and sur-
mounted, with the help of Judge Bernstein * before the authentic
life at home can be resumed.

Covertly and in fact, the wartime episode with Maria is offered as
the one authentic moment, the high tide of Rath's life. It is clear
enough that the Roman idyll with Maria sans pajamas and cul-
minating in the scene in the ruined villa (!) is regarded as the
highest moment to which mortal Rousseauian man may attain.
Postwar life with the family and community projects, far from
being an advance into the good life as advertised, are unmistakably
set forth as making the best of a sorry situation.

Charles Gray's most authentic moment is the Return: repetition;
Tom Rath's is rotation, the coming upon the Real Thing among
the ruins—a moment which needn't have been disguised, since, for
one thing, it has honorable literary forebears, as when Prince Andrei transcended everydayness and came to himself for the first time
only when he lay wounded on the field of Borodino. This is a true
existential reversal, the discovery of the pearl of great price at the
very heart of the objective-empirical disaster. Yet even if Tom
Rath's rotation with Maria had been offered at its face value, it
would not have rung true. For Tom's adventure is not, in fact, a
rotation but a desperate impersonation masquerading as rotation.

The second reverse: Overtly the adventure with Maria is offered
as rotation, an untrammeled exploration of *la solitude à deux* amid
the smoking ruins of the *en soi*.

Covertly and in fact, Tom Rath is taking refuge in the standard
rotation of the soap opera, the acceptable rhythm of the Wellsian-
Huxleyan-Nathanian romance of love among the ruins. His happiness with Maria as they lie in the ruined villa warmed by the burning piano, far from being a free exploration, is in reality a conform-
ing to the most ritualistic of gestures: that which is thought to be
proper and fitting for a sexual adventure. The motto of Tom's hap-

* In the character of Judge Bernstein, who is like Herman Wouk's Barney Green-
wald, and in the character of the sympathetic Negro sergeant, the author shows his
true affiliation as a compulsive liberal novelist of the Merle Miller school, which
lays down the strict condition that no Negro or Jew may be admitted to fiction unless
he has been previously canonized.

piness is "Now I am really living," which does not mean now I am truly myself but rather, now at last I am doing the acceptable-thing-which-an-American-officer-in-Europe-is-supposed-to-do. He has at last achieved a successful impersonation, the role-taking of the American-at-war. It would have been more interesting if Rath's adventure could have been explored as a repetition, a re-experiencing of what his father had done with the Mademoiselle from Armentières. As it is, finding himself in the situation of alienation, the familiar I estranged from the It, Tom Rath, instead of becoming a self, a free individual, solves the dilemma by a dismal impersonation, a fading into the furniture of the It.

Tom Rath's dream is the sexual dream of the commuter, the longing for a Pepper Young rotation which can only come about through the agency of war or amnesia. The inhibition of the sexual longing of the commuter occurs far below the level of sin. It is not the scruple of sin which deters the commuter from sexual rotation but the implicit threat to his self-system of defenses against anxiety. What if he is turned down? What if he is premature in his performance? (What if Destry misses?) In Harry Stack Sullivan's words, the mark of success in the culture is how much one can do to another's genitals without risking one's self-esteem unduly. But when the Bomb falls, the risk is at a minimum. When the vines sprout in Madison Avenue and Radio City lies greening like an Incan temple in the jungle, and when Maria develops amnesia, there is hardly any risk at all.

5

NOTES FOR A NOVEL

ABOUT THE END OF THE WORLD

A SERIOUS NOVEL about the destruction of the United States and the end of the world should perform the function of prophecy in reverse. The novelist writes about the coming end in order to warn about present ills and so avert the end. Not being called by God to be a prophet, he nevertheless pretends to a certain prescience. If he did not think he saw something other people didn't see or at least didn't pay much attention to, he would be wasting his time writing and they reading. This does not mean that he is wiser than they. Rather might it testify to a species of affliction which sets him apart and gives him an odd point of view. The wounded man has a better view of the battle than those still shooting. The novelist is less like a prophet than he is like the canary that coal miners used to take down into the shaft to test the air. When the canary gets unhappy, utters plaintive cries, and collapses, it may be time for the miners to surface and think things over.

But perhaps it is necessary first of all to define the sort of novel and the sort of novelist I have in mind. By a novel about "the end of the world," I am not speaking of a Wellsian fantasy or a science-fiction film on the Late Show. Nor would such a novel presume to predict the imminent destruction of the world. It is not even interested in the present very real capacity for physical destruction: that each of the ninety-odd American nuclear submarines carries sixteen Polaris missiles, each of which in turn has the destructive capacity of all the bombs dropped in World War II. Of more concern to the novelist are other signs, which, if he reads them correctly, portend a different kind of danger.

It is here that the novelist is apt to diverge from the general population. It seems fair to say that most people are optimistic with qualifications—or rather that their pessimism has specific causes. If the students and Negroes and Communists would behave, things wouldn't be so bad. The apprehension of many novelists, on the other hand, is a more radical business and cannot be laid to particular evils such as racism, Vietnam, inflation. The question which must arise is whether most people are crazy or most serious writers are crazy. Or to phrase the alternatives more precisely: Is the secular city in great trouble or is the novelist a decadent bourgeois left over from a past age who likes to titivate himself and his readers with periodic doom-crying?

The signs are ambiguous. The novelist and the general reader agree about the nuclear threat. But when the novelist begins behaving like a man teetering on the brink of the abyss here and now, or worse, like a man who is already over the brink and into the abyss, the reader often gets upset and even angry. One day an angry lady stopped me on the street and said she did not like a book I wrote but that if I lived up to the best in me I might write a good Christian novel like *The Cardinal* by Henry Morton Robinson or perhaps even *The Foundling* by Cardinal Spellman.

What about the novelist himself? Let me define the sort of novelist I have in mind. I locate him not on a scale of merit—he is not necessarily a good novelist—but in terms of goals. He is, the novelist we speak of, a writer who has an explicit and ultimate concern with the nature of man and the nature of reality where man finds himself. Instead of constructing a plot and creating a cast of characters from a world familiar to everybody, he is more apt to set forth with a stranger in a strange land where the signposts are enigmatic but which he sets out to explore nevertheless. One might apply to the novelist such adjectives as "philosophical," "metaphysical," "prophetic," "eschatological," and even "religious." I use the word "religious" in its root sense as signifying a radical *bond*, as the writer sees it, which connects man with reality—or the failure of such a bond—and so confers meaning to his life—or the absence of meaning. Such a class might include writers as diverse as Dostoevsky, Tolstoy, Camus, Sartre, Faulkner, Flannery O'Connor. Sartre, one might object, is an atheist. He is, but his atheism is "religious" in the sense intended here: that the novelist betrays a passionate conviction about man's nature, the world, and man's obligation in the world. By the same token I would exclude much of the English novel—without prejudice: I am quite willing to believe that Jane Austen and Samuel Richardson are better novelists than Sartre and O'Connor. The nineteenth-century Russian novelists were haunted by God; many of the French existentialists are haunted by his absence. The English novelist is not much interested one way or another. The English novel traditionally takes place in a society as everyone sees it and takes it for granted. If there are vicars and churches prominent in the society, there will be vicars and churches in the novel. If not, not. So much for vicars and churches.

What about American novelists? One would exclude, again without prejudice, social critics and cultural satirists like Steinbeck and Lewis. The Okies were too hungry to have "identity crises." Dodsworth was too interested in Italy and *dolce far niente* to worry about God or the death of God. The contemporary novel deals with the sequelae. What happens to Dodsworth after he lives happily ever after in Capri? What happens to the thousand Midwesterners who settle on the Riviera? What happens to the Okie who succeeds in Pomona and now spends his time watching Art Linkletter? Is all well with them or are they in deeper trouble than they were on Main Street and in the dust bowl? If so, what is the nature of the trouble?

We have a clue to the preoccupation of the American novelist in the recurring complaint of British critics. A review of a recent novel spoke of the Americans' perennial disposition toward "philosophical megalomania." Certainly one can agree that if British virtues lie in tidiness of style, clarity and concision, a respect for form, and a native embarrassment before "larger questions," American failings include pretension, grandiosity, formlessness, Dionysian excess, and a kind of metaphysical omnivorousness. American novels tend to be about everything. Moreover, at the end, everything is disposed of, God, man, and the world. The most frequently used blurb on the dust jackets of the last ten thousand American novels is the sentence "This novel investigates the problem of evil and the essential loneliness of man." A large order, that, but the American novelist usually feels up to it.

This congenital hypertrophy of the novelist's appetites no doubt makes for a great number of very bad novels, especially in times when, unlike in nineteenth-century Russia, the talent is not commensurate with the ambition.

2

Since true prophets, i.e., men called by God to communicate something urgent to other men, are currently in short supply, the novelist may perform a quasi-prophetic function. Like the prophet, his news is generally bad. Unlike the prophet, whose mouth has been purified by a burning coal, the novelist's art is often bad, too. It is fitting that he should shock and therefore warn his readers by speaking of last things—if not the Last Day of the Gospels, then of a possible coming destruction, of a laying waste of cities, of vineyards reverting to the wilderness. Like the prophet, he may find himself in radical disagreement with his fellow countrymen. Unlike the prophet, he does not generally get killed. More often he is ignored. Or, if he writes a sufficiently dirty book, he might become a best seller or even be bought by the movies.

What concerns us here is his divergence from the usual views of the denizens of the secular city in general and in particular from the new theologians of the secular city.

While it is important to take note of this divergence, extreme care must be taken not to distort it and especially not to fall prey to the seduction of crepe-hanging for its own sake. Nothing comes easier than the sepulchral manifestoes of the old-style café existentialist and the new-style hippie who professes to despise the squares and the technology of the Western city while living on remittance checks from the same source and who would be the first to go for his shot of penicillin if he got meningitis.

Yet even after proper precautions are exercised, it is impossible to overlook a remarkable discrepancy. It would appear that most serious novelists, to say nothing of poets and artists, find themselves out of step with their counterparts in other walks of life in the modern city, doctor, lawyer, businessman, technician, laborer, and now the new theologian.

It's an old story with novelists. People are always asking, Why don't you write about pleasant things and normal people? Why all the neurosis and violence? There are many nice things in the world. The reader is offended. But if one replies, "Yes, it's true; in fact there seem to be more nice people around now than ever before, but somehow as the world grows nicer it also grows more violent. The triumphant secular society of the Western world, the nicest of all worlds, killed more people in the first half of this century than have been killed in all history. Travelers to Germany before the last war reported that the Germans were the nicest people in Europe"—then the reader is even more offended.

If one were to take a Gallup poll of representative denizens of the megalopolis on this subject, responses to a question about the future might run something like this:

Liberal politician: If we use our wealth and energies constructively to provide greater opportunities for all men, there is unlimited hope for man's well-being.

Conservative politician: If we defeat Communism and revive old-time religion and Americanism, we have nothing to worry about.

Businessman: Business is generally good; the war is not hurting much, but the Negroes and the unions and the government could ruin everything.

Laborer: All this country needs is an eight-hour week and a guaranteed minimum income.

City planner: If we could solve international problems and spend our yearly budget on education and housing, we could have a paradise on earth.

Etc., etc.

Each is probably right. That is to say, there is a context within which it is possible to agree with each response.

But suppose one were to ask the same question of a novelist who, say, was born and raised in a community which has gone far to satisfy the lists of city needs, where indeed housing, education, recreational and cultural facilities, are first class; say some such place as Shaker Heights, Pasadena, or Bronxville. How does he answer the poll? In the first place, if he was born in one of these places, he has probably left since. It might be noted in passing that such communities (plus Harvard, Princeton, Yale, Bennington, Sarah Lawrence, and Vassar) have produced remarkably few good novelists lately, which latter are more likely to come from towns in south Georgia or the Jewish sections of New York and Chicago.

But how, in any case, is the refugee novelist from Shaker Heights likely to respond to the poll? I venture to say his response might be something like: *Something is wrong here; I don't feel good.*

Now of course, if all generalizations are dangerous, perhaps the most dangerous of all is a generalization about novelists, who are a perverse lot and don't even get along with each other, and who, moreover, speak an even more confused Babel nowadays than usual. But if there is a single strain that runs through the lot, whether Christian or atheist, black or white, Greek or Jew, it is a profound disquiet.

Is it too much to say that the novelist, unlike the new theologian, is one of the few remaining witnesses to the doctrine of original sin, the imminence of catastrophe in paradise?

If, anyhow, we accept this divergence as a fact, that the serious American artist is in dissent from the current American proposition, we are faced with some simple alternatives by way of explanation.

Either we must decide that the artist is mistaken and in what sense he is mistaken: whether he is a self-indulged maniac or a harmless eccentric or the culture's court jester whom everyone expects to cut the fool and make scandalous sallies for which he is well paid.

Or the novelist in his confused Orphic way is trying to tell us something we would do well to listen to.

Again it is necessary to specify the dissent, the issue and the parties to it. One likes to pick the right enemies and unload the wrong allies.

The issue, one might say at the outset, is not at all the traditional confrontation between the "alienated" artist and the dominant business-technological community. For one thing, the novelist, even the serious novelist who doesn't write dirty books, never had it so good. It is businessmen, or rather their wives, who are his best customers. Great business foundations compete to give him money. His own government awards him cash prizes. For another thing, the old self-image of the artist as an alien in a hostile society seems increasingly to have become the chic property of those writers who have no other visible claim to distinction. Nothing is easier than to set up as a two-bit hippie Cassandra crying havoc in bad verse.

It is the grossness of conventional distinctions which makes the case difficult. The other day I received a questionnaire from a sociologist who had evidently compiled a list of novelists. The first question was something like "Do you, as a novelist, feel alienated from the society around you?" I refused to answer the question on the grounds that any answer would be certain to be misunderstood. To have replied yes would embrace any one of several ambiguities. One "yes" might mean "Yes, I find the entire Western urban-technological complex repugnant, and so I have dropped out, turned on, and tuned in." Another "yes" might mean "Yes, since I am a Christian and therefore must to some degree feel myself an alien and wayfarer in any society, so do I feel myself in this society, even though I believe that Western democratic society is man's best hope on this earth." Another "yes" might mean "Yes, being a John Bircher, I am convinced the country has gone mad."

The novelist's categories are not the same as the sociologist's. So his response to the questionnaire is apt to be perverse: Instead of responding to the questions, he wonders about the questioner. Does the questionnaire imply that the sociologist is not himself alienated? Having achieved the transcending objective stance of science, has he also transcended the mortal condition? Or is it even possible that if the sociologist should reply to his own question- naire, "No, I do not feel alienated"—that such an answer, though given in good faith, could nevertheless conceal the severest sort of alienation. One thinks of the alienation Søren Kierkegaard had in mind when he described the little Herr Professor who has fitted the entire world into a scientific system but does not realize that he himself is left out in the cold and cannot be accounted for as an in- dividual.

If the scientist's vocation is to clarify and simplify, it would seem that the novelist's aim is to muddy and complicate. For he knows that even the most carefully contrived questionnaire cannot dis- cover how it really stands with the sociologist or himself. What will be left out of even the most rigorous scientific formulation is noth- ing else than the individual himself. And since the novelist deals first and last with individuals and the scientist treats individuals only to discover their general properties, it is the novelist's responsi- bility to be chary of categories and rather to focus upon the mys- tery, the paradox, the *openness* of an individual human existence. If he is any good, he knows better than to speak of the "business- man," as if there were such a genus. It was useful for Sinclair Lewis to create George Babbitt, but it has served no good purpose for bad novelists to have created all businessmen in the image of George Babbitt.

Here is the sort of businessman the "religious" novelist is inter- ested in, i.e., the novelist who is concerned with the radical ques- tions of man's identity and his relation to God or to God's absence. He sketches out a character, a businessman-commuter who, let us say, is in some sense or other *lost* to himself. That is to say, he feels that something has gone badly wrong in the everyday round of business activity, in his office routine, in the routine life at home, in his Sunday-morning churchgoing, in his coaching of the Little League. Even though by all objective criteria all is well with him, he knows that all is not well with him. What happens next? Of course he can opt out. But thanks to Sinclair Lewis, we now know better than Sinclair Lewis. One is not content to have him opt out

and take up the thong-sandaled life in Capri. Perhaps we do have
better sense in some matters. Or perhaps it is only that Capri is too
available. As a matter of fact it would be easier nowadays to write a
satirical novel about some poor overaged hippie who did drop out
and try to turn on. But the present-day novelist is more interested
in catastrophe than he is in life among the flower people. Uncertain himself about what has gone wrong, he feels in his bones that
the happy exurb stands both in danger of catastrophe and somehow
in need of it. Like Thomas More and Saint Francis he is most
cheerful with Brother Death in the neighborhood. Then what happens to his businessman? One day he is on his way home on the
five-fifteen. He has a severe heart attack and is taken off the train at
a commuters' station he has seen a thousand times but never vis-
ited. When he regains consciousness, he finds himself in a strange
hospital surrounded by strangers. As he tries to recall what has happened, he catches sight of his own hand on the counterpane. It is
as if he had never seen it before: He is astounded by its complexity,
its functional beauty. He turns it this way and that. What has happened? Certainly a kind of natural revelation, which reminds one
of the experiences induced by the psychedelic drugs. (It is interesting to note that this kind of revelation, which can only be called a
revelation of being, is viewed by the "religious" novelist as exhila-
rating or disgusting depending on his "religion." Recall Sartre's
Roquentin catching sight of his own hand, which reminds him of a
great fat slug with red hairs.) At any rate I cite this example to show
the kind of character, the kind of predicament, the kind of event
with which the novelist is nowadays more likely to concern himself
than was Hemingway or Lewis. Is it not reasonable to say that, in
some sense or other, the stricken commuter has "come to himself"?
In what sense he has come to himself, how it transforms his relationship with his family, his business, his church, is of course the
burden of the novel.

3

In view of the triumphant and generally admirable democratic-
technological transformation of society, what is the ground of the

novelist's radical disquiet? Can the charge be brought against him, as Harvey Cox has accused the existentialists, of being an anachronism, one of the remnant of nineteenth-century "cultivated personalities" who, finding no sympathetic hearing from either technician or consumer, finds it convenient to believe that the world is going to the dogs?

Might not the novelist follow the new theologian in his embrace of the exurb and the computer? Evidently the former does not think so. Offhand I cannot think of a single first-class novelist who has any use for the most "successful" American society, namely life in the prosperous upper-middle-class exurb, in the same sense that Jane Austen celebrated a comparable society. Rather is the novelist more apt to be a refugee from this very society.

The curious fact is that it is the new novelist who judges the world and not the new theologian. It is the novelist who, despite his well-advertised penchant for violence, his fetish of freedom, his sexual adventurism, pronounces anathemas upon the most permissive of societies, which in fact permits him everything.

How does the novelist judge the new theologian? One might expect that since one of the major burdens of the American novel since Mark Twain has been a rebellion against Christendom, the emancipated novelist might make common cause with the emancipated theologian. The truth is, or so it appears to me, that neither novelists nor anybody else is much interested in *any* theologians, and least of all in God-is-dead theologians. The strenuous efforts of the latter to baptize the computer remind one of the liberal clergyman of the last century who used to wait, hat in hand so to speak, outside the scientific laboratories to assure the scientist there was no conflict between science and religion. The latter could not have cared less.

Yet the contemporary novelist is as preoccupied with catastrophe as the orthodox theologian with sin and death.

Why?

Perhaps the novelist, not being a critic, can only reply in the context of his own world view. All issues are ultimately religious, said Toynbee. And so the "religion" of the novelist becomes relevant if he is writing a novel of ultimate concerns. It would not have mattered a great deal if Margaret Mitchell were a Methodist or an atheist. But it does matter what Sartre's allegiance is, or Camus's or Flannery O'Connor's. For what his allegiance is is what he is writing about.

As it happens, I speak in a Christian context. That is to say, I do not conceive it my vocation to preach the Christian faith in a novel, but as it happens, my world view is informed by a certain belief about man's nature and destiny which cannot fail to be central to any novel I write.

Being a Christian novelist nowadays has certain advantages and disadvantages. Since novels deal with people and people live in time and get into predicaments, it is probably an advantage to subscribe to a world view which is incarnational, historical, and predicamental, rather than, say, Buddhism, which tends to devalue individual persons, things, and happenings. What with the present dislocation of man, it is probably an advantage to see man as by his very nature an exile and wanderer rather than as a behaviorist sees him: as an organism in an environment. Despite Camus's explicit disavowal of Christianity, his Stranger has blood ties with the wayfarer of Saint Thomas Aquinas and Gabriel Marcel. And if it is true that we are living in eschatological times, times of enormous danger and commensurate hope, of possible end and possible renewal, the prophetic-eschatological character of Christianity is no doubt peculiarly apposite.

It is also true, as we shall presently see, that the Christian novelist suffers special disabilities.

But to return to the question: What does he see in the world which arouses in him the deepest forebodings and at the same time kindles excitement and hope?

What he sees first in the Western world is the massive failure of Christendom itself. But it is a peculiar failure and he is apt to see it quite differently from the scientific humanist, for example, who may quite frankly regard orthodox Christianity as an absurd anachronism. The novelist, to tell the truth, is much more interested in the person of the scientific humanist than in science and religion.

Nor does he set much store by the usual complaint of Christians that the enemies are materialism and atheism and Communism. It is at least an open question whether the world which would follow a total victory of the most vociferous of the anti-Communists would be an improvement over the present world with all its troubles.

No, what the novelist sees, or rather senses, is a certain quality of the postmodern consciousness as he finds it and as he incarnates it in his own characters. What he finds—in himself and in other people—is a new breed of person in whom the potential for catastrophe—and hope—has suddenly escalated. Everyone knows about the awesome new weapons. But what is less apparent is a comparable realignment of energies within the human psyche. The psychical forces presently released in the postmodern consciousness open unlimited possibilities for both destruction and liberation, for an absolute loneliness or a rediscovery of community and reconciliation.

The subject of the postmodern novel is a man who has very nearly come to the end of the line. How very odd it is, when one comes to think of it, that the very moment he arrives at the threshold of his new city, with all its hard-won relief from the sufferings of the past, happens to be the same moment that he runs out of meaning! It is as if he surrenders his ticket, arrives at his destination, and gets off his train—and then must also surrender his passport and become a homeless person! The American novel in past years has treated such themes as persons whose lives are blighted by social evils, or reformers who attack these evils, or perhaps the dislocation of expatriate Americans, or of Southerners living in a region haunted by memories. But the hero of the postmodern novel is a man who has forgotten his bad memories and conquered his present ills and who finds himself in the victorious secular city. His only problem now is to keep from blowing his brains out.

Death-of-God theologians are no doubt speaking the truth when they call attention to the increasing irrelevance of traditional religion. Orthodox theologians claim with equal justification, though with considerably more dreariness, that there is no conflict between Christian doctrine and the scientific method. But to the novelist it looks as if such polemics may be overlooking the *tertium quid* within which all such confrontations take place, the individual consciousness of postmodern man.

The wrong questions are being asked. The proper question is not whether God has died or been superseded by the urban-political complex. The question is not whether the Good News is no longer relevant, but rather whether it is possible that man is presently undergoing a tempestuous restructuring of his consciousness which does not presently allow him to take account of the Good News. For what has happened is not merely the technological transformation of the world but something psychologically even more portentous. It is the absorption by the layman not of the scientific method but rather of the magical aura of science, whose credentials he accepts for all sectors of reality. Thus in the lay culture of a scientific society nothing is easier than to fall prey to a kind of seduction which sunders one's very self from itself into an all-transcending "objective" consciousness and a consumer-self with a list of "needs" to be satisfied. It is this monstrous bifurcation of man into angelic and bestial components against which old theologies must be weighed before new theologies are erected. Such a man could not take account of God, the devil, and the angels if they were standing before him, because he has already peopled the universe with his own hierarchies. When the novelist writes of a man "coming to himself" through some such catalyst as catastrophe or ordeal, he may be offering obscure testimony to a gross disorder of consciousness and to the need of recovering oneself as neither angel nor organism but as a wayfaring creature somewhere between.

And so the ultimate question is what is the *term* or historical outcome of this ongoing schism of the consciousness. Which will be more relevant to the "lost" man of tomorrow who knows he is lost: the new theology of politics or the renewed old theology of Good News? What is most noticeable about the new theology, despite the somber strains of the funeral march, is the triviality of the postmortem proposals. After the polemics, when the old structures are flattened and the debris cleared away, what is served up is small potatoes indeed. What does the Christian do with his God dead and

His name erased? It is proposed that he give more time to the political party of his choice or perhaps make a greater effort to be civil to
salesladies and shoe clerks. To the "religious" novelist, whether it
be Sartre or O'Connor, the positive proposals of the new theology
must sound like a set of resolutions passed at the P.T.A.

The man who writes a serious novel about the end of the
world—i.e., the passing of one age and the beginning of another—
must reckon not merely like H. G. Wells with changes in the environment but also with changes in man's consciousness which
may be quite as radical. Will this consciousness be more or less
religious? The notion of man graduating from the religious stage to
the political is after all an unexamined assumption. It might in fact
turn out that the modern era, which is perhaps three hundred years
old and has already ended, will be known as the Secular Era,
which came to an end with the catastrophes of the twentieth century.

The contrast between the world views of denizens of the old
modern world and of the postmodern world might be sketched
novelistically.

Imagine two scientists of the old modern world, perhaps a pair of
physicists at Los Alamos in the 1940's. They leave the laboratory
one Sunday morning after working all night and walk past a church
on their way home. The door is open, and as they pass, they hear a
few words of the gospel preached. "Come, follow me," or something of the sort. How do they respond to the summons? What do
they say to each other? What can they do or say? Given the exhila-
rating climate of the transcending objectivity and comradeship
which must have existed at the high tide of physics in the early
twentieth century, it is hard to imagine a proposition which would
have sounded more irrelevant than this standard sermon preached,
one allows, with all the characteristic dreariness and low spirits of
Christendom at the same time in history. If indeed the scientists
said anything, what they said would not even amount to a rejection
of the summons—*Come!*—a summons which is only relevant to a
man in a certain predicament. Can one imagine these scientists
conceiving themselves in a predicament other than a *Schadenfreude*

about creating the ultimate weapon? Rather would the words heard
at the open door be received as a sample of a certain artifact of culture. Scientist A might say to Scientist B, "Did you know there is a
local cult of Penitentes not five miles from here who carry whips
and chains in a pre-Lenten procession?" Nor can one blame them
for attending such a spectacle in the same spirit with which they attend the corn dance at Tesuque. The fact is that some of the Los
Alamos physicists became quite good amateur ethnologists.

Imagine now a third scientist, perhaps a technician, fifty years
later. Let us suppose that the world has not even blown up—it is
after all too easy to set the stage so that the gospel is preached to a
few ragamuffins in the ruins. Rather has it happened that the high
culture of twentieth-century physics has long since subsided to a
routine mop-up of particle physics—something like a present-day
botanist who goes to Antarctica in the hopes of discovering an
overlooked lichen. The technician, employed in the Santa
Fe–Taos Senior Citizens Compound, is doing routine radiation
counts on synthetic cow's milk. But let us suppose that the schism
and isolation of the individual consciousness has also gone on
apace so that mankind is presently divided into two classes: the
consumer long since anesthetized and lost to himself in the rounds
of consumership, and the stranded objectivized consciousness, a
ghost of a man who wanders the earth like Ishmael. Unlike the
consumer he knows his predicament. He is the despairing man
Kierkegaard spoke of, for whom there is hope because he is aware
of his despair. He is a caricature of the contemporary Cartesian
man who has objectified the world and his body and sets himself
over against both like the angel at the gates of Paradise. All crea-
turely relations crumble at his touch. He has but to utter a word—
achieving intersubjectivity, interpersonal relations, meaningful be-
havior—and that which the word signifies vanishes.

Such a man leaves his laboratory on a workaday Wednesday feeling more disembodied than usual and passes the same church,
which is now in ruins, ruined both by the dreariness of the old
Christendom and by the nutty reforms of the new theologians.
From the ruins a stranger emerges and accosts him. The stranger is

himself a weary, flawed man, a wayfarer. He is a priest, say, someone like the whisky priest in Graham Greene's *The Power and the
Glory*, who has been sent as yet another replacement into hostile
territory. The stranger speaks to the technician. "You look unwell,
friend." "Yes," replies the technician, frowning. "But I will be all
right as soon as I get home and take my drug, which is the best of
the consciousness-expanding community-simulating self-integrating
drugs." "Come," says the priest, "and I'll give you a drug which
will integrate your self once and for all." "What kind of a drug is
that?" "Take this drug and you will need no more drugs." Etc.

How the technician responds is beside the point. The point concerns modes of communication. It is possible that a different kind
of communication-event occurs in the door of the church than occurred fifty years earlier.

                                    4

The American Christian novelist faces a peculiar dilemma today. (I
speak, of course, of a dilemma of the times and not of his own per-
sonal malaise, neuroses, failures, to which he is at least as subject
as his good heathen colleagues, sometimes I think more so.) His
dilemma is that though he professes a belief which he holds saves
himself and the world and nourishes his art besides, it is also true
that Christendom seems in some sense to have failed. Its vocabulary is worn out. This twin failure raises problems for a man who is
a Christian and whose trade is with words. The old words of grace
are worn smooth as poker chips and a certain devaluation has occurred, like a poker chip after it is cashed in. Even if one talks only
of Christendom, leaving the heathens out of it, of Christendom
where everybody is a believer, it almost seems that when everybody
believes in God, it is as if everybody started the game with one
poker chip, which is the same as starting with none.

The Christian novelist nowadays is like a man who has found a
treasure hidden in the attic of an old house, but he is writing for
people who have moved out to the suburbs and who are bloody sick
of the old house and everything in it.

The Christian novelist is like a starving Confederate soldier who finds a hundred-dollar bill on the streets of Atlanta, only to discover that everyone is a millionaire and the grocers won't take the money.

The Christian novelist is like a man who goes to a wild lonely place to discover the truth within himself and there after much ordeal and suffering meets an apostle who has the authority to tell him a great piece of news and so tells him the news with authority. He, the novelist, believes the news and runs back to the city to tell his countrymen, only to discover that the news has already been broadcast, that this news is in fact the weariest canned spot announcement on radio-TV, more commonplace than the Exxon commercial, that in fact he might just as well be shouting Exxon! Exxon! for all anyone pays any attention to him.

The Christian novelist is like a man who finds a treasure buried in a field and sells all he has to buy the field, only to discover that everyone else has the same treasure in his field and that in any case real estate values have gone so high that all field-owners have forgotten the treasure and plan to subdivide.

There is besides the devaluation of its vocabulary the egregious moral failure of Christendom. It is significant that the failure of Christendom in the United States has not occurred in the sector of theology or metaphysics, with which the existentialists and new theologians are also concerned and toward which Americans have always been indifferent, but rather in the sector of everyday morality, which has acutely concerned Americans since the Puritans. Americans take pride in doing right. It is not chauvinistic to suppose that perhaps they have done righter than any other great power in history. But in the one place, the place which hurts the most and where charity was most needed, they have not done right. White Americans have sinned against the Negro from the beginning and continue to do so, initially with cruelty and presently with an indifference which may be even more destructive. And it is the churches which, far from fighting the good fight against man's native inhumanity to man, have sanctified and perpetuated this indifference.

To the eschatological novelist it even begins to look as if this single failing may be the tragic flaw in the noblest of political organisms. At least he conceives it as his duty to tell his countrymen how they can die of it, so that they will not.

What is the task of the Christian novelist who mirrors in himself the society he sees around him—who otherwise would not be a novelist—whose only difference from his countrymen is that he has the vocation to be a novelist? How does he set about writing, having cast his lot with a discredited Christendom and having inherited a defunct vocabulary?

He does the only thing he can do. Like Joyce's Stephen Dedalus, he calls on every ounce of cunning, craft, and guile he can muster from the darker regions of his soul. The fictional use of violence, shock, comedy, insult, the bizarre, are the everyday tools of his trade. How could it be otherwise? How can one possibly write of baptism as an event of immense significance when baptism is already accepted but accepted by and large as a minor tribal rite somewhat secondary in importance to taking the kids to see Santa at the department store? Flannery O'Connor conveyed baptism through its exaggeration, in one novel as a violent death by drowning. In answer to a question about why she created such bizarre characters, she replied that for the near-blind you have to draw very large, simple caricatures.

So too may it be useful to write a novel about the end of the world. Perhaps it is only through the conjuring up of catastrophe, the destruction of all Exxon signs, and the sprouting of vines in the church pews, that the novelist can make vicarious use of catastrophe in order that he and his reader may come to themselves.

Whether or not the catastrophe actually befalls us, or is deserved—whether reconciliation and renewal may yet take place—is not for the novelist to say.

6

THE MESSAGE

IN THE BOTTLE

The act of faith consists essentially in knowledge and there we find its
formal or specific perfection.
                              —Thomas Aquinas, *De Veritate*

Faith is not a form of knowledge; for all knowledge is either knowledge
of the eternal, excluding the temporal and the historical as indifferent,
or it is pure historical knowledge. No knowledge can have for its object
the absurdity that the eternal is the historical.
                              —Søren Kierkegaard, *Philosophical Fragments*

SUPPOSE A MAN IS a castaway on an island. He is, moreover, a
special sort of castaway. He has lost his memory in the shipwreck
and has no recollection of where he came from or who he is. All
he knows is that one day he finds himself cast up on the beach. But
it is a pleasant place and he soon discovers that the island is inhab-
ited. Indeed it turns out that the islanders have a remarkable culture with highly developed social institutions, a good university,
first-class science, a flourishing industry and art. The castaway is
warmly received. Being a resourceful fellow, he makes the best of
the situation, gets a job, builds a house, takes a wife, raises a family, goes to night school, and enjoys the local arts of cinema,
music, and literature. He becomes, as the phrase goes, a useful
member of the community.

The castaway, who by now is quite well educated and curious
about the world, forms the habit of taking a walk on the beach early

in the morning. Here he regularly comes upon bottles which have been washed up by the waves. The bottles are tightly corked and each one contains a single piece of paper with a single sentence written on it.

The messages are very diverse in form and subject matter. Naturally he is interested, at first idly, then acutely—when it turns out that some of the messages convey important information. Being an alert, conscientious, and well-informed man who is interested in the advance of science and the arts, and a responsible citizen who has a stake in the welfare of his island society, he is anxious to evaluate the messages properly and so take advantage of the information they convey. The bottles arrive by the thousands and he and his fellow islanders—by now he has told them of the messages and they share his interest—are faced with two questions. One is, Where are the bottles coming from?—a question which does not here concern us; the other is, How shall we go about sorting out the messages? which are important and which are not? which are more important and which less? Some of the messages are obviously trivial or nonsensical. Others are false. Still others state facts and draw conclusions which appear to be significant.

Here are some of the messages, chosen at random:

Lead melts at 330 degrees.
2 + 2 = 4.
Chicago, a city, is on Lake Michigan.
Chicago is on the Hudson River or Chicago is not on the Hudson River. *
At 2 p.m., January 4, 1902, at the residence of Manuel Gómez in Matanzas, Cuba, a leaf fell from the banyan tree.
The British are coming.
The market for eggs in Bora Bora [a neighboring island] is very good.
If water John brick is.
Jane will arrive tomorrow.
The pressure of a gas is a function of heat and volume.
Acute myelogenous leukemia may be cured by parenteral administration of metallic beryllium.

* Some of the bottles must have been launched by Rudolf Carnap, since the sentences are identical with those he uses in the article "Formal and Factual Science."

> In 1943 the Russians murdered 10,000 Polish officers in the Katyn forest.
> A war party is approaching from Bora Bora.
> It is possible to predict a supernova in the constellation Ophiuchus next month by using the following technique—
> The Atman (Self) is the Brahman.
> The dream symbol, house with a balcony, usually stands for a woman.
> Tears, idle tears, I know not what they mean.
> Truth is beauty.
> Being comprises essence and existence.

As the castaway sets about sorting out these messages, he would, if he followed conventional logical practice, separate them into two large groups. There are those sentences which appear to state empirical facts which can only be arrived at by observation. Such are the sentences

> Chicago is on Lake Michigan.
> Lead melts at 330 degrees.

Then there are those sentences which seem to refer to a state of affairs implicit in the very nature of reality (or some would say in the very structure of consciousness). Certainly they do not seem to depend on a particular observation. Such are the sentences

> Chicago is on the Hudson River or Chicago is not on the Hudson River.
> $2 + 2 = 4$.

These two types of sentences are usually called synthetic and analytic.

For the time being I will pass over the positivist division between sense and nonsense, a criterion which would accept the sentence about the melting point of lead because it can be tested experimentally but would reject the sentences about the dream symbol and the metaphysical and poetic sentences because they cannot be tested. I will also say nothing for the moment about another possible division, that between those synthetic sentences which state repeatable events, like the melting of lead, and those which state nonrepeatable historical events, like the murder of the Polish officers.

It is possible, however, to sort out the messages in an entirely different way. To the islander indeed it must seem that this second way is far more sensible—and far more radical—than the former. The sentences appear to him to fall naturally into two quite different groups.

There are those sentences which are the result of a very special kind of human activity, an activity which the castaway, an ordinary fellow, attributes alike to scientists, scholars, poets, and philosophers. Different as these men are, they are alike in their withdrawal from the ordinary affairs of the island, the trading, farming, manufacturing, playing, gossiping, loving—in order to discover underlying constancies amid the flux of phenomena, in order to take exact measurements, in order to make precise inductions and deductions, in order to arrange words or sounds or colors to express universal human experience. (This extraordinary activity is first known to have appeared in the world more or less simultaneously in Greece, India, and China around 600 B.C., a time which Jaspers calls the axial period in world history.)

In this very large group, which the islander might well call "science" in the broadest sense of knowing, the sense of the German word *Wissenschaft*, the islander would put both synthetic and analytic sentences, not only those accepted by positive scientists, but the psychoanalytic sentence, the metaphysical sentence, and the lines of poetry. (He might even include paintings as being, in a sense, sentences.) If the physicist protests at finding himself in the company of psychoanalysts, poets, Vedantists, and Scholastics, the islander will reply that he is not saying that all the sentences are true but that their writers appear to him to be engaged in the same sort of activity as the physicist, namely, withdrawal from the ordinary affairs of life to university, laboratory, studio, mountain eyrie, where they write sentences to which other men assent (or refuse assent), saying, Yes, this is indeed how things are. In some sense or other, the sentences can be verified by the readers even if not testable experimentally—as when the psychiatric patient hears his analyst explain a dream symbol and suddenly realizes that this is indeed what his own dream symbol meant.

In the second group the islander would place those sentences which are significant precisely in so far as the reader is caught up in the affairs and in the life of the island and in so far as he has *not* withdrawn into laboratory or seminar room. Such are the sentences

> *There is fresh water in the next cove.*
> *A hostile war party is approaching.*
> *The market for eggs in Bora Bora is very good.*

These sentences are highly significant to the islander, because he is thirsty, because his island society is threatened, or because he is in the egg business. Such messages he might well call "news."

It will be seen that the criteria of the logician and the positive scientist are of no use to the islander. They do not distinguish between those messages which are of consequence for life on the island and those messages which are not. The logician would place these two sentences

> *A hostile war party is approaching.*
> *The British are coming [to Concord].*

in the same pigeonhole. But to the islander they are very different. The islander lumps together synthetic and analytic, sense and nonsense (to the positivist) sentences under the group "science." Nor is the division tidy. Some sentences do not seem to be provided for at all. The islander is fully aware of the importance of the sentence about the melting point of lead and he puts it under "science." He is fully aware of the importance of the sentence about the hostile war party and he puts it under "news." But where does he put the sentence about the approach of the British to Concord? He does not really care; he would be happy to put it in the "science" pigeonhole if the scientists want it. All he knows is that it is not news to him or the island.

If the islander was asked to say what was wrong with the first division of the logician and scientist, he might reply that it unconsciously assumes that this very special posture of "science" (including poetry, psychoanalysis, philosophy, etc.) is the only attitude that yields significant sentences. People who discover how to strike this attitude of "science" seem also to decide at the same time that they will only admit as significant those sentences which have been written by others who have struck the same attitude. Yet there are times when they act as if this were not the case. If a group of island logicians are busy in a seminar room sifting through the messages from the bottles and someone ran in crying, "The place is on fire!" the logicians would not be content to classify the message as a protocol sentence. They would also leave the building. The castaway will observe only that their classification does take account of the extraordinary significance which they as men have attributed to the message.

To the castaway it seems obvious that a radical classification of the sentences cannot abstract from the concrete situation in which one finds oneself. He is as interested as the scientist in arriving at a rigorous and valid classification. If the scientist should protest that one can hardly make such a classification when each sentence may have a different significance for every man who hears it, the castaway must agree with him. He must agree, that is, that you cannot classify without abstracting. But he insists that the classification be radical enough to take account of the hearer of the news, of the difference between a true piece of news which is not important and a true piece of news which is important. In order to do this, we do not have to throw away the hard-won objectivity of the scientist. We have only to take a step further back so that we may see objectively not only the sentences but the positive scientist who is examining them. After all, the objective posture of the scientist is in the world and can be studied like anything else in the world.

If the scientist protests that in taking one step back to see the scientist at work, the castaway is starting a game of upstaging which has no end—for why not take still another step back and watch the castaway watching the scientist—the castaway replies simply that this is not so. For if you take a step back to see the castaway classifying the messages, you will only see the same thing he sees as he watches the scientist, a man working objectively.

Then, if the castaway is a serious fellow who wants to do justice both to the scientists and to the news in the bottle, he is obliged to become not less but more objective and to take one step back of the

scientist, so that he can see him at work in the laboratory and seminar room—and see the news in the bottle too.

What he will see then is not only that there are two kinds of sentences in the bottles but that there are two kinds of postures from
which one reads the sentences, two kinds of verifying procedures by
which one acts upon them, and two kinds of responses to the sentences.

The classification of the castaway would be something like this:

The Difference between a Piece of Knowledge and a Piece of News

(1) The Character of the Sentence

By "piece of knowledge" the castaway means knowledge *sub
specie aeternitatis*. By *sub specie aeternitatis* he means not what the
philosopher usually means but rather knowledge which can be arrived at anywhere by anyone and at any time. The islanders may
receive such knowledge in the bottle and be glad to get it—if they
have not already gotten it. But getting this knowledge from across
the seas is not indispensable. By its very nature the knowledge can
also be reached, in principle, by the islander on his island, using
his own raw materials, his own scientific, philosophical, and artistic efforts.

Such knowledge would include not only the synthetic and analytic propositions of science and logic but also the philosophical
and poetic sentences in the bottle. To the logician the sentence
"Lead melts at 330 degrees" seems to be empirical and synthetic. It
cannot be deduced from self-evident principles like the analytic
sentence "2 + 2 = 4." It cannot be arrived at by reflection, however strenuous. Yet to the castaway this sentence is knowledge *sub
specie aeternitatis*. It is a property of lead on any island at any time
and for anyone.

The following sentences the castaway would consider knowledge
sub specie aeternitatis even though they might not have been so
considered in the past. Notice that the list includes a mixture of
synthetic, analytic, normative, poetic, and metaphysical sentences.

Lead melts at 330 degrees.
Chicago is on the Hudson River or Chicago is not on the Hudson River.
2 + 2 = 4.
The pressure of a gas is a function of temperature and volume.
*Acute myelogenous leukemia may be cured by parenteral administration
   of metallic beryllium.*
The dream symbol, house and balcony, usually represents a woman.
Men should not kill each other.
Being comprises essence and existence.

He is not saying that all the sentences are true—at least one (the one about leukemia) is probably not. But they are all pieces of knowledge which can be arrived at (or rejected) by anyone on any island at any time. If true they will hold true for anyone on any island at any time. He has no quarrel with the positivist over the admissibility of poetic and metaphysical statements. Admissible or not, it is all the same to him. All he is saying is that this kind of sentence may be arrived at (has in fact been arrived at) independently by people in different places and can be confirmed (or rejected) by people in still other places.

By a "piece of news" the castaway generally means a synthetic sentence expressing a contingent and nonrecurring event or state of affairs which event or state of affairs is peculiarly relevant to the concrete predicament of the hearer of the news.

It is a knowledge which cannot possibly be arrived at by any effort of experimentation or reflection or artistic insight. It may not be arrived at by observation on any island at any time. It may not even be arrived at on this island at any time (since it is a single, nonrecurring event or state of affairs).

Both these sentences are synthetic empirical sentences open to verification by the positive method of the sciences. Yet one is, to the castaway, knowledge *sub specie aeternitatis* and the other is a piece of news.

Water boils at 100 degrees at sea level.
There is fresh water in the next cove.

The following sentences would qualify as possible news to the castaway.

> At 2 p.m., January 4, 1902, at the residence of Manuel Gómez in Ma-
>   tanzas, Cuba, a leaf fell from the banyan tree.
> The British are coming.
> The market for eggs in Bora Bora [a neighboring island] is very good.
> Jane will arrive tomorrow.
> In 1943 the Russians murdered 10,000 Polish officers in the Katyn
>   forest.
> A war party is approaching from Bora Bora.
> There is fresh water in the next cove.

What does the positive scientist think of the sentences which the castaway calls news? Does he reject them as being false or absurd? No, he is perfectly willing to accept them as long as they meet his standard of verification. By the use of the critical historical method he attaches a high degree of probability to the report that the British were approaching Concord. As for the water in the next cove, he goes to see for himself and so confirms the news or rejects it. But what sort of significance does he assign these sentences as he sorts them out in the seminar room? To him they express a few of the almost infinite number of true but random observations which might be made about the world. The murder of the Polish officers may have been a great tragedy, yet in all honesty he cannot assign to it a significance qualitatively different from the sentence about the leaf falling from the banyan tree (nor may the castaway necessarily). This is not to say that these sentences are worthless as scientific data. For example, the presence of water in the next cove might serve as a significant datum for the descriptive science of geography, or as an important clue in geology. This single observation could conceivably be the means of verifying a revolutionary scientific theory—just as the sight of a star on a particular night in a particular place provided dramatic confirmation of Einstein's general theory of relativity.

The sentences about the coming of the British and the murder of the Polish officers might serve as significant data from which, along with other such data, general historical principles might be drawn—just as Toynbee speaks of such and such an event as being a good example of such and such a historical process.

In summary, the castaway will make a distinction between the sentences which assert a piece of knowledge *sub specie aeternitatis* and the sentences announcing a piece of news which bears directly on his life. The scientist and logician, however, cannot, in so far as they are scientists and logicians, take account of the special character of these news sentences. To them they are empirical observations of a random order and, if significant, they occupy at best the very lowest rung of scientific significance: they are the particular instances from which hypotheses and theories are drawn.

(2) The Posture of the Reader of the Sentence

The significance of the sentences for the reader will depend on the reader's own mode of existence in the world. To say this is to say nothing about the truth of the sentences. Assuming that they are all true, they will have a qualitatively different significance for the reader according to his own placement in the world.

(a) The posture of objectivity. If the reader has discovered the secret of science, art, and philosophizing, and so has entered the great company of Thales, Lao-tse, Aquinas, Newton, Keats, Whitehead, he will know what it is to stand outside and over against the world as one who sees and thinks and knows and tells. He tells and hears others tell how it is there in the world and what it is to live in the world. In so far as he himself is a scientist, artist, or philosopher, he reads the sentences in the bottles as stating (or coming short of stating) knowledge *sub specie aeternitatis*. It may be trivial knowledge; it may be knowledge he has already arrived at; it may be knowledge he has not yet arrived at but could arrive at in time; it may be false knowledge which fails to be verified and so is rejected. It cannot be any other kind of knowledge.

(b) The posture of the castaway. The reader of the sentences may or may not be an objective-minded man. But at the moment of finding the bottle on the beach he is, we will say, very far from being objective-minded. He is a man who finds himself in a certain situation. To say this is practically equivalent, life being what it is, to saying that he finds himself in a certain predicament. Let us say his predicament is a simple organic need. He is thirsty. In his predicament the sentence about the water is received not as a datum from which, along with similar data, more general scientific conclusions might be drawn. Nor is it received as stating a universal human experience, even though the announcement were composed by Shakespeare at the height of his powers. The sentence is received as news, news strictly relevant to the predicament in which the hearer of the news finds himself.

So with other kinds of news, ranging from news relevant to the most elementary organic predicament to news of complex cultural significance.

Here are some other examples of news and their attending contexts.

Mackerel here!	(*Malinowski's Trobriand Island fisherman announcing a strike to his fellows*)
Jane is home!	(*I love Jane and she has been away*)
The market is up $2.00.	(*I am in the market*)
The British are coming!	(*I am a Minute Man. The context here is not organic but cultural. I thrive under British rule but I throw in my lot with the Revolution for patriotic reasons*)
The light has turned green!	(*I have stopped at a red light*)
Eisenhower is elected!	(*I voted for Stevenson*)

News sentences, in short, are drawn from the context of everyday life and indeed to a large extent comprise this context.

Insofar as a man is objective-minded, no sentence is significant as a piece of news. For in order to be objective-minded one must stand outside and over against the world as its knower in one mode or another. As empirical scientists themselves have noticed, one condition of the practice of the objective method of the sciences is the exclusion of oneself from the world of objects one studies.* The absent-minded professor, the inspired poet, the Vedic mystic, is indifferent to news, sometimes even news of high relevance for him, because he is in a very real sense "out of this world." †

---

* See, for example, the physicist Erwin Schrödinger in *What Is Life?* and the psychiatrist C. G. Jung in *Der Geist der Psychologie.*

† I wish to make an objective distinction here without pejoration to castaways on the one hand or scientists, scholars, mystics, and poets, on the other—while at the same time readily admitting we could use a few more of the absent-minded variety at this time.

In summary, the hearer of news is a man who finds himself in a predicament. News is precisely that communication which has bearing on his predicament and is therefore good or bad news.

The question arises as to whether news is not the same thing as a sign for an organism, a sign directing him to appropriate need-satisfactions, like the buzzer to Pavlov's dog, or warning him of a threat, like the lion's scent to a deer. The organism experiences needs and drives and learns to respond to those signs in its environment which indicate the presence of food, opposite sex, danger, and so on.

This may very well be a fair appraisal of the status of the news we are talking about here—providing the notions of "organism" and "sign" be allowed sufficiently broad interpretation. For the organism we speak of here is not only the physiological mechanism of the body but the encultured creature, the economic creature, and so on. The sign we speak of here is not merely the environmental element; it is the sentence, the symbolic assertion made by one man and understood by another.

The scientist—I use the word in the broadest possible sense to include philosophers and artists as well as positive scientists—has abstracted from his own predicament in order to achieve objectivity.* His objectivity is indeed nothing else than his removal from his own concrete situation. No sentence can be received by him as a piece of news, therefore, because he does not stand in the way of hearing news.

(3) The Scale of Significance

The scale of significance by which the scientist evaluates the sentences in the bottles may be said to range from the particular to the general. The movement of science is toward unity through abstraction, toward formulae and principles which embrace an ever

---

* If the depth psychologist objects that the scientist and artist is no different from anyone else: he undertakes his science and his art so that he may satisfy the deepest unconscious needs of his personality by "sublimating" and so on— the castaway will not quarrel with him. He will observe only that, whatever his psychological motivation may be, the scientist and artist—and depth analyst—undertake a very extraordinary activity in virtue of which they stand over against the world as its knowers.

greater number of particular instances. Thus the sentence "Hydrogen and oxygen combine in the ratio of two to one to form water" is a general statement covering a large number of particular cases. But Mendeleev's law of periodicity covers not merely water but all other cases of chemical combination. A theory of gravitation and a theory of radiation are conceived at very high levels of abstraction. But a unified field theory which unites the two occurs at an even higher level.

The scale of significance by which the castaway evaluates news is its relevance for his own predicament. The significance of a piece of knowledge is abstracted altogether from the concrete circumstances which attended the discovery of the knowledge, its verification, its hearing by others. The relationship of Mendeleev's law of periodicity to Lavoisier's discovery of the composition of water is a relation *sub specie aeternitatis*. Its significance in no way depends upon Lavoisier's or Mendeleev's circumstance in life or on the circumstance of him who hears it.

But in judging the significance of a piece of news, everything depends on the situation of the hearer. The question is not merely, What is the nature of the news? but, Who is the hearer? If a man has lost his way in a cave and hears the cry "Come! This way out!" the communication qualifies as news of high significance. But if another man has for reasons of his own come to the cave to spend the rest of his life, the announcement will be of no significance. To a man dying of thirst the news of diamonds over the next dune is of no significance. But the news of water is.

The abstraction of the scientist from the affairs of life may be so great that he even ignores news of the highest relevance for his own predicament. When a friend approached Archimedes and announced, "Archimedes, the soldiers of Marcellus are coming to kill you," Archimedes remained indifferent. He attributed no significance to a contingent piece of news in comparison with the significance of his geometrical deductions. In so doing it may be that he acted as an admirable martyr for science or it may be that he acted foolishly. All that we are concerned here to notice are the traits of objectivity.

The castaway, on the other hand, can only take account of knowledge *sub specie aeternitatis* if it is significant also as news. If his island stands to win international honor providing one of its scientists discovers the secret of atomic energy, or if indeed such a discovery means survival, then the announcement of his scientist friend

$$E = MC^2!$$

is news of the highest significance.

In summary, the scale of significance by which one judges sentences expressing knowledge *sub specie aeternitatis* is the scientific scale of particular–general. The scale of significance by which a castaway evaluates the news in the bottle is the degree of relevance for his own predicament.

(4) Canons of Acceptance

The operation of acceptance of a piece of knowledge *sub specie aeternitatis* is synonymous with the procedure of verification.

We need not review the verification procedures of formal logic or positive science. The truth of analytic sentences is demonstrated by a disclosure of the deductive process by which they are inferred. The truth or probability of synthetic sentences is demonstrated by a physical operation repeatable by others.

What about the verification procedures of our other "scientific" sentences, those of psychoanalysts, artists, philosophers, *et al.?* For example, a neurotic physicist is able to verify the suggestion of his analyst that his dream symbol means such and such, and to do so without resorting to a physical operation. These and other such sentences, I suggest, are verifiable not experimentally but experientially by the hearer on the basis of his own experience or reflection. These sentences

Your dream symbol, house and balcony, represents a woman.
The whole is greater than the part.
We are such stuff as dreams are made on, and our little life is rounded with a sleep.

can only be verified (or rejected) by the immediate assent or assent after reflection of him who hears, on the basis of his own experience.

The criteria of acceptance of a news sentence are not the same as those of a knowledge sentence. This is not a pejorative judgment. To say this is not to say that news is of a lower cognitive order than knowledge—such a judgment presupposes the superiority of the scientific posture. It is only to say that once a piece of news is subject to the verification procedures of a piece of knowledge, it simply ceases to be news.

If I am thirsty and you appear on the next sand dune and shout, "Come with me! I know where water is!" it is not open to me to apply any of the verification procedures mentioned above, experimental operations, deduction, or interior recognition and assent to the truth of your statement. A piece of news is neither deducible, repeatable, or otherwise confirmable *at the point of hearing.*

You may deny this, saying that the thirsty man is not really different from the scientist: The only way to verify a report in either case is to go and see for yourself. Very true! But what we are concerned with is not the act, going and seeing for yourself, as a verification procedure, but how one decides to heed the initial "Come!" The scientist does not need to heed the "Come!" For he does not have to come. He is in no predicament whatever and any knowledge that he might wish to arrive at can be arrived at anywhere and at any time and by anyone. Whatever he wants to find out can be found out in his laboratory, on his field trip, in his studio, on his grass mat.

But the castaway must act by a canon of acceptance which is usable *prior* to the procedure of verification. He is obliged to contrive some standard. Otherwise he is easy prey for any clever scoundrel who knows how to take advantage of his predicament to lead him into a den of thieves. What is this standard? What elements does it comprise?

Clearly there are at least two elements. One is the relevance of the news to my predicament. If the stranger in the desert approaches me and announces, "I know what your need is. It is diamonds. Come with me. I know where they are"—I reject him on two counts. One, because it is not diamonds I need; two, because, if he is such a fool or knave as to believe it is diamonds I want, he is probably lying anyway. But if he announces instead, "Come! I know your need. I will take you to water"—then this very announcement is an earnest of his reliability. Yet he might still be a knave or a fool.

Two men are riding a commuter train. One is, as the expression goes, fat, dumb, and happy. Though he lives the most meaningless sort of life, a trivial routine of meals, work, gossip, television, and sleep, he nevertheless feels quite content with himself and is at home in the world. The other commuter, who lives the same kind of life, feels quite lost to himself. He knows that something is dreadfully wrong. More than that, he is in anxiety; he suffers acutely, yet he does not know why. What is wrong? Does he not have all the goods of life?

If now a stranger approaches the first commuter, takes him aside, and says to him earnestly, "My friend, I know your predicament; come with me; I have news of the utmost importance for you"— then the commuter will reject the communication out of hand. For he is in no predicament, or if he is, he does not know it, and so the communication strikes him as nonsense.

The second commuter might very well heed the stranger's "Come!" At least he will take it seriously. Indeed it may well be that he has been waiting all his life to hear this "Come!"

The canon of acceptance by which one rejects and the other heeds the "Come!" is its relevance to his predicament. The man who is dying of thirst will not heed news of diamonds. The man at home, the satisfied man, he who does not feel himself to be in a predicament, will not heed good news. The objective-minded man, he who stands outside and over against the world as its knower, will not heed news of any kind, good or bad—in so far as he remains objective-minded. The castaway will heed news relevant to his predicament. Yet the relevance of the news is not in itself sufficient warrant.

A second canon of acceptance of news is the credentials of the newsbearer. Such credentials make themselves known through the reputation or through the mien of the newsbearer. The credentials of the bearer of knowledge *sub specie aeternitatis* are of no matter to the scientist. It doesn't matter whether Wagner, in writing his music, is a rascal or whether Lavoisier, in speaking of oxygen, is a thief. The knowledge sentence carries or fails to carry its own credentials in so far as it is in some fashion affirmable. If the newsbearer is my brother or friend and if I know that he knows my predicament and if he approaches me with every outward sign of sobriety and good faith, and if the news is of a momentous nature, then I have reason to heed the news. If the newsbearer is known to me as a knave or a fool, I have reason to ignore the news.

If the newsbearer is a stranger to me, he is not necessarily disqualified as a newsbearer. In some cases indeed his disinterest may itself be a warrant, since he does not stand to profit from the usual considerations of friendship, family feelings, and so on. His sobriety or foolishness, good faith or knavery may be known through his mien. Even though he may bring news of high relevance to my predicament, yet a certain drunkenness of spirit—enthusiasm in the old sense of the word—is enough to disqualify him and lead me to suspect that he is concerned not with my predicament but only with his own drunkenness. If a Jehovah's Witness should ring my doorbell and announce the advent of God's kingdom, I recognize the possibly momentous character of his news but must withhold acceptance because of a certain lack of sobriety in the newsbearer.*

If the newsbearer is a stranger and if he meets the requirements of good faith and sobriety and, extraordinarily enough, knows my predicament, then the very fact of his being a stranger is reason enough to heed the news. For if a perfect stranger puts himself to

---

* If one thinks of the Christian gospel primarily as a communication between a newsbearer and a hearer of news, one realizes that the news is often not heeded because it is not delivered soberly. Instead of being delivered with the sobriety with which other important news would be delivered—even by a preacher—it is spoken either in a sonorous pulpit voice or at a pitch calculated to stimulate the emotions. But emotional stimuli are not news. The emotions can be stimulated on any island and at any time.

some trouble to come to me and announce a piece of news relevant to my predicament and announce it with perfect sobriety and with every outward sign of good faith, then I must say to myself, What manner of man is this that he should put himself out of his way for a perfect stranger—and I should heed him. It was enough for Jesus to utter the one word *Come!* to a stranger—yet when he uttered the same word in Nazareth, no one came.

The message in the bottle, then, is not sufficient credential in itself as a piece of news. It is sufficient credential in itself as a piece of knowledge, for the scientist has only to test it and does not care who wrote it or whether the writer was sober or in good faith. *But a piece of news requires that there be a newsbearer.* The sentence written on a piece of paper in the bottle is sufficient if it is a piece of knowledge but it is hardly sufficient if it is a piece of news.

A third canon of acceptance is the possibility of the news. If the news is strictly relevant to my predicament and if the bearer of the news is a person of the best character, I still cannot heed the news if (1) I know for a fact that it cannot possibly be true or (2) the report refers to an event of an unheralded, absurd, or otherwise inappropriate character. If I am dying of thirst and the newsbearer announces to me that over the next dune I will discover molten sulfur and that it will quench my thirst, I must despair of his news. If the castaway arrived at his South Sea island in 1862 and found his adoptive land in bondage to a tyrant and if a newsbearer arrived and announced that Robert E. Lee and the Army of Northern Virginia were on their way to deliver the island—such a piece of news would lie within the realm of possibility yet be so intrinsically inappropriate that the most patriotic of islanders could hardly take it seriously. If, however, there had been promises of deliverance for a hundred years from a neighboring island and if, further, signs had been agreed upon by which one could recognize the deliverer, and if, finally, a newsbearer from this very island arrived and announced a piece of news of supreme relevance to the predicament of the islanders and announced it in perfect sobriety and with every outward sign of good faith, then the islander must himself be a fool or a knave if he did not heed the news.

(5) Response of the Reader of the Sentence

The response of a reader of a sentence expressing a piece of knowledge is to confirm it (or reject it). The response of a hearer of a piece of news is to heed it (or ignore it) by taking action appropriate to one's predicament. In the sphere of pure knowledge, knowledge in science, philosophy, or art, the act of knowing is complete when the sentence (or formula or insight or poem or painting) is received, understood, and confirmed as being true. Other consequences may follow. Physics may lead to useful inventions; a great philosopher may invigorate his civilization and prolong its life for hundreds of years; a great artist may lower the incidence of neurosis. But science is not necessarily committed to technics; philosophers do not necessarily philosophize in order to preserve the state; art is not a form of mental hygiene. There is a goodness and a joy in science and art apart from the effects of science and art on ordinary life. These effects may follow and may be good, but if the effect is made the end, if science is enslaved to technics, philosophy to the state, art to psychiatry—one wonders how long we would have a science, philosophy, or art worthy of the name.

The appropriate response of the reader of a sentence conveying a piece of knowledge—a piece of knowledge which, let us say, falls in the vanguard of the islander's own knowledge—is to know this and more. The movement of science is toward an ever-more-encompassing unity and depth of vision. The movement of the islander who has caught the excitement of science, art, or philosophy is toward the attainment of an ever-more-encompassing unity and depth of vision. The man who finds the bottle on the beach and who reads its message conveying a piece of knowledge undertakes his quest, verification and extension of the knowledge, on his own island or on any island at any time. His quest takes place *sub specie aeternitatis* and, in so far as he is a scientist, he does not care who he is, where he is, or what his predicament may be.

The response of a hearer of a piece of news is to take action appropriate to his predicament. The news is not delivered to be confirmed—for then it would not be a piece of news but a piece of knowledge. There would be no pressing need to deliver it for it is not relevant to the predicament of the islander and it can, theoretically, be arrived at by the islander himself on his own island. The piece of news is delivered to be heeded and acted upon. There is a criterion of acceptance of a piece of news but this acceptance procedure is strictly ancillary to the action to be taken. In science, however, the technical invention which may follow the discovery is optional.*

If a congress of scientists, philosophers, and artists is convening in an Aspen auditorium in order to take account of the recent "sentences" of their colleagues (hypotheses, theories, formulae, logics, geometries, poems, symphonies, etc.), and if during the meeting a fire should break out, and if then a man should mount the podium and utter the sentence "Come! I know the way out!"—the conferees will be able to distinguish at once the difference between this sentence and all the other sentences which have been uttered from the podium. Different as a bar of music is from a differential equation, it will be seen at once that the two share a generic likeness when compared with a piece of news. A radical shift of posture by both teller and hearer has taken place. The conferees will attach a high importance to the sentence even though it conveys no universal truth and *even though it may not be verified on hearing*. A different criterion of acceptance becomes appropriate. It is not an inferior or makeshift criterion—as when a castaway makes do with a raft but would rather have a steamship. It is the criterion appropriate to news as a category of communication. If a criterion of verification could be used, then the communication would cease to be news relevant to my predicament; it would become instead a piece of knowledge *sub specie aeternitatis.†*

---

* Einstein's discovery of the equivalence of matter and energy and of the ratio of the equivalence was a momentous advance of science. As it happened, it was also a piece of good news for the Allies in World War II. Indeed, pure science, research *sub specie aeternitatis*, may be undertaken under the pressure of a historical predicament. But the point is that it may also be undertaken—and Einstein's research was undertaken—with no thought of its possible bearing on politics.

† True, after the announcement, the way out could then be seen by the conferee from where he sits, and so the news verified before it is heeded and acted upon. The event then takes place at an organic level of animal response. But the difference still holds: the prime importance which the hearer attaches to the announcement, even

The conferees at Aspen apply an appropriate criterion. They are not gullible—for bad advice at this juncture could get them killed. If the newsbearer had announced, not that he knew the way out, but that world peace had been achieved, they would hardly heed him. If he commanded them to flap their arms and fly out through the skylight, they would hardly heed him. If he spoke like a fool with all manner of ranting and raving, they would hardly heed him. If they knew him to be a liar, they would hardly heed him. But if he spoke with authority, in perfect sobriety, and with every outward sign of good faith and regard for them, saying that he knew the way out and they had only to follow him, they would heed him. They would heed him with all dispatch. They would, unless there were an Archimedes present, give his news priority over the most momentous and exciting advance in science. They would heed him at any cost, even though as scientists they must preserve a low regard for sentences bearing news of a contingent event.

The Mistaking of a Piece of Knowledge for a Piece of News from across the Seas

What if it should happen that a scientist should assign a high order of significance to a piece of knowledge and a low order of significance to a piece of news? He could make a serious mistake. Having assigned all news sentences to a low order of significance, he could make the mistake of attending only to scientific sentences in the belief that since they are so important in the sphere of knowledge, they might also do duty as pieces of news. Thus, if it should happen that he experiences a predicament of homelessness or of anxiety without cause, he may seek for its cause and cure within the sphere of scientific and artistic knowledge or from the satisfaction of his island needs. He may resort to analysis or drugs or group therapy or creative writing or reading creative writing, all of which may assuage this or that symptom of his loneliness or anxiety. Or he

though it is of no greater scientific significance than the sentence "There is a fly on your nose"; the response of the hearer of the sentence, the getting out rather than the verification in situ.

may seek a wife or new friends or more meaningful relationships. But what if it should be the case that his symptoms of homelessness or anxiety do not have their roots in this or that lack of knowledge or this or that malfunction which he may suffer as an islander but rather in the very fact that he is a castaway and that as such he stands not in the way of one who requires a piece of island knowledge or a technique of island treatment or this or that island need satisfaction but stands rather in the way of one who is waiting for a piece of news from across the seas? Then he has deceived himself and, even if his symptoms are better, is worse off then he was.

The Difference between Island News and News from across the Seas

My purpose here is not apologetic. We are not here concerned with the truth of the Christian gospel or with the career in time of that unique Thing, the Jewish-People-Jesus-Christ-Catholic-Church. An apologetic would deal with the evidences of God's entry into history through His covenant with the Jews, through His own incarnation, and through His institution of the Catholic Church as the means of man's salvation. It would also deal with philosophical approaches to God's existence and nature. My purpose is rather the investigation of news as a category of communication.

In the light of the distinction we have made, however, it is possible to shed light on some perennial confusions which arise whenever Christianity is misunderstood as a teaching *sub specie aeternitatis*. As Kierkegaard put it, the object of the student is not the teacher but the teaching, while the object of the Christian is not the teaching but the teacher.* I say perennial because the misunderstanding by the Athenians of Saint Paul and the offense they took is not essentially different from the misunderstanding of modern eclectics like Whitehead, Huxley, and Toynbee, and the offense they take. Not being an apostle and, as Kierkegaard again would say, having no authority to preach, I should hope not to give

* Although primarily a teacher, a Person, Christianity, of course, involves a teaching too.

further offense and to propose only a small clarifying distinction—
not a piece of news in the bottle but only a minor "scientific" sentence—which should offend neither believer nor unbeliever.
Whitehead, for one, should not take offense. He pronounced that
generality is the salt of religion just as it is the salt of science. And if
one should propose therefore that Christianity is not a teaching but
a teacher, not a piece of knowledge *sub specie aeternitatis* but a
piece of news, not a member in good standing of the World's Great
Religions but a unique Person-Event-Thing in time—then the
eclectic should not mind, because to say this is hardly to advance
the case of Christianity in his eyes; it is rather to admit the worst
that he has suspected all along. I do not mean that a mistaking of
the Judeo-Christian Thing for a piece of knowledge *sub specie aeternitatis* leads always to hostility and rejection. Indeed it is more
common nowadays to accept Christianity on such grounds—as
being confirmed by Buddhism in this respect or by psychiatry in
some other respect—or as in the case of the *Look* magazine article
which announced that one might now believe in miracles because
the Law of Probability allowed that once in a great while a body
might fly straight up instead of falling down.

We might then be content here to agree to disagree about what
salt is and whether or not in becoming general it loses its savor.
Nevertheless the peculiar character of the Christian claim, its staking everything on a people, a person, an event, a thing existing
here and now in time—and on the news of this Thing—and its relative indifference to esoteric philosophical truths such as might be
arrived at by Vedantists, Buddhists, idealists, existentialists, or by
any islanders anywhere or at any time—might serve here to
quicken our interest in news as a category of communication.

But to return to the castaway and the message in the bottle. The
castaway has, we have seen, classified the messages differently from
the scientist and logician. Their classifications would divide the sentences accordingly as they were analytic or synthetic, necessary or
contingent, repeatable or historic, etc. But the castaway's classification divides them accordingly as some express a knowledge which
can be arrived at anywhere and at any time, given the talent, time,

and inclination of the student—and as others tell pieces of news which cannot be so arrived at by any effort of observation or reflection however strenuous and yet which are of immense importance to the hearer. Has the castaway's classification exhausted the significant communications which the bottles contain? If this is the case, then we seem to be saying that the news which the islander finds significant is nothing more than signs of various need-satisfactions which the organism must take account of to flourish. These needs and their satisfactions are readily acknowledged by the objective-minded man. Indeed, the main concern of the biological, medical, and psychological sciences is the discovery of these various needs and the satisfying of them. If a man is thirsty, then he had better pay attention to news of water. If a culture is to survive, it had better heed the news of the approach of the British or a war party from a neighboring island. Also, if a man is to live a rich, full, "rewarding" life, he should have his quota of myths and archetypes.

Are we saying in short that the predicament which the islander finds himself in and the means he takes to get out of it are those very needs and drives and those very satisfactions and goals which the objective-minded man recognizes and seeks to provide for every island everywhere? It is not quite so simple. For we have forgotten who it is we are talking about. As we noted earlier, the significance of news depends not only on the news but on the hearer, who he is and what his predicament is.

Our subject is not only an organism and a culture member; he is also a castaway. That is to say, he is not in the world as a swallow is in the world, as an organism which is what it is, never more or less. Our islander may choose his mode of being. Thus, he may choose to exist as a scientist, outside and over against the world as its knower, or he may choose to exist as a culture member, that is, an organism whose biological and psychological needs are more or less satisfied by his culture. But however he chooses to exist, he is in the last analysis a castaway, a stranger who is in the world but who is not at home in the world.

A castaway, everyone would agree, would do well to pay attention to knowledge and news, knowledge of the nature of the world and news of events that are relevant to his life on the island. Such news, the news relevant to his survival as an organism, his life as a father and husband, as a member of a culture, as an economic man, and so on—we can well call *island news*. Such news is relevant to the everyday life of any islander on any island at any time.

Yet even so all is not well with him. Something is wrong. For with all the knowledge he achieves, all his art and philosophy, all the island news he pays attention to, something is missing. What is it? He does not know. He might say that he was homesick except that the island is his home and he has spent his life making himself at home there. He knows only that his sickness cannot be cured by island knowledge or by island news.

But how does he know he is sick, let alone homesick? He may not know. He may live and die as an islander at home on his island. But if he does know, he knows for the simple reason that in his heart of hearts he can never forget who he is: that he is a stranger, a castaway, who despite a lifetime of striving to be at home on the island is as homeless now as he was the first day he found himself cast up on the beach.

But then do you mean that his homesickness is one final need to be satisfied, that the island news has taken care of 95 per cent of his needs and that there remains one last little need to be taken care of—these occasional twinges of nostalgia? Or, as the church advertisements would say, one must have a "church home" besides one's regular home? No, it is much worse than that. I mean that in his heart of hearts there is not a moment of his life when the castaway does not know that life on the island, being "at home" on the island, is something of a charade. At that very moment when he should feel most at home on the island, when needs are satisfied, knowledge arrived at, family raised, business attended to, at that very moment when by every criterion of island at-homeness he should feel most at home, he feels most homeless. Not one moment of his life passes but that he is aware, however faintly, of his own predicament: that he is a castaway.

Nor would it avail to say to him simply that he is homesick and that all he needs is to know who he is and where he came from. He would only shake his head and turn away. For he knows nothing of any native land except the island and such talk anyhow reminds him of Sunday school. But if we say to him only that something is very wrong and that after fifty years on the island he is still a stranger and a castaway, he must listen, for he knows this better than anyone else.

Then what should he do? It is not for me to say here that he do this or that or should believe such and such. But one thing is certain. He should be what he is and not pretend to be somebody else. He should be a castaway and not pretend to be at home on the island. To be a castaway is to be in a grave predicament and this is not a happy state of affairs. But it is very much happier than being a castaway and pretending one is not. This is despair. The worst of all despairs is to imagine one is at home when one is really homeless.

But what is it to be a castaway? To be a castaway is to search for news from across the seas. Does this mean that one throws over science, throws over art, pays no attention to island news, forgets to eat and sleep and love—does nothing in fact but comb the beach in search of the bottle with the news from across the seas? No, but it means that one searches nevertheless and that one lives in hope that such a message will come, and that one knows that the message will not be a piece of knowledge or a piece of island news but news from across the seas.

It is news, however, this news from across the seas, and it is as a piece of news that it must be evaluated. Faith is the organ of the historical, said Kierkegaard. Faith of a sort is the organ for dealing with island news, and faith of a sort is the organ for dealing with news from across the seas.

But what does it mean to say that faith is the organ of the historical? For Kierkegaard it means two things. For an ordinary historical truth—what we here call "island news"—faith is the organ of the historical because the organ of the historical must have a structure analogous to the historical. The nature of the historical is becoming. The nature of belief is a "negated uncertainty which corresponds to the uncertainty of becoming." By historical Kier-

kegaard means the existing thing or event, not only that which
existed in the past, but that which exists here and now before our
very eyes. One sees that star rightly enough, but one must also confirm by another act that the star has come into existence. Faith is
the organ which confirms that an existing thing has come into existence.* The Christian faith, however—the news from across the
seas—is an embrace of the Absolute Paradox as such, a setting aside
of reason, a *credo quia absurdum est*. It is well known that Kierkegaard, unlike Saint Thomas, denies a cognitive content to faith—
faith is not a form of knowledge. His extreme position is at least
in part attributable to his anxiety to rescue Christianity from the
embrace of the Hegelians.

Yet we must ask whether Kierkegaard's antinomy of faith versus
reason is any more appropriate to the situation of the castaway than
the logician's classification of synthetic and analytic. For the castaway, or anyone who finds himself in a predicament in the world,
there are two kinds of knowledge, knowledge *sub specie aeternitatis*
and news bearing on his own predicament. The classification of the
castaway would correspond roughly to the two knowledges of Saint
Thomas: (1) scientific knowledge, in which assent is achieved by
reason, (2) knowledge of faith, in which scientific knowledge and
assent are undertaken simultaneously. The fact is that Kierkegaard, despite his passionate dialectic, laid himself open to his
enemies. For his categories of faith, inwardness, subjectivity, and
Absolute Paradox seem to the objective-minded man to confirm the
worst of what he had thought all along of the Christian news.

To Kierkegaard the Absolute Paradox was that one's eternal happiness should depend on a piece of news from across the seas. He
still remained Hegelian enough ("scientist" enough in our terminology) to accept the scientific scale of significance which ranks
general knowledge *sub specie aeternitatis* very high and contingent
historical knowledge very low. Yet the curious fact is that the philosophical movement of which he has been called the founder has
developed an anthropology, a view of man, which is very much

---

* A similar distinction is made by Newman between real assent and notional assent.

more receptive to such news than Kierkegaard ever allowed one could be—*even though this movement has in most cases disavowed the Christian setting Kierkegaard gave it*. The Jasperian notion of shipwrecked man, Heidegger's notion of man's existence as a *Geworfenheit*, the state of being a castaway, allows the possibility of such news as a significant category of communication, as indeed the most significant.

To put it briefly: When Kierkegaard declares that the deliverance of the castaway by a piece of news from across the seas rather than by philosophical knowledge is the Absolute Paradox, one wonders simply how the castaway could be delivered any other way. *It is this news and this news alone that he has been waiting for*. Christianity cannot appear otherwise than as the Absolute Paradox once one has awarded total competence to knowledge *sub specie aeternitatis*, once one has disallowed the cognitive content of news as a category of communication.

The stumbling block to the scientist-philosopher-artist on the island is that salvation comes by hearing, by a piece of news, and not through knowledge *sub specie aeternitatis*. But scandalized or not, he might at least realize that it could not be otherwise. For no knowledge which can be gained on the island, on any island anywhere at any time, can be relevant to his predicament as a castaway. The castaway is he who waits for news from across the seas.

It is interesting to see what criteria of acceptance Kierkegaard does allow to faith. Clearly he removes faith from the sphere of knowledge and science in any sense of these words. Is it not then simply a matter of God's gift, a miraculous favor which allows one to embrace the Absolute Paradox and believe the impossible? No, there is more to be said. Kierkegaard recognizes that a category of communication is involved. Faith comes from God, but it also comes by hearing. It is a piece of news and there is a newsbearer. But why should we believe the newsbearer, the apostle? Must the apostle first prove his case to the scientist in the seminar room? No, because this would mean that God and the apostle must wait in the porter's lodge while the learned upstairs settle the matter.

Why then do we believe the apostle? We believe him because he has the authority to deliver the message. The communication of the genius (the scientific message in the bottle) is in the sphere of immanence. "A genius may be a century ahead of his time and therefore appear to be a paradox but ultimately the race will assimilate what was once a paradox in such a way that it is no longer a paradox." Given time, knowledge may be arrived at independently on any island. It is otherwise with the apostle. His message is in the sphere of transcendence and is therefore paradoxical. It cannot be arrived at by any effort and not even eternity can mediate it.

How then may we recognize the divine authority of the apostle? What, in other words, are the credentials of the newsbearer? The credential of the apostle is simply the gravity of his message: "I am called by God; do with me what you will, scourge me, persecute me, but my last words are my first; I am called by God and I make you eternally responsible for what you do against me."

Kierkegaard recognized the unique character of the Christian gospel but, rather than see it as a piece of bona fide news delivered by a newsbearer, albeit news of divine origin delivered by one with credentials of divine origin, he felt obliged to set it over against knowledge as paradox. Yet to the castaway who becomes a Christian, it is not paradox but news from across the seas, the very news he has been waiting for.

Kierkegaard, of all people, overlooked a major canon of significance of the news from across the seas—the most "Kierkegaardian" canon. One canon has to do with the news and the newsbearer, the nature of the news, and the credentials of the newsbearer. But the other canon has to do with the hearer of the news. Who is the hearer when all is said and done? Kierkegaard may have turned his dialectic against the Hegelian system, but he continued to appraise the gospel from the posture of the Hegelian scientist—and pronounced it absurd that a man's eternal happiness should depend not on knowledge *sub specie aeternitatis* but on a piece of news from across the seas. But neither the Hegelian nor any other objective-minded man is a hearer of news. For he has struck a posture and removed himself from all predicaments for which news might be relevant. Who is the hearer? The hearer is the castaway, not the man in the seminar, but the man who finds himself cast into the world. For whom is the news not news? It is not news to a swallow, for a swallow is what it is, no more and no less; it is at home in the world and no castaway. It is not news to unfallen man because he too is at home in the world and no castaway. It is not news to a fallen man who is a castaway but believes himself to be at home in the world, for he does not recognize his own predicament. It is only news to a castaway who knows himself to be a castaway.

Once it is granted that Christianity is the Absolute Paradox, then, according to Kierkegaard, the message in the bottle is all that is needed. It is enough to read "this little advertisement, this *nota bene* on a page of universal history—'We have believed that in such and such a year God appeared among us in the humble figure of a servant, that he lived and taught in our community, and finally died.' "

But the message in the bottle is not enough—if the message conveys news and not knowledge *sub specie aeternitatis*. There must be, as Kierkegaard himself saw later, someone who delivers the news and who speaks with authority.

Is this someone then anyone who rings the doorbell and says "Come!" No indeed, for in these times everyone is an apostle of sorts, ringing doorbells and bidding his neighbor to believe this and do that. In such times, when everyone is saying "Come!" when radio and television say nothing else but "Come!" it may be that the best way to say "Come!" is to remain silent. Sometimes silence itself is a "Come!"

Since everyone is saying "Come!" now in the fashion of apostles—Communists and Jehovah's Witnesses as well as advertisers—the uniqueness of the original "Come!" from across the seas is apt to be overlooked. The apostolic character of Christianity is unique among religions. No one else has ever left or will ever leave his island to say "Come!" to other islanders for reasons which have nothing to do with the dissemination of knowledge *sub specie aeternitatis* and nothing to do with his own needs. The Communist is disseminating what he believes to be knowledge *sub specie aeterni-*

tatis—and so is the Rockefeller scientist. The Jehovah's Witness and the Holy Roller are bearing island news to make themselves and other islanders happy. But what if a man receives the commission to bring news across the seas to the castaway and does so in perfect sobriety and with good faith and perseverance to the point of martyrdom? And what if the news the newsbearer bears is the very news the castaway had been waiting for, news of where he came from and who he is and what he must do, and what if the newsbearer brought with him the means by which the castaway may do what he must do? Well then, the castaway will, by the grace of God, believe him.

7

THE MYSTERY OF LANGUAGE

LANGUAGE IS an extremely mysterious phenomenon. By mysterious I do not mean that the events which take place in the brain during an exchange of language are complex and little understood—although this is true too. I mean, rather, that language, which at first sight appears to be the most familiar *sort* of occurrence, an occurrence which takes its place along with other occurrences in the world—billiard balls hitting other billiard balls, barkings of dogs, cryings of babies, sunrises, and rainfalls—is in reality utterly different from these events. The importance of a study of language, as opposed to a scientific study of a space-time event like a solar eclipse or rat behavior, is that as soon as one scratches the surface of the familiar and comes face to face with the nature of language, one also finds himself face to face with the nature of man.

If you were to ask the average educated American or Englishman or Pole, or anyone else acquainted with the scientific temper of the last two hundred years, what he conceived the nature of language to be, he would probably reply in more or less the following way:

When I speak a word or sentence and you understand me, I utter a series of peculiar little sounds by which I hope to convey to you the meaning I have in mind. The sounds leave my mouth and travel through the air as waves. The waves strike the tympanic membrane of your outer ear and the motion of the membrane is carried to the inner ear, where it is transformed into electrical impulses in the auditory nerve. This nerve impulse is transmitted to your brain, where a very complex series of events takes place, the upshot of which is that you "understand" the words; that is, you ei-

ther respond to the words in the way I had hoped you would or the
words arouse in you the same idea or expectation or fear I had in
mind. Your understanding of my sounds depends upon your having heard them before, upon a common language. As a result of
your having heard the word *ball* in association with the thing ball,
there has occurred a change in your brain of such a character that
when I say *ball* you understand me to mean ball.

This explanation of language is not, of course, entirely acceptable to a linguist or a psychologist. But it is the *sort* of explanation
one would give to a question of this kind. It is the sort of explanation to be found in the *Book of Knowledge* and in a college psychology textbook. It may be less technical or a great deal more technical—no doubt modern philosophers of meaning would prefer the
term *response* to *idea* in speaking of your understanding of my
words—but, technical or not, we agree in general that something of
the kind takes place. The essence of the process is a series of events
in space-time: muscular events in the mouth, wave events in the
air, electrocolloidal events in the nerve and brain.

The trouble is that this explanation misses the essential
character of language. It is not merely an oversimplified explanation; it is not merely an incomplete or one-sided explanation. It
has nothing at all to do with language considered as language.

What I wish to call attention to is not a new discovery, a new
piece of research in psycholinguistics which revolutionizes our concept of language as the Michelson-Morley experiment revolu-
tionized modern physics. It is rather the extraordinary sort of thing
language is, which our theoretical view of the world completely
obscures. This extraordinary character of language does not depend
for its unveiling upon a piece of research but is there under our
noses for all to see. The difficulty is that it *is* under our noses; it is
too close and too familiar. Language, symbolization, is the stuff of
which our knowledge and awareness of the world are made, the
medium through which we see the world. Trying to see it is like
trying to see the mirror by which we see everything else.

There is another difficulty. It is the fact that language cannot be
explained in the ordinary terminology of explanations. The termi-

nology of explanations is the native attitude of the modern mind toward that which it does not understand—and is its most admirable trait. That attitude is briefly this: Here is a phenomenon . . . how does it work? The answer is given as a series of space-time events. This is how C works; you see, this state of affairs A leads to this state of affairs B, and B leads to C. This attitude goes a long way toward an understanding of billiards, of cellular growth, of anthills and sunrises. But it cannot get hold of language.

All of the space-time events mentioned in connection with the production of speech do occur, and without them there would be no language. But language is something else besides these events. This does not mean that language cannot be understood but that we must use another frame of reference and another terminology. If one studies man at a so-to-speak sublanguage level, one studies him as one studies anything else, as a phenomenon which is susceptible of explanatory hypothesis. A psychologist timing human responses moves about in the same familiar world of observer and data-to-be-explained as the physiologist and the physicist. But as soon as one deals with language not as a sequence of stimuli and responses, not as a science of phonetics or comparative linguistics, but as the sort of thing language is, one finds himself immediately in uncharted territory.

The usual version of the nature of language, then, turns upon the assumption that human language is a marvelous development of a type of behavior found in lower animals. As Darwin expressed it, man is not the only animal that can use language to express what is passing in his mind: "The *Cebus azarae* monkey in Paraguay utters at least six distinct sounds which excite in other monkeys similar emotions." More recent investigations have shown that bees are capable of an extraordinary dance language by which they can communicate not only direction but distance.

This assumption is of course entirely reasonable. When we study the human ear or eye or brain we study it as a development in continuity with subhuman ears and eyes and brains. What other method is available to us? But it is here that the radical difference between the sort of thing that language is and the sort of thing that the transactions upon the billiard table are manifests itself to throw us into confusion. This method of finding our way to the nature of language, this assumption, does not work. It not only does not work; it ignores the central feature of human language.

The oversight and the inability to correct it have plagued philosophers of language for the past fifty years. To get to the heart of the difficulty we must first understand the difference between a sign and a symbol.

A sign is something that directs our attention to something else. If you or I or a dog or a cicada hears a clap of thunder, we will expect rain and seek cover. It will be seen at once that this sort of sign behavior fits in very well with the explanatory attitude mentioned above. The behavior of a man or animal responding to a natural sign (thunder) or an artificial sign (Pavlov's buzzer) can be explained readily as a series of space-time events which takes place because of changes in the brain brought about by past association.

But what is a symbol? A symbol does not direct our attention to something else, as a sign does. It does not direct at all. It "means" something else. It somehow comes to contain within itself the thing it means. The word *ball* is a sign to my dog and a symbol to you. If I say *ball* to my dog, he will respond like a good Pavlovian organism and look under the sofa and fetch it. But if I say *ball* to you, you will simply look at me and, if you are patient, finally say, "What about it?" The dog responds to the word by looking for the thing; you conceive the ball through the word *ball*.

Now we can, if we like, say that the symbol is a kind of sign, and that when I say the word *ball*, the sound strikes your ear drum, arrives in your brain, and there calls out the idea of a ball. Modern semioticists do, in fact, try to explain a symbol as a kind of sign. But this doesn't work. As Susanne Langer has observed, this leaves out something, and this something is the most important thing of all.

The thing that is left out is the relation of denotation. The word *names* something. The symbol symbolizes something. Symbolization is qualitatively different from sign behavior; the thing that distinguishes man is his ability to symbolize his experience rather than simply respond to it. The word *ball* does all the things the psychologist says it does, makes its well-known journey from tongue to brain. But it does something else too: it names the thing.

So far we have covered ground which has been covered much more adequately by Susanne Langer and the great German philosopher of the symbol, Ernst Cassirer. The question I wish to raise here is this: What are we to make of this peculiar act of naming? If we can't construe it in terms of space-time events, as we construe other phenomena—solar eclipses, gland secretion, growth—then how can we construe it?

The longer we think about it, the more mysterious the simplest act of naming becomes. It is, we begin to realize, quite without precedent in all of natural history as we know it. But so, you might reply, is the emergence of the eye without precedent, so is sexual reproduction without precedent. These are nevertheless the same *kinds* of events which have gone before. We can to a degree understand biological phenomena in the same terms in which we understand physical phenomena, as a series of events and energy exchanges, with each event arising from and being conditioned by a previous event. This is not to say that biology can be reduced to physical terms but only that we can make a good deal of sense of it as a series of events and energy exchanges.

But naming is *generically* different. It stands apart from everything else that we know about the universe. The collision of two galaxies and the salivation of Pavlov's dog, different as they are, are far more alike than either is like the simplest act of naming. Naming stands at a far greater distance from Pavlov's dog than the latter does from a galactic collision.

Just what is the act of denotation? What took place when the first man uttered a mouthy little sound and the second man understood it, not as a sign to be responded to, but as "meaning" something they beheld in common? The first creature who did this is almost by minimal empirical definition the first man. What happened is of all things on earth the one thing we should know best. It is the one thing we do most; it is the warp and woof of the fabric of our consciousness. And yet it is extremely difficult to look *at* instead of through and even more difficult to express once it is grasped.

Naming is unique in natural history because for the first time a being in the universe stands apart from the universe and affirms some other being to be what it is. In this act, for the first time in the history of the universe, "is" is spoken. What does this mean? If something important has happened, why can't we talk about it as we talk about everything else, in the familiar language of space-time events?

The trouble is that we are face to face with a phenomenon which we can't express by our ordinary phenomenal language. Yet we are obliged to deal with it; it happens, and we cannot dismiss it as a "semantical relation." We sense, moreover, that this phenomenon has the most radical consequences for our thinking about man. To refuse to deal with it because it is troublesome would be fatal. It is as if an astronomer developed a theory of planetary motion and said that his theory holds true of planets A, B, C, and D but that planet E is an exception. It makes zigzags instead of ellipses. Planet E is a scandal to good astronomy; therefore we disqualify planet E as failing to live up to the best standards of bodies in motion.

This is roughly the attitude of some modern semanticists and semioticists toward the act of naming. If the relation of symbol to thing symbolized be considered as anything other than a sign calling forth a response, then this relation is "wrong." Say whatever you like about a pencil, Korzybski used to say, but never say it is a pencil. The word is not the thing, said Chase; you can't eat the word *oyster*. According to some semanticists, the advent of symbolization is a major calamity in the history of the human race. Their predicament is not without its comic aspects. Here are scientists occupied with a subject matter of which they, the scientists, disapprove. For the sad fact is that we shall continue to say "This is a pencil" rather than "This object I shall refer to in the future by the sound *pencil*."

By the semanticists' own testimony we are face to face with an extraordinary phenomenon—even though it be "wrong." But if, instead of deploring this act of naming as a calamity, we try to see it for what it is, what can we discover?

When I name an unknown thing or hear the name from you, a remarkable thing happens. In some sense or other, the thing is said to "be" its name or symbol. The semanticists are right: this round thing is certainly not the word *ball*. Yet unless it becomes, in some sense or other, the word *ball* in our consciousness, we will never know the ball! Cassirer's thesis was that everything we know we know through symbolic media, whether words, pictures, formulae, or theories. As Mrs. Langer put it, symbols are the vehicles of meaning.

The transformation of word into thing in our consciousness can be seen in the phenomenon of false onomatopoeia. The words *limber*, *flat*, *furry*, *fuzzy*, *round*, *yellow*, *sharp* sound like the things they signify, not because the actual sounds resemble the thing or quality, but because the sound has been transformed in our consciousness to "become" the thing signified. If you don't believe this, try repeating one of these words several dozen times: All at once it will lose its magic guise as symbol and become the poor drab vocable it really is.

This modern notion of the symbolic character of our awareness turns out to have a very old history, however. The Scholastics, who incidentally had a far more adequate theory of symbolic meaning in some respects than modern semioticists, used to say that man does not have a direct knowledge of essences as do the angels but only an indirect knowledge, a knowledge mediated by symbols. John of St. Thomas observed that symbols come to contain within themselves the thing symbolized *in alio esse*, in another mode of existence.

But what has this symbolic process got to do with the "is" I mentioned earlier, with the unprecedented affirmation of existence? We know that the little copula "is" is a very late comer in the evolution of languages. Many languages contain no form of the verb "to be." Certainly the most primitive sentence, a pointing at a particular thing and a naming, does not contain the copula. Nevertheless it is a *pairing*, an apposing of word and thing, an act the very essence of which is an "is-saying," an affirming of the thing to be what it is for both of us.

Once we have grasped the nature of symbolization, we may begin to see its significance for our view of man's place in the world. I am assuming that we share, to begin with, an empirical-realistic view of the world, that we believe that there are such things as rocks, planets, trees, dogs, which can be at least partially known and partially explained by science, and that man takes his place somewhere in the scheme. The faculty of language, however, confers upon man a very peculiar position in this scheme—and not at all the position we establish in viewing him as a "higher organism."

The significance of language may be approached in the following way. In our ordinary theoretical view of the world, we see it as a process, a dynamic succession of energy states. There are subatomic particles and atoms and molecules in motion; there are gaseous bodies expanding or contracting; there are inorganic elements in chemical interaction; there are organisms in contact with an environment, responding and adapting accordingly; there are animals responding to each other by means of sign behavior.

This state of affairs we may think of as a number of terms in interaction, each with all the others. Each being is in the world, acting upon the world and itself being acted upon by the world.

But when a man appears and names a thing, when he says this is water and water is cool, something unprecedented takes place. What the third term, man, does is not merely enter into interaction with the others—though he does this too—but stand apart from two of the terms and say that one "is" the other. The two things which he pairs or identifies are the *word* he speaks or hears and the *thing* he sees before him.

This is not only an unprecedented happening; it is also, as the semanticists have noted, scandalous. A is clearly not B. But were it not for this cosmic blunder, man would not be man; he would never be capable of folly and he would never be capable of truth. Unless he says that A is B, he will never know A or B; he will only respond to them. A bee is not as foolish as man, but it also cannot tell the truth. All it can do is respond to its environment.

What are the consequences for our thinking about man? There are a great many consequences, epistemological, existential, religious, psychiatric. There is space here to mention only one, the effect it has on our *minimal* concept of man. I do not mean our concept of his origin and his destiny, which is, of course, the province of religion. I mean, rather, our working concept, as our minimal working concept of water is a compound of hydrogen and oxygen.

An awareness of the nature of language must have the greatest possible consequences for our minimal concept of man. For one thing it must reveal the ordinary secular concept of man held in the West as not merely inadequate but quite simply mistaken. I do not refer to the Christian idea of man as a composite of body and soul, a belief which is professed by some and given lip service by many but which can hardly be said to be a working assumption of secular learning. We see man—when I say we, I mean 95 per cent of those who attend American high schools and universities—as the highest of the organisms: He stands erect, he apposes thumb and forefinger, his language is far more complex than that of the most advanced *Cebus azarae*. But the difference is quantitative, not qualitative. Man is a higher organism, standing in direct continuity with rocks, soil, fungi, protozoa, and mammals.

This happens not to be true, however, and in a way it is unfortunate. I say unfortunate because it means the shattering of the old dream of the Enlightenment—that an objective-explanatory-causal science can discover and set forth all the knowledge of which man is capable. The dream is drawing to a close. The existentialists have taught us that what man is cannot be grasped by the sciences of man. The case is rather that man's science is one of the things that man does, a mode of existence. Another mode is speech. Man is not merely a higher organism responding to and controlling his environment. He is, in Heidegger's words, that being in the world whose calling it is to find a name for Being, to give testimony to it, and to provide for it a clearing.

8

TOWARD A TRIADIC
THEORY OF MEANING

IT IS A MATTER for astonishment, when one comes to think of it, how little use linguistics and other sciences of language are to psychiatrists. When one considers that the psychiatrist spends most of his time listening and talking to patients, one might suppose that there would be such a thing as a basic science of listening-and-talking, as indispensable to psychiatrists as anatomy to surgeons. Surgeons traffic in body structures. Psychiatrists traffic in words. Didn't Harry Stack Sullivan say that psychiatry properly concerns itself with transactions between people and that most of these transactions take the form of language? Yet if there exists a basic science of listening-and-talking I have not heard of it. What follows is a theory of language as behavior. It is not new. Its fundamentals were put forward by the American philosopher Charles Peirce three-quarters of a century ago. It shall be the contention of this article that, although Peirce is recognized as the founder of semiotic, the theory of signs, modern behavioral scientists have not been made aware of the radical character of his ideas about language. I also suspect that the state of the behavioral sciences vis-à-vis language is currently in such low spirits, not to say default, that Peirce's time may have come.

If most psychiatrists were asked why they don't pay much attention to the linguistic behavior, considered as such, of their patients, they might give two sorts of answers, both reasonable enough. One runs as follows: "Well, after all, I have to be more interested in

what the patient is saying than in the words and syntax with which
he says it." And if, like most of us, he has been exposed to the standard academic behavioral sciences, he might add, again reasonably
enough: "Well, of course we know that conversation is a series of
learned responses, but these are very subtle events, occurring
mostly inside the head, and so there is not much we can say about
them in the present state of knowledge."

Both explanations are familiar, reasonable, and dispiriting. But
what is chiefly remarkable about them is that they are contradictory. No one has ever explained how a psychiatrist can be said to
be "responding" to a patient when he, the psychiatrist, listens to the
patient tell a dream, understands what is said, and a year later
writes a paper about it. To describe the psychiatrist's behavior as a
response is to use words loosely.

Charles Peirce was an unlucky man. His two most important
ideas ran counter to the intellectual currents of his day, were em-
braced by his friends—and turned into something else. William
James took one idea and turned it into a pragmatism which, whatever its value, is not the same thing as Peirce's pragmaticism.
Peirce's triadic theory has been duly saluted by latter-day semioticists—and turned into a trivial instance of learning theory. Freud
was lucky. The times were ready for him and he had good enemies.
It is our friends we should beware of.

What follows does not pretend to offer the psychiatrist an adequate theory of language sprung whole and entire like Minerva
from Jove's head. It is offered as no more than a sample of another
way of looking at things. I hope that it might either stimulate or ir-
ritate behavioral scientists toward the end that they will devise operational means of confirming or disconfirming these statements—or
perhaps even launch more fruitful studies than this very tentative
investigation. What follows is adapted freely from Peirce, with all
credit to Peirce, and space will not be taken to set down what was
originally Peirce and what are the adaptations. Here again Peirce
was unlucky, in that his views on language were put forward as part
of a metaphysic, i.e., a theory of reality, and in a language

uncongenial to modern behavioral attitudes. To say so is not to put down Peirce's metaphysic. But the problem here is to disentangle from the metaphysic those insights which are germane to a view of language as behavior.

First I shall give a brief statement of what I take to be Peirce's theory of language considered as a natural phenomenon, i.e., not as a logic or a formal structure but as overt behavior open to scientific inquiry. There shall follow a loose list of postulates which I take to be implied by Peirce's triadic theory of signs. These "postulates," unlike the arbitrary postulates of a mathematical system, are empirical statements which are more or less self-evident. From them certain other statements can be deduced. Their value will depend both on the degree to which the postulates are open to confirmation and the usefulness of the deduced statements to such enterprises as the psychiatrist's understanding of his own transactions with his patients.

Peirce believed that there are two kinds of natural phenomena. First there are those events which involve "dyadic relations," such as obtain in the "physical forces . . . between pairs of particles." The other kind of event entails "triadic relations":

> All dynamical action, or action of brute force, physical or psychical, either takes place between two subjects . . . or at any rate is a resultant of such action between pairs. But by "semiosis" I mean, on the contrary, an action, or influence, which is, or involves, a cooperation of *three* subjects, such as a sign, its object, and its interpretant, this tri-relative influence not being in any way resolvable into actions between pairs.

If A throws B away and B hits C in the eye, this event may be understood in terms of two dyadic relations, one between A and B, the other between B and C. But if A *gives* B to C, a genuine triadic relation exists. "Every genuine triadic relation involves meaning." An index sign is part of a dyadic relation. An index refers to the object it denotes by virtue of really being affected by that object. Examples of indexes: a low barometer as an index of rain, the cry of warning of a driver to a pedestrian. A symbol, however, is something which stands to somebody for something in some respect or capacity. "The index is physically connected with its object . . . but the symbol is connected with its object by virtue of . . . the symbol-using mind."

Dyadic events are, presumably, those energy exchanges conventionally studied by the natural sciences: subatomic particles colliding, chemical reactions, actions of force-fields on bodies, physical and chemical transactions across biological membranes, neuron discharges, etc.

Triadic events, on the other hand, characteristically involve symbols and symbol users. Moreover, a genuine triadic relation cannot be reduced to a series of dyadic relations. Peirce seems to be saying that when a symbol user receives a symbol as "meaning" such and such an object, we may *not* understand this event as a sequence of dyadic events or energy exchanges even though dyadic events and energy exchanges are involved: sound waves in air, excitation of sensory end-organ, afferent nerve impulse, electro colloidal synaptic event, efferent nerve impulse, muscle contraction, or glandular secretion.

Peirce's distinction between dyadic and triadic behavior has been noted before, but so pervasive has been the influence of what might be called dyadic behaviorism that Peirce's "triadic relation" has been recognized only to the degree that it can be set forth as a congeries of dyads. Morris, for example, interprets Peirce's triad as implying that in addition to response and stimulus there is a third factor, a "reinforcing" state of affairs. This is like saying that Einstein's special theory will be accepted only to the degree that it can be verified by Newtonian mechanics. Like Newtonian mechanics, dyadic theory can account for perhaps 98 per cent of natural phenomena. Unfortunately the phenomenon of talking-and-listening falls in the remaining 2 per cent.

What would happen if we took Peirce seriously? That is to say, if we retain the posture of behavioral science which interests itself only in the overt behavior of other organisms, what are we to make of observable behavior which cannot be understood as a series of dyadic energy transactions? What has happened in the past is that we have admitted of course that there is such a thing as symbol-mongering, as naming things, as uttering sentences which are true or false, as "rules" by which names are assigned and sentences formed. We have admitted that such activity is a natural phenomenon and as such is open to scientific investigation. But what kind of scientific investigation? We have gotten around the difficulty by treating the products of symbol-mongering *formally,* by what Carnap calls the formal sciences (logic, mathematics, syntax), while assigning the activity itself to a *factual* science, in this case learning theory, which has not, however, been able to give an account of it. It is no secret that learning theorists will have no truck with symbols and meaning. Most textbooks of psychology do not list the word *symbol* in their indexes. Indeed, how can learning theory, as we know it, give an account of symbolic activity? If we are to believe Peirce, it cannot. For the empirical laws of learning theory are formulations of dyadic events of the form $R = f(O)$, in which R = response variables and O = stimulus variables.*

The question must arise then: If triadic activity is overt behavior and as such is the proper object of investigation of a factual behavioral science and is not formulable by the postulates and laws of conventional behaviorism, what manner of "postulates" and "laws," if any, would be suitable for such a science? Or is the game worth the candle? For, as George Miller says, whenever the behavioral scientist confronts language as behavior, he is generally nagged by the suspicion that the rule-governed normative behavior of naming, of uttering true and false sentences, may somehow be beyond the scope of natural science. Shall we as behavioral scientists accordingly surrender all claim to language as a kind of behavior and yield the field to formalists, logicians, and transformational linguists? Have we not indeed already settled for a kind of tacit admission that there exists a behavior for which there is no behavioral science?

To give some simple examples:

* Actually the dyads should be segmented in some such order as $O = f(S)$, in which O = the organic variables and S = the stimulus variables; $I_b = f(I_a)$, in which I = the intervening neurophysiological variables within the organism; and $R = f(O)$, in which R = response variables, or measurement of behavior properties.

Two events occurred in Helen Keller's childhood. One can be reasonably well understood by learning theory. The other cannot.

Helen, we know from Miss Sullivan, learned to respond to the word *cake* spelled in her hand by searching for a piece of cake.

Even though we were not present and could not have seen the events inside Helen's head if we had been, we nevertheless feel confident that learning theory can give a fairly adequate account of the kind of events which occurred. B. F. Skinner would have no difficulty explaining what happened and most of us would find his explanation useful.

But a second event occurred. One day Helen learned in great excitement that the word *water* spelled in one hand was the *name* of the liquid flowing over the other hand. She then wanted to know the names of other things.

Theorists of language behavior have been unable to give a coherent account of this event. When one tries to fit this triadic event onto a dyadic model, queer things happen. Ogden and Richards, for example, found themselves with a triangle, two sides of which represented proper "causal" relations between symbol and reference and between reference and referent. A dotted line was drawn between symbol and referent. The dotted line stood for an "imputed relation" between word and thing as contrasted with the "real" relation between word and organism, and organism and referent. The next step was to see man's use of symbols as somehow deplorable. Korzybski constructed a curious quasi-ethical science of "general semantics" in which he berated people for the wrong use of symbols. Stuart Chase compared symbol-using man unfavorably with his cat Hobie.

One might suppose that a science of language behavior must first determine what sort of behavior is taking place before issuing moral judgments about it.

Three men have a toothache.

One man groans.

The second man say, "Ouch!"

The third man says, "My tooth aches."

Now it may be unexceptionable to say that all three men emitted responses, the first a wired-in response, the second and third learned responses.* But if one wishes to give a nontrivial account of language behavior, it does not suffice to describe the second and third utterances as learned responses. What kind of a learned response is a sentence and how does it differ from other responses?

Nor does it suffice to describe the two events in Helen Keller's childhood as instances of learning by reinforcement.

The greatest obstacle to progress in semiotic has been the loose use of analogical terms to describe different events without specifying wherein lies the similarity and wherein lies the difference. To use a term like *response* analogically is to risk a spurious understanding of matters that are in fact little understood and difficult to investigate.

One recalls Chomsky's reaction to Skinner's *Verbal Behavior:*

> Anyone who seriously approaches the study of linguistic behavior, whether linguist, psychologist, or philosopher, must quickly become aware of the enormous difficulty of stating a problem which will define the area of his investigation, and which will not be either trivial or hopelessly beyond the range of present-day understanding and technique.

The following is a loose set of postulates and definitions which I take to be suitable for a behavioral schema of symbol use and which might be adapted from Peirce's theory of triads. Recognizing the peculiar difficulties that regularly attend such enterprises—not the least source of confusion is the fact that unlike any other field of inquiry language is fair game for everybody, for formal and factual scientists, for logicians, linguists, learning theorists, semanticists, syntacticians, information theorists, and, alas, even for philosophers—I accordingly offer these propositions with the minimal expectation that they will at least suggest an alternative, a way of thinking about man's use of signs which is different from the standard treatment and, I trust also, less dispiriting.

The Peirce scholar will note certain omissions and divergencies. There are two main departures from Peirce's theory. (1) No ac-

---

* "Ouch" is a learned response. A German wouldn't say "Ouch" but perhaps "Aie," a Yiddish speaker "Oy."

count whatever is given here of Peirce's ontology of Firstness, Secondness, and Thirdness in terms of which his semiotic is expressed. This omission I take to be justified by the desirability of using only those concepts which have operational significance for behavioral science. Accordingly, what is offered is not a comprehensive theory of signs but only a very tentative account of sentence utterance, that is, sentences considered as items of behavior. (2) The emphasis is clinical, that is, upon *mistakes*, misperceptions of sentences in their transmission from sender to receiver. There are two reasons for this emphasis. One is that the clinical encounter, that of therapist and patient, is the recurring paradigm in this essay. The other is that mistakes suggest a useful method of exploring this treacherous terrain. There are different kinds of mistakes and there are different kinds of variables in the communication process. Perhaps one may be taken as evidence of the other. A good way to study auto mechanics is to study auto breakdowns. Vapor locks, short circuits, transmission failures may be the best evidence that there are such things as carburetors, electrical systems, and gears—especially if the mechanic can't lift the hood.

1. The basic unit of language behavior is the sentence.

A word has no meaning except as part of a sentence. Single-word utterances are either understood as sentences or else they are not understood at all. For example, when Wittgenstein's Worker A says to Worker B, "Slabs!" Worker B understands him to mean, send slabs!—or perhaps misunderstands him to mean, I already have slabs.

If I say the word *pickle* to you, you must either understand the utterance as a sentence—this is a pickle, this is a picture of a pickle, pass the pickles, tastes like a pickle—or you will ask me what I mean or perhaps say, "What about pickles?"

1.1. A sentence utterance is a coupling of elements by a coupler.

The subject-predicate division * is not the only kind of coupling

---

* Or the NP-VP division of transformational linguists. Or Strawson's division of a sentence into what you are talking about and what you are saying about it.

which occurs in sentences.* Not only can symbols be coupled with symbols; symbols can also be coupled with things or classes of things. Peirce's example: A father catches his child's eye, points to an object, and says, "Balloon."

1.2. A sentence utterance is a triadic event involving a coupler and the two elements of the uttered sentence.†

1.21. If a dyadic relation is abstracted from a triadic relation and

---

* Nor are language couplings the only kind of couplings which occur. There are other kinds of symbols and other kinds of sentences, e.g., the coupling of a map with the territory, the coupling of van Gogh's painting *The Cypresses* with what is symbolized (which is not merely the cypresses but forms of feeling as well). But here we are concerned primarily with language sentences.

† In Chapter 9 I describe symbol-using behavior as characterized by a tetradic structure. Thus, if one were to observe an utterance of a symbol—or, as I would say here, of a sentence—one would notice that there is not only an utterer and a coupling of sentence elements, but also a listener or receiver of the sentence. "The second person is required as an element not merely in the genetic event of learning language but as the *indispensable and enduring condition of all symbolic behavior.* The very act of symbolic formulation, whether it be language, logic, art, or even thinking, is of its very nature a formulation for a *someone else.* Even Robinson Crusoe, writing in his journal after twenty years on the island, is nevertheless performing a through-and-through social and intersubjective act."

Today, ten years later, I would broaden the notion of coupling "symbol" and "object" to the utterance of sentences in general, whether symbol and object, naming sentences, or traditional declarative sentences with subject and predicate.

This "tetradic behavior," involving an utterer, a receiver, symbol and object, is contrasted with the "semiotic triangle" of Ogden and Richards, involving a *sign* which affects an *interpreter* which in turn responds with behavior relevant to an *object* or referent.

I find it convenient here, however, to observe Peirce's distinction between *dyadic* relations and *triadic* relations. It will be seen that no substantial change has been made. What matters is the difference in "valence" between the semiotic relations encountered in symbol use and those in signal use, whether the difference is between triads and tetrads or dyads and triads.

Thus, the "semiotic triangle of Ogden and Richards with its "causal" relations between sign and interpreter and between interpreter and referent is clearly, in Peirce's scheme of things, a pair of dyads.

The tetrad I proposed can, if one wishes to deal with atomic rather than molecular events, be split apart along its interface between utterer and receiver of a sentence, yielding a coupling of sentence elements by utterer and a subsequent coupling by receiver. The tetradic model, I see now, is appropriate only in successful communication, i.e., those transactions in which the same elements are coupled by both utterer and receiver and in the same mode of coupling. Unfortunately this is not always the case.

In short, in Chapter 9 I deal with the "molecular" structure of the communication process, whereas I am here dealing with the "atomic" structure.

studied as such, the study may have validity as a science, but the science will not be a science of triadic behavior.

For example, a neurologist may study the dyadic events which occur in the acoustic nerve of a person who hears the sentence *The King of France is bald*. The result of such a study may be a contribution to the science of neurology, but it will not be a contribution to the science of triadic behavior.

A logician may abstract from the speaker of a sentence, study the formal relation between the terms of the sentence and what is entailed by its assertion. His study may contribute to the science of logic, but it will not contribute to the science of triadic behavior.

A professor writes a sentence on the blackboard: *The King of France is bald*. The class reads the sentence.

If one wishes to study this sentence utterance as an item of behavior, it does not suffice to abstract from the professor and the class and to study the semantics and syntax of the sentence. If one considers the sentence utterance as an item of behavior, one quickly perceives that it is a pseudo sentence. The sentence may have been uttered but it does not assert anything. For one thing, the phrase *the King of France* does not refer to anything, since there does not presently exist a king of France. For another thing, a second condition of bona fide sentence utterance is lacking. As Peirce said, asserting a sentence is something like going before a notary and assuming responsibility for it. No one imagines that the professor has done this.

Many of the philosophical puzzles about sentences have arisen from the failure to distinguish between actual sentence utterances and professors uttering pseudo sentences in classrooms.

1.3. A name is a class of sounds coupled with a thing or class of things.

There is no necessary relationship between a name and that which is named beyond the coupling of name and thing by namer.

1.31. It is the peculiar property of a name, a class of sounds, not only that it can be coupled with a class of things but also that in the coupling the sound is transformed and "becomes" the thing.*

The word *glass* sounds brittle but it is not. The word *brittle* sounds brittle but it is not.

The word *sparkle* seems to sparkle for English-speakers but not for Germans. The word *funkeln* seems to sparkle for Germans but not for English-speakers.†

1.311. A symbol must be unlike what it symbolizes in order that it may be transformed and "become" what is symbolized.

The sound *cup* can become a symbol for cup. A cup cannot be a symbol for cup.

1.4. The coupling relation of a sentence is not like any other world relation. Yet—indeed for this very reason—it may symbolize any world relation whatever, subject only to the context of utterance and the rules of sentence formation.

1.41. A sentence may mean anything it is used to mean.

Thus, the sentence *baby chair* uttered by a two-year-old can be

---

* It is this transformation of symbols and their subsequent confusion with things that Count Korzybski used to rage against. "Whatever you choose to say about this object," he would say, holding a pencil aloft, "don't say 'this *is* a pencil.'" "Whatever you say the object 'is,' well it is not" (p. 35).

In point of fact, I have never seen anyone mistake a word for a thing or try to write with the word *pencil*, though the magic use of words undoubtedly occurs in primitive societies and perhaps an analogous misuse in modern technological societies.

Korzybski tended to treat the peculiar features of symbol use as misbehavior to be gotten rid of by a therapeutic semantics which was almost an ethical science.

In a triadic theory of meaning it is to be hoped that symbolic transformations and sentence couplings with the verb *is* will not be put down as instances of bad behavior or human stupidity but rather will be regarded as a fundamental property of sentence utterance.

What needs to be explored is not human perversity as such but rather a parameter variable of symbol use. All sentences entail couplings. The mode of coupling is a *normative* dimension in which couplings may be used truly or falsely in propositions, well or badly in poetry, as a transparent vehicle of meaning or as an opaque simulacrum which distorts meaning.

† Werner and Kaplan note that the word *chair* is not merely a sign or label for chairs: ". . . the material, phonemically unique sequence, *ch-ai-r*, is articulated into a production whose expressive features parallel those ingredients in the percept 'chair.' . . . Only when the vocable has become imbedded in an organismic matrix, regulated and directed by an activity of schematizing or form-building, does it enter into a semantic correspondence with the object (referent) and does it become transformed from the status of a sign to that of symbolic vehicle."

reliably understood by its mother as asserting within different contexts any number of different relationships. It can also be understood as a command or a question. Some possible meanings of the two-word telegraph sentence *baby chair:*

> That is a baby chair (chair for the baby).
> That is a little chair.
> Baby is in his chair.
> Baby wants his chair.
> Where is baby chair?
> Bring baby chair.
> Bring chair for baby.*

* Cf. Braine: He and others have noted that an early stage of language acquisition in children features two-word utterances comprising a "pivot" word and an "open" word. Thus a child using the "pivot" word *there* might combine it with any number of "open" words and say *there ball*, *there man*, *there doggie*, etc. Then in a few months a second stage is reached in which the child combines two "open" words. Thus instead of saying *there car* or *there man*, the child might say *man car*, meaning "A man is in the car."

Braine noted a pause or juncture between the two "open" words. Thus *baby chair* or *baby book*, uttered without a juncture, is presumably a pivot-open construction meaning "(There is) a little chair" or "(There is) a little book." Whereas the utterance *baby#chair*, uttered in a certain context, is reliably understood by the mother to mean "The baby is in his chair." The symbol # represents a juncture or pause.

This open-open construction is a very large class and represents, to my way of thinking, nothing less than the child's graduation from the naming sentence (*there ball*) to the syntactical, "subject-predicate" sentence.

Let us agree with Chomsky that a child's linguistic behavior cannot possibly be accounted for by traditional learning theory with its notions of "stimulus control," "conditioning," "generalization and analogy," "patterns," "habit structures," or "dispositions to respond."

The question, however, is whether the sole alternative to learning theory is Chomsky's "innate ideas and innate principles," specifically in this case a "language acquisition device," a kind of magic black box interposed between input and output which contains not only the principles of universal grammar but the capacity of generating the grammar of one's own language.

I wonder whether Chomsky's LAD (language acquisition device) is nothing more nor less than the unique human ability to couple sentence elements, to couple symbols with things, symbols with symbols, which couplings may be understood to mean whatever context allows them to mean.

Indeed, may not grammar itself be defined as the primitive coupling plus whatever inflection, particles, and patterns may be required to supplant the diminishing context and the intuitive grasp by the mother of the child's couplings? Thus the child's sentence *baby#chair* may be understood infallibly by the mother to mean *The baby is now in his chair*. But as the intimate mother-child relationship declines and as it becomes necessary for people to talk to strangers over telephones about

1.42. The coupling relation of a sentence is not isomorphic with the world relation it symbolizes.

It is true that the sentence *John loves Mary* is a coupling of sentence elements (a child could say *John Mary* and be understood if John was loving Mary at the time) referring to a dyadic relationship between John and Mary.

But it is also true that although the sentence *John gives a ring to Mary* refers to a triadic relation obtaining between John, the ring, and Mary, the sentence is still a coupling of elements: (1) we are speaking about John; (2) we are saying something about him.

It is also true that although the sentence *John plays bridge with Mary and Ted and Alice* refers to a tetradic relation obtaining between John and Mary and Ted and Alice, the sentence is still a coupling of elements: (1) we are speaking about John; (2) we are saying something about him.*

1.5. When one studies dyadic behavior, i.e., the learned response of an organism to stimuli, it is proper to isolate certain parameters and variables. These include: amplitude of response, latency of response, frequency of stimulus, reinforcement, extinction, discrimination, and so on.

babies and chairs which at least one party cannot see, it becomes necessary to add such words as *the*, *is*, *in*, *his*, etc.

If one must speak of a universal grammar, it is surely impossible to avoid the basic phenomenon of the sentence as a coupling and the basic division of couplings into two sorts, whether the language be English or Algonquin: (1) an object beheld by both speaker and hearer and pointed at and understood as one of a class of like objects and named by a sound which is understood as a class of like sounds—thus the pointing at and the utterance of the single-word sentence by father to son: *balloon*. (2) the coupling of symbol and symbol, e.g., *baby#chair* to signify whatever world relation or event is beheld in common by speaker and hearer.

* According to Veatch, mathematical logicians habitually confuse logical relations with "real" relations—here we would say sentence relations with world relations. Veatch calls the sentence coupling "an intentional relation of identity." Thus the relation of John to Bill asserted in the sentence *John is larger than Bill* is a world relation which can be expressed by the isomorphic form xRy. Mathematical logicians persist in setting forth the *sentence* in the form xRy, whereas in truth the sentence relation is of the form S *is* P.

Lord Russell and the early Wittgenstein of the *Tractatus* believed that the sentence must be in some sense isomorphic with the fact asserted by the sentence. The later Wittgenstein changed his mind and came to believe that sentences were plays in a language game and could mean whatever they were used to mean.

But if one considers triadic behavior, i.e., the coupling of a sentence by a coupler, a different set of parameters and variables must be considered.

There follow below some of these parameters and variables.

1.51. Every sentence is uttered in a *community*.

The community of discourse is a necessary and nontrivial parameter of triadic behavior.

This is not the case in dyadic behavior. For example, to speak of a "community" of organisms responding to each other by signals may be true enough, but it is also to use words trivially, analogically, and contingently. Thus, it may not be false to say that an exchange of growls between polar bears takes place in a community of polar bears. It is trivial to say so, however, because it is possible to think of bears responding to stimuli outside a community, e.g., to the sound of splitting ice, in the same way we think of bears responding to growls.

But it is impossible to think of an exchange of sentences occurring otherwise than between two or more persons.

1.511. In triadic behavior, the dimension of community can act as either parameter or variable.

It is a parameter, for example, in an ongoing encounter between therapist and patient: the community does not change.

It is a variable when the community varies. The meaning of a sentence can very well be a dependent variable, depending on the independent variable, the changing community.

For example, the patient utters the following sentence to the therapist: *My wife bugs me*. This sentence may be uttered as a constative sentence asserting a state of affairs between patient and wife.

On the following day, however, at a group session at which both patient and wife are present, the same sentence is both uttered by patient and received by all present with another or at least an added meaning. The new meaning, moreover, is a function of the new community. Thus, it not only asserts a relation between patient and wife; it is also delivered and received as an attack, a bugging of wife and a wife being bugged.

1.52. A signal is received by an organism in an *environment*. A sentence is received and uttered in a *world*.

When Helen Keller learned that water was *water*, she then wished to know what other things "were"—until the world she knew was named.

1.521. An environment has gaps for an organism, but the world is global, that is, it is totally accounted for, one way or another, rightly or wrongly, by names and sentences.

A chicken will respond to the sight of a hawk but not to the sight of a tree. But a child wishes to know what a tree "is."

A chicken does not know whether the earth is flat or round or a bowl, but a man, primitive or technological, will account for the earth one way or another.

1.522. Sentences refer to different worlds.

A sentence may refer to the here-and-now world, a past world, a future world, an imaginary world, a theoretical world.

There are often cues or referring words in the sentence which indicate its world.

> That is a balloon. (Present world)
> President Kennedy was assassinated. (Past world)
> Communism will disappear. (Future world)
> Once upon a time there lived a king. (Fictional past world)
> There was this traveling salesman. (Fictional world, joke)
> In this dream I saw a burning house. (Dream world)
> If wishes were horses, beggars would ride. (Hypothetical world)
> The square of the hypotenuse equals the sum of the squares of the opposite sides. (Abstract world)

Once upon a time is a referring phrase which clearly specifies its world for the listener. *That* in *That is a balloon* is a referring word which indicates something being looked at or pointed at. But not all sentences have referring words which specify the world of the sentence. In any case a world must be supplied by the listener. Some sentences are ambiguous. Thus a patient may say to his therapist:

> This traveling salesman was hoping to meet a farmer's daughter.

The sentence may be: (1) the beginning of a joke, (2) an account of a dream, (3) a facetious but nonetheless true declaration of lust by the patient, who is in fact a traveling salesman.*

1.523. Since a sentence entails a world for both utterer and receiver, both utterer and receiver necessarily see themselves as being *placed* vis-à-vis the world. A sentence utterer cannot not be placed vis-à-vis the world of the sentence. If he is not placed, then his relation to the world of the sentence is the relation of not being placed.

Some sentences are uttered and received in the everyday world of marketplace and fireside.

> Broker: IBM is up two points.
> Husband: The baby is crying, dear.

Other sentences, e.g., scientific propositions, are uttered, so to speak, out of the world, that is to say, from a posture abstracted from the everyday world, or as the scholastics used to say, *sub specie aeternitatis.* From this posture world items tend to be seen not as consumer articles or sources of need-satisfactions but rather as specimens to be classified or events to be arrayed in causal chains. Even concrete sentences, uttered from this posture, are received as propositions in hypothetico-deductive systems.

> Chemist A to Chemist B: The temperature is now 102!

This sentence is not a comment on the weather but is rather an evidential sentence, perhaps an observation of a pointer reading at the end of an experiment which serves to confirm a hypothetico-deductive system.†

---

* Transactions between analyst and patient are especially open to sudden shifts of context, missing referring words, uncued worlds, since the rules of this language game require the patient to say "what comes to mind."

† Here again, the uncritical use of analogical terms has impeded inquiry into distinctively human modes of meaning. Thus, when instrumentalists like Dewey describe scientific research as socially useful activity like farming and marketing, they state a not very interesting similarity at the expense of a much more interesting difference. What concerns us here is how the farmer sees himself vis-à-vis the world, and how the scientist sees himself. The two are not necessarily the same.

More interesting still is how the layman sees himself vis-à-vis the world of science. Is it possible, for example, for a layman to benefit in one sense from the goods and

The peculiar vocation of the therapist requires that he listen to both kinds of sentences, distinguish one from the other, and respond accordingly.

Thus the sentence

After what happened yesterday, I've decided that life is not worth living.

is open to one of several readings. It may be the serious expression of a decision by one man in the world to another. Perhaps the patient intends to commit suicide. More likely, it is uttered by way of a general complaint and to pass the time of day. But perhaps also it could be uttered as a data sentence, i.e., a product of the joint patient-therapist investigation of the patient's illness. The patient is saying: I have indeed reached a decision but rather than act on it by committing suicide I am going to play the language game of analysis and offer it as data. The therapist in turn is required to decide on the spot whether the sentence (1) is a cry for help, (2) asserts commonplace low spirits, (3) offers data for the language game of analysis, or (4) is all three.

It will be seen in this context that Sullivan's description of the psychiatrist as a participant-observer is in fact an accurate characterization of the semiotic options available in the therapist-patient encounter.

1.53. Every sentence is uttered and received in a *medium*.

The medium is a nontrivial parameter or variable in every transaction in which sentences are used. The medium is not necessarily the message, but the message can be strongly influenced by the medium.

In learned or instinctive behavior, stimulus S_1 is received by an organism which in turn responds as it has learned or been wired to respond. To a similar stimulus S_2 it responds similarly according as S_2 resembles S_1. A dog responds to his master's whistle or to a recording of his master's whistle in the same way.

services of scientific technology while in another sense falling prey to them, e.g., coming to see himself as a consumer of these same goods and services as a passive beneficiary of a more or less esoteric, not to say magic, enterprise? "They will soon come up with a cure for cancer," one hears. The question is, Who is "they," and how does the speaker see himself in relation to "them"?

But the sentence utterance *I need you* can provoke varying responses according as the medium varies through which it is transmitted.

If the President says to me, "I need you!" my response will vary according as the message reaches me over television or by way of a person-to-person phone call—even though the acoustic and phonemic properties of the two utterances may be identical.

1.54. Every sentence has a *normative* dimension.

The true-or-false property which Aristotle ascribed to propositions is only one of the norms of sentence utterances. A sentence may be true or false, significant or nonsensical, trite or fresh, bad art or good art, etc.

Behavioral scientists are uncomfortable with the normative because natural science has traditionally had nothing to do with norms. As a consequence, behavioral scientists are usually content to yield the field, to leave true-or-false propositions to logicians, bad sentences to grammarians, metaphors to poets.

Yet sentences are items of behavior and these items have normative dimensions. Therefore a behavioral account of sentence utterances must give an account of these norms.

Behavioral scientists need not have made themselves so miserable. For the fact is that the normative dimension of language behavior is not an awkward addendum to be stuck onto the elegant corpus of behavioral science. No, the normative dimension of sentence utterance is a fundamental property of the coupling of the elements of the sentence, whether the sentence be a true-or-false proposition or a good-or-bad work of art.

A sentence utterance is not like other world events and is not isomorphic with the world event or relation the sentence is about. A world event or relation is generally either an energy exchange (sodium reacting with water) or a real relation (China being bigger than Japan). But a sentence is a coupling of elements by a coupler. It is bothersome to call a world event or relation good or bad. What is good or bad about sodium reacting with water or China being bigger than Japan? But, since a sentence is a coupling of elements by a coupler, these elements can be coupled well or badly.*

World events and relations are neither true nor false but sentences can be. Yet true-or-false is only one normative dimension of sentences.

Here are some others.

Clouds are fleece is false as a literal statement, true in a sense as a metaphor, bad in the sense of being a trite metaphor.

That is a sparrow may be a true assertion of class relationship but it may also be perfunctory, a bored assignment of a commonplace object (English sparrow) to a commonplace class.

That is a dusky seaside sparrow may assert a similar relationship, yet it may be uttered with all the excitement and sense of discovery of a bird-watcher coming upon an occasional species.

Even nondeclarative sentences have normative dimensions.

Patient says to therapist, "Don't you dare plot against me!" An imperative sentence and therefore neither true nor false but inappropriate because, let us stipulate, the therapist harbors no such plot.

---

* Here I am making the case that sentence utterances are triadic events about dyadic events. My utterance *Sodium reacts with water* is a triadic event about a dyadic event.

It is also true, of course, that a sentence utterance, a triadic event, can be about another sentence utterance, also a triadic event.

Thus, a coupling can be about another coupling. A therapist makes an analysis of a patient's dream, to which the patient replies, "That's a lie!" The patient is making a coupling about the therapist's coupling. Note that the patient's sentence addresses itself to a normative dimension of the analyst's sentence. Sentences about other sentences tend characteristically to be judgments about the norms of the latter. E.g.: "That's a lousy painting," "Nixon's speech last night was not his best," "Kennedy wowed them in Berlin," "Stalin lied," "That's a bad metaphor," "So that's a sparrow. So what?"

The only point is that a sentence coupling, being what it is, can be about anything whatever. Since the coupling *China is larger than Japan* is wholly unlike the relationship of China and Japan, it can assert that relationship. Note that a map cannot. A map is isomorphic but it asserts nothing, unless some assertory claim is appended, e.g., the signature of the cartographer.

Note that those mathematical logicians who believe that propositions are isomorphic with the reality they refer to have found it necessary to invent another mark which shows that the propositional relation is *asserted*, e.g., Frege's assertion mark.

But it is of the very nature of a sentence coupling that it not only signifies a relation which is unlike itself but also asserts it.

Said Emperor Henry IV to Pope Gregory VII at Canossa, "I apologize." A performative sentence, hence neither true nor false but possibly sincere or insincere.

Patient to therapist: "I see what you mean." It is possible that the norm in question here is not whether the patient is telling the truth but whether he is uttering a sentence or a nonsentence, i.e., making a polite sound.

2. The receiver of a sentence can take or mistake the sentence.

Note that an organism cannot in this sense be said to make a mistake in responding to a stimulus in its environment, unless the word *mistake* is used in an analogical sense.

But can't a bass be said to make a mistake in taking an artificial lure? Yes, but the bass does not mis-take the lure except in a trivial analogical sense, however tragic the consequences for the bass. For the bass responds to the lure willy-nilly according as the lure resembles what the bass has learned or been wired to respond to.

An organism responds to a stimulus S_n according as it has learned to respond to S, a class of stimuli. The probability of response to S_n can be expressed statistically by a bell curve. The response to S_n is the more likely as S_n resembles S.

If, however, you say to me, "The Russians are coming!" it can happen that I can perfectly understand the sentence according as I have learned to understand English syntax and semantics. Yet I can utterly mis-take your sentence. I may understand you to be reporting an invasion, whereas in truth you are reading a movie marquee.

In this use of the word *mistake*, I also exclude other errors, for example, slips, misconceptions, lies, false propositions.

A Freudian slip might be described as a dyadic irruption of unconscious forces into triadic behavior and as such does not concern us here. A slip is intrapsychic. A mistake is interpersonal. A mistake is a miscoupling of sentence elements in which I couple the elements of your sentence in some fashion other than the way you coupled them. If you say to me, "I enjoyed beating you" instead of "I enjoyed meeting you," no mistaking of sentences has occurred. I understand you well enough. What has occurred is an irruption of your feelings into your polite triadic behavior. Such an event is interesting enough but is not germane to a study of triadic behavior as such.

If I see a piece of paper in the woods, take it for a rabbit, and say, "Look, there's a rabbit," haven't I made a mistake?

Also, isn't a lie a mistake? Suppose I did in fact see a rabbit but do not want you to shoot it and accordingly say, "Oh, that's just a piece of paper." Wouldn't you be telling the truth if you replied, "You are mistaken"?

Perhaps these are mistakes and perhaps it is true enough to say that a bass mistakes an artificial lure for a minnow.

Rather than argue the semantics of the word *mistake*, let us simply define the word for our present purposes. We shall understand the word in its root sense of taking amiss. More specifically, a mistake is the coupling of a sentence by its receiver in some fashion other than its coupling by its utterer. I wish, in short, to set apart triadic mistakes, the taking amiss by one person of another person's utterances.

2.1. A sentence may be mistaken by mistaking any one of the parameters of the sentence. A parameter of a sentence utterance is a variable which is constant for a particular discourse but may vary from one discourse to another.

Some of the parameters of sentence utterances are: the mode of coupling of its elements, the community of discourse, the medium of communication, the world to which the sentence refers, the placement of utterer and receiver of the sentence vis-à-vis its world, the normative mode (true-false, stale-fresh, appropriate-inappropriate, crazy-sane, etc.).

2.11. The receiver of a sentence can mistake it by miscoupling its elements, that is, by coupling the wrong elements or by coupling the right elements in the wrong mode or parameter.

Wrong elements:

Wittgenstein's Worker A: "Five slabs!" (meaning, send up five slabs).
Wittgenstein's Worker B (a new man who, unaccustomed to A's orders, supposes that A is taking inventory and is reporting that he has five slabs): "Very good! I'll check them off!"

Wrong parameter:

NASA scientist on Wallops Island to native islander: "Look, the sky is violet!"
Islander, receiving the sentence as an ordinary world-news item, whereas in truth the scientist is making an observation which confirms the success of an experiment—the discharge by rocket of strontium chloride into the upper atmosphere: "Yes, it's a lovely sunset."

2.111. The receiver of a naming sentence can receive the name correctly and look at the same object the namer looks at yet nevertheless mistake the sentence by making the wrong world-slice (abstraction) of the class of objects named.

Father (pointing to a half dollar with an eagle on it): "That's a half dollar."
Child (later, pointing to chicken): "Half dollar!"

2.112. There is an interface between scientist and layman such that a sentence uttered by the former is subject to characteristic miscouplings by the latter.

Professor of medicine on grand rounds approaching the bed of a patient and picking up the chart: "Hm, a case of sarcoidosis."

The sentence—[This is] a case of sarcoidosis—is coupled one way by its utterer, another way by a medical student who hears it, and yet another way by the patient himself. A proposition asserting class membership, logically speaking, the sentence is so understood by the three persons. Yet, triadically speaking, each understands it differently.

Professor's coupling: This is a case of sarcoidosis. Which is to say, this patient is a man who has something wrong with him, a disorder of unknown etiology and uncertain course but with sufficient signs and symptoms and pathology in common with other such cases to warrant the class name sarcoidosis, a name however which serves as nothing better than a shorthand method of speaking of an ill-defined illness.

Medical student's coupling: This is a case of sarcoidosis. Which is to say, the patient is assigned to the disease-class sarcoidosis Platonically. The patient is understood to participate in a higher reality than himself, namely, his disease. Later the student will refer to the patient by some such sentence as "I have a case of sarcoidosis on the third floor."

Patient's coupling: *This is a case of sarcoidosis.* I have been invaded by an entity, a specter named *sarcoidosis.*

2.1121. The lay-science interface often leads to a reversal of roles wherein the scientist-therapist "laicizes" his sentences, while the layman-patient "scientizes" his, with characteristic miscouplings attendant upon both.

> Patient: "I've been looking forward to our beating—er, meeting today."
> Therapist: "You were thinking of beating me?"
> Patient: "Well, I have been reacting negatively lately."
> Therapist: "I wonder who is beating up on who.*

Freud of course would have been concerned with the slip and the intrapsychic mechanism which produced it. In Peircean terms he was interested in the dyadics which irrupted into triadic behavior. But what increasingly interests us is how patient and therapist talk about the slip and how one understands or misunderstands the other.

Perhaps no one trait of patient-psychiatrist talk is more commonplace than this lay-science reversal, the patient Platonizing his sentences by a *Good Housekeeping* psychological jargon ("reacting negatively"), the therapist vulgarizing his ("who is beating up on who") in the reverse expectation that the real is to be found in the common tongue. In a kind of minuet, patient and therapist change places. The question is, How does the switch work? What kind of a scientist does the layman become by his Platonizing? Does the common tongue bring the real closer for the therapist?

Freud was thinking about unresolved and disabling conflicts within the psyche. But what is beginning to dawn on us is that the very technique designed to probe and resolve such conflicts may *in itself* loom so large for the patient, be offered with such dazzling credentials, that he may fall prey to a technique and be further impoverished. In speaking of the earlier transaction, the Freudian slip, one is accustomed to using a traditional dyadic language: conflict, intrapsychic dynamism, repression, cathexis, resolution, etc. In the later transaction across the lay-science interface one

---

* For the spirit if not the letter of this conversation I am indebted to Gottschalk.

finds oneself using such expressions as: falling prey to, impoverishment, loss of sovereignty, inauthentic, etc.

2.12. The receiver of a sentence can mistake it by mistaking the world to which it refers.

Thus it is not enough for the receiver to "know what the sentence means," in the sense that a professor can write a sentence on the blackboard and every student can explain its syntax and semantics, that it is a declarative sentence, etc. One must also know whether it is a report, a story, an account of a dream, a joke, a quotation.

> Salesman to boss: "There was this traveling salesman who met a farmer's daughter—"
> Boss: receives sentence as the beginning of a joke whereas in truth it is a report, the salesman's seriocomic explanation of how he happened to lose an account.

By its very nature classical psychoanalysis with its encouragement of the analysand to "say what comes to mind" is peculiarly susceptible to sudden and uncued shifts of contexts and attendant misunderstandings. Miscouplings of sentences are more apt to occur here because parameters are more apt to become variables. The patient can shift "worlds" and communities at his pleasure. Indeed he is obliged to.

> Therapist (after a long silence): "What comes to mind?"
> Patient: "The center does not hold."

Is the patient misquoting Yeats, describing his mental health, talking about the state of the union, or doing all three? Is the sentence uttered seriously or in a playful allusive way? It is the analyst's business to know—that is, to catch on to the world mode of the sentence.

2.13. The receiver of a sentence can mistake it by mistaking the placement of the utterer vis-à-vis the world of the sentence.

> Scene: a room under the University of Chicago stadium in 1943, during the early days of the Manhattan Project.
> Fermi's assistant: "Dr. Fermi, the radiation count of the pile is two forty-two!"
> Fermi: "Very good!"

The assistant is uttering an alarm, calling attention to danger to life and limb. The sentence calls for appropriate behavior: turn the pile off, let's get out of here. Other such sentences might be "Vesuvius is about to erupt," or "The safety valve is stuck."

Fermi, however, receives the sentence as having been uttered, not in the ordinary world of predicaments, but rather as a confirmatory report of a pointer reading.*

If one diagrammed each triadic event, Fermi's coupling and his assistant's coupling, one could depict the assistant speaking to Fermi within the world and calling his attention to an imminent threat from one sector of the world. Fermi's reading of the sentence, however, would place both Fermi and the assistant *outside* this world in a transcending abstracted posture from which world events are read as data for theory.

Similarly:

Therapist (after a long silence): "What comes to mind?"
Patient: "I've decided to break off the analysis."
Therapist: "Tell me about it."
Instead of replying, the patient rises, shakes hands, and leaves.

The therapist mistakes the placement of the patient vis-à-vis the world of the sentence *I've decided to break off the analysis.* He, the analyst, assumes that the patient has uttered one more sentence in the language game of analysis, i.e., a game where sentences are reports of data to be examined rather than announcements of actions to be taken. Whereas in truth the patient has shifted the world of discourse from the language game of analysis to the language of the everyday world, where, when one announces his departure, one departs.

2.14. A sentence can be mistaken in its normative mode, that is, by being received in a normative mode other than that in which it was uttered.

---

* The classical world-mistake involving a lay-science interface was the Roman soldier's mistaking Archimedes' complaint when the former spoiled Archimedes' geometric figures in the sand:

Archimedes (concerned about the mathematical world represented by his figure in the sand): "Don't step on my right-angle triangle!"

Soldier (receiving the remark as a calculated insult to the Roman empire): "Take this!" (And runs him through with his sword.)

Therapist (after a long silence): "What comes to mind?"

Patient (seeing the curtain at the window stir in the breeze): "There's a rat behind the arras."

Therapist: "Who's the rat?"

Patient: "Polonius."

Therapist: "Don't forget that Hamlet mistook Polonius for the king."

Patient (agitated): "You mean—it's oedipal? Hm. No. Yes. It is!"

Note that it is impossible to characterize the sentence *There's a rat behind the arras* by the conventional propositional norm of true-or-false. There is no rat behind the curtain. But neither patient nor analyst supposes that the sentence asserts anything about a rat. The sentence is rather, like so much of the talk in analysis, an allusive ambiguous assertion with more than one referent. It is, let us stipulate, (1) a playful allusion to the circumstance that both patient and analyst saw a performance of *Hamlet* the night before, (2) a reference to a dream, (3) a surfacing of unconscious oedipal feelings.

A mistake in the triadic sense can occur here if the therapist mistakes one of the parameters of the patient's sentences, e.g., a normative parameter: suppose he had taken the sentence about the rat as a true-or-false proposition and gotten up to look for the rat. Or suppose he took the sentence as no more than an allusion to last night's playgoing when in truth it may refer to far more serious matters.

Up to this point we have not diverged from the conventional analytical quest: the decoding of the patient's sentence toward the end of identifying and resolving unconscious conflicts. One does not dispute the validity of this enterprise. But we have other fish to fry. We want to observe this conversation not through the analyst's eyes, which see the patient as a psychic malfunction, but through a zoom camera which zooms back in order to see the encounter as it occurs, between two sentence couplers, in a world, in an office where a certain language game is played, next to a street where other language games are played.

Through such a zoomed-back camera, we fancy we can see things a bit differently. Thus, instead of seeing the patient through the analyst's eyes as a dyadic creature whose distress may be traced to "repression" and "resistance" to the disclosure of unconscious contents, we see a certain sort of educated lay person who is very much aware of the language game being played here, very much aware of the analyst's theories, very much aware of the difference between being in the world of the analyst's office and being in the world of the street outside.

We suspect by the same token that the agitation manifested by the patient in the last sentence of the conversation may have a very different source than the dyadic distress ordinarily attributed to him. Conventionally the patient is supposed to resist the attribution to him of oedipal feelings. But is it not possible that in this case what was thought to be dyadic misery may turn out to be triadic delight? So that, far from being like one of Freud's Victorian patients who "resisted" the disclosure of such unconscious contents, this patient may be a horse of an entirely different color, namely, late-twentieth-century man who likes nothing better than to exhibit the proper pathology, in this case the central pathology of the Master himself. "It's oedipal!" exclaims the patient with every sign of delight.

Our business is to say what is right and what is wrong here. What is right is that Freud was right and that the patient does indeed do well to confront his oedipal feelings. What is wrong is a certain loss of sovereignty by the patient. We must trace out the connection between valid theory and falling prey to valid theory. For is it not true that the patient's chief claim to humanity here rests on the honorable credentials of his pathology? "Hurray!" he is saying. "I am certified human after all! I have oedipal feelings!"

A Tertium Quid:
The Lady Novelist?

Tolstoy once said that a talented lady novelist could spend five minutes looking through the window of a barracks and know all she needed to know about soldiering.

If she can see so much in five minutes, how much more must the talented therapist see after, say, a hundred hours with his patient?

So here is the real question, or rather the main specter which haunts every inquiry into language as behavior. Granted the short-comings of the two major methodological approaches to the talking patient—the analytic-psychical and the organismic-behavioristic—is not the sole remaining alternative the novelistic? Instead of "nov-elistic" we could say phenomenological, for the novelist must first and last be a good phenomenologist, and to most behavioral scien-tists phenomenologists are closer to novelists than to scientists. But is it not the case that when all is said and done and all theories aside, what happens is that the therapist gets to know his patient pretty well, understands him, intuits him, can talk with him and about him—and that behavioral theory can never say much about it?

Let us at least articulate our unhappiness. Unhappiness changes. We are no longer miserable about the old quarrel between classical behaviorism and classical psychoanalysis or about the more in-tricate quarrels and rapprochements of their followers. For it has become more and more evident that our main emotion when con-fronted by both Freud and Skinner, say, is not partisan feelings—for both are "right" in their way—but rather epistemological em-barrassment. Both men put forward dyadic models, one for orga-nisms interacting in an environment, the other for invisible "forces" interacting within a psyche. The question now is not which approach is right but how both can be right at the same time. To us now, Freud's and Skinner's models stand to each other like the two worlds on each side of Alice's looking-glass. Both worlds are demonstrably right and useful in their way, but how do you get from one to the other?

Is the lady novelist the only *tertium quid*?

But first, what does the lady novelist see if we put her down, not outside a barracks window, but on the other side of a viewing mir-ror through which she can see therapist and patient who were talk-ing about the rat behind the arras and related oedipal feelings? She notices first off, let us say, that the patient does get excited. But far from its being the case that he is upset and is "resisting" the disclo-sure of unpleasant unconscious contents, she has the distinct impression that the patient is delighted. Moreover, being a good novelist and well attuned to the intellectual fashions of the day, she has the distinct impression that the patient's pleasure has something to do with the fact that he has produced a kind of behavior which measures up to, or fits in with, the very theory to which he and his analyst subscribe. Perhaps it also occurs to her that the patient is in a sorry fix indeed if his chief claim to happiness is that occasion when he manages to be sick in the right way.

Suppose that the lady novelist is right. Is she then the *tertium quid?* Is her way the only way to get at what is going on? And if it is, has not all the fun gone out of the game of behavioral science and the scientific method itself lost its splendid rigor?

Have we not in fact come back to George Miller's original misgiving, which haunts all behavioral scientists when the subject of words and meanings is raised? Must we not then let it go at that, surrender the field to Tolstoy's lady novelist, or to Husserl, which is to say the same thing?

Perhaps. But Charles Peirce did propose a radical theory of signs which undertook to give an account of those transactions in which symbols are used to name things and to assert sentences about things. In view of the heroic and generally unavailing attempts during the past fifty years to give such an account through one or another dyadic theory, it might be worthwhile for once to approach triadic behavior with a genuine triadic theory.

Such a theory might bestow order and system upon the phenomenologizing which to the behavioral scientist must seem closer to novel writing than to a science of behavior.

For example, the oedipal patient's agitation may be given some such preliminary reading as follows:

The patient's agitation is not dyadic misery—resistance to the disclosure of unacceptable unconscious contents—but triadic delight. This delight, moreover, is quite as fundamental a trait of triadic behavior as organismic "need-satisfaction" is in dyadic behavior. It is a naming delight which derives from the patient's discovery that his own behavior, which until now he had taken to be the unformulable, literally unspeakable, vagary of one's self, has turned out not merely to be formulable, that is to say, namable by a theory to which both patient and therapist subscribe, but to be namable with a name which is above all names: *oedipal!*

As such, the patient's delight has good and bad, authentic and inauthentic components, which must be traced out and identified within an adequate triadic theory. Thus, the patient's sentence *It's oedipal!* must be investigated for Platonic and even magical components in its mode of coupling as well as for its valid intersubjective celebration of an important discovery. Perhaps the patient's sentence can be paraphrased in some such terms as: "At last I have succeeded! At last I have produced a proper, even a classical, piece of psychopathology!"

Accordingly, the patient's behavior with its strong normative components must be evaluated on a normative scale which is in turn an integral part of the triadic theory in question. It is impossible in other words to avoid the subject of the patient's impoverishment and loss of sovereignty.

In his astounding achievement of applying the scientific method to the irrational contents of the unconscious, Freud did not have time to consider what goes on between doctor and patient, nor how a technique itself can loom large as part of the intellectual furniture of a later age, much less how it could come to pass that one can fall prey to the very technique one seeks help from.

But that does not excuse us from investigating these matters.

9

THE SYMBOLIC STRUCTURE
OF INTERPERSONAL PROCESS

NOWADAYS ONE frequently hears the relation between psychiatrist and patient described as a field of interaction in which the psychiatrist plays the dual role of participant and observer. The concept of the prime role of social interaction in the genesis of the psyche, largely the contribution of Mead in social psychology and Sullivan in psychiatry, is a valid and fruitful notion and marks an important advance over older psychologies of the individual psyche. Yet it presently conceals a deep ambiguity, and, as ordinarily understood, tends to perpetuate a divorce between theory and practice which cannot fail to impede the progress of psychiatry as an empirical science. It is the thesis of this essay that this ambiguity in both psychiatry and social psychology can be traced to an equivocation of behavioral terms such as *sign, stimulus, interaction,* and so forth, in which they are applied to two generically different communication events. It is further proposed (1) to call into question the behavioristic or sign theory of interpersonal process, (2) to outline the generic structure of symbolic behavior, and (3) to examine briefly its relevance for the therapist-patient relation.

The ambiguity is found in the way such behavioral terms as interpersonal reflexes, social interaction, and response are applied to what seem to be two different kinds of interpersonal events. This usage leads to confusion because it is not made clear whether the writers mean that the events are different and the terms are used broadly, or that the events are really alike and the terms are used strictly. On the one hand, the phrase *interpersonal relation* is often used with the clear assumption that what is designated is an interaction between organisms describable in the terms of a behavioristic social psychology.* On the other hand, the same term is extended to activities which are even recognized by the writers as being in some sense different from the directly observable behavior of organisms. The ambiguity appears in the description of the behavior of both psychiatrist and patient. Thus those studying the patient find it natural to speak of the objective study of his behavior and also of an "interpretive content analysis" of what he says.† And the behavior of the psychiatrist is described as "participant observation." The psychiatrist not only enters into a conversation as other people do; he also preserves a posture of objectivity from which he takes note of the patient's behavior, and his own, according to the principles of his science. One is free, of course, to designate all these activities by some such term as behavior or interaction. But if it is meant that these activities are really alike, it is not clear in what ways they are alike. Or if it is allowed that they are different, it is not clear wherein they differ or under what larger canon they may be brought into some kind of conceptual order.

The anomalous position of empirical scientists vis-à-vis intersubjective phenomena has been noticed before. Even Mead declared that an ideally refined behaviorism could explain the behavior of the observed subject but not that of the observing behaviorist. The social psychologist, it seems fair to say, sets out to understand social behavior as a species of interaction between organisms.‡ Yet by his

* See, for example, David McK. Rioch: "The theory [Sullivan's theory of interpersonal relations] is very effective in dealing with the *behavior* of organisms, as it provides a comprehensive framework for dealing with the interaction of multiple factors, including the observer."

† See, for example, Joseph Jaffe: "The measurement of human interaction has recently been approached through a variety of techniques, ranging from interpretive content analyses to objective recording of temporal patterns in behavioral interaction."

‡ "Social psychology, considered as a branch of psychology, is the study of individual responses as conditioned by stimuli arising from social or collective situations;

own behavior he seems to allow for a kind of interpersonal activity which can be called "interaction" only by the most Pickwickian use of language. For the social psychologist observes, theorizes, and writes papers which he expects his colleagues not merely to respond to but to understand as well.* His behaviorism does not give an account of his own behavior. The awkward fact is that *verstehen*, that indispensable technique by which the social scientist discovers what another person "means," is not provided for by neobehavioristic psychology. The anomaly is implicit in social psychology but explicit and acute in psychiatry because of the peculiar nature of the therapist-patient encounter. It is not possible to ignore the role of the scientist when he comprises one half of the social dyad under study. The social psychologist studies the interactions of persons and groups. But the psychiatrist is very largely concerned with the "interaction" between the patient and himself. And so the psychiatrist has come to be called the "participant observer."

But the term *participant observation* expresses rather than clarifies a dilemma of the social sciences, and it should be accepted heuristically rather than as an explanation of what the psychiatrist is doing. The persistent ambiguity, however, is not occupationally peculiar to psychiatrists, and is not to be resolved by psychiatric theory. It comes about not as a result of some peculiar exigency of the therapist-patient relation but rather as a result of a fundamental incoherence in the attitude of empirical scientists toward that generic phenomenon of which the therapist-patient encounter is but a special instance: human communication. And it is to communication theory, considered both as the empirical science of symbolic behavior (psycholinguistics) and as a unified theory of signs (semiotic), that one must look for the source of the confusion and its resolution.

---

considered as a branch of sociology or as collective psychology, it is the study of collective responses or of the behavior of groups and other collectivities." (L. L. Bernard, "Social Psychology.")

   * See Chapter 12.

The Incoherence of a Behavioristic
Theory of Meaning

About thirty-five years ago Edward Sapir called attention to a serious oversight in the then current psychology of language, writing, ". . . psychologists have perhaps too narrowly concerned themselves with the simple psychophysical bases of speech and have not penetrated very deeply into its symbolic nature." He called for an empirical study of speech as a mode of symbolic behavior. Ten years later another great linguist, Benjamin Lee Whorf, took issue with his colleagues' practice of "recording hairsplitting distinctions of sound, performing phonetic gymnastics, and writing complex grammars which only grammarians read." "Linguistics," he reminded them, "is essentially the quest of *meaning*."

The warnings of Sapir and Whorf have not been heeded. On the contrary. The trend of theoretical linguistics in recent years has been in precisely the opposite direction. Linguists are quite frank about their aversion to meaning, to symbolic behavior, as a fit subject for empirical investigation. As Carroll has summed it up, the trend has been away from a psychology of verbal behavior—that is, the empirical investigation of the language event as a natural phenomenon; the trend instead has been toward "communication theory," which abstracts from the event itself and concerns itself with a statistical analysis of the capacity of various systems of communication, and "discourse analysis," which is a formal determination of the recurrence of morphemes in connected speech. The upshot has been an incoherent attitude toward symbolic behavior. Language is held to be a kind of sign response and so understandable in behavioristic terms as an interaction between an organism and its environment—which consists, in this case, of other organisms.* At the same time, the peculiar status of symbolic behavior is recognized by treating it *formally*—there are no formal

---

* A symbol, according to Charles Morris, is a sign produced by its interpreter which acts as a substitute for some other sign with which it is synonymous. Thus hunger cramps might take the place of the buzzer announcing the food and become a symbol for the dog.

sciences, as far as I know, devoted to the syntax or semantics of animal utterances. Thus, there is a natural science devoted to the study of reaction times and learning behavior; there are formal sciences which treat the logic and grammar of sentences. But where is the natural science which treats sentence events—not a sentence written on a blackboard, but the happening in which a father, replying to his son's question, utters the following sounds: "That is a balloon"?

A good example of this incoherence is to be found in the otherwise valuable discipline of semiotic, which seeks to unite the several disciplines of symbolic logic, psychological behaviorism, and semantics into a single organon.* Semiotic is divided into three levels or dimensions: syntactics, pragmatics, and semantics. Syntactics is, as one might expect, a formal science having to do with the logico-grammatical structure of signs and with the formation and transformation rules of language. Pragmatics is the natural science of organisms responding to signs in their environments—psychiatry would be considered a branch of pragmatics. Semantics, which has to do with the relation of signs and their designata, is not a natural science of symbolic behavior, as one might have hoped. It is a formal deductive discipline in which "semantic rules" are proposed, designating the conditions under which a sign is applied to its object or designatum.† Thus, in semiotic, symbolic behavior is studied *formally* in syntactics and semantics, but is disqualified in the natural empirical science of pragmatics—or written off as a refinement of sign-response behavior.

The embarrassing fact is that there does not exist today, as far as I am aware, a natural empirical science of symbolic behavior *as such.*‡ Yet communication, the language event, is a real happen-

---

* See Chapter 11.

† See also Alfred Tarski. Other writers interpret semantics not merely as a formal science but as a quasi-ethical science in which users of words are scolded for not using them at the proper level of abstraction. See, for example, Alfred Korzybski, *Science and Sanity*.

‡ General linguistics is, of course, an empirical science, but, except for acoustics, only at the comparative level. In phonetics, phonemics, morphophonemics, syntax, and lexicography, the linguist describes the structure of the languages of the

ing; it is as proper a subject for a natural science as nuclear fission or sexual reproduction.

Neobehavioristic social psychology is not able to take account of symbolic behavior, let alone provide a heuristically fruitful basis of investigation. To say so is in no wise to challenge the accomplishments of the behavioristic approach. Learning theory is still valid as far as it goes. Reaction times still stand. It is still quite true to say that when a conversation takes place between two people, a stimulus or energy exchange makes its well-known journey as a wave disturbance in the air, through the solids of the middle ear, as an afferent nerve impulse, as an electrocolloidal change in the central nervous system, as an efferent nerve impulse, as a muscle movement in the larynx of the second speaker, as a wave disturbance, and so on. One is still justified in calling the interpersonal process what Mead called it fifty years ago: a conversation of gesture in which my speech stimulus "calls out a response" from you. It is not enough to say this, however. For, as Susanne Langer rather drily observed, to set forth language as a sequence of stimuli and responses overlooks the salient trait of symbolic behavior: Symbols, words, not only call forth responses; they also denote things, name things for both speakers. Furthermore, behavioristic psychology is not able to take account of another universal trait of connected speech: Words are not merely aggregates of sound, however significant; in sentences or in agglutinative forms they also *assert* a state of affairs (or deny it or question it or command it). No alternative remains to the behaviorist semanticist but to disqualify the phenomenon of symbolization—to call it "an unreal but imputed relation between word and thing" or simply "wrong." Again one is free to call symbolic behavior wrong or unreal or anything one likes, but such epithets hardly settle its status for the empirical scientist. It remains the task of empirical science to investigate phenomena as they happen, and everyone would agree that symbolic

earth as they are found to occur. What one fails to find in the literature, however, is an empirical study of the language event in itself as a generic event. It is much as if biologists were interested in describing the various kinds of mitotic division among different species, but were not interested in studying the process of mitosis.

behavior does happen: People talk together, name things, make assertions about states of affairs, and to a degree understand each
other.

The real task is how to study symbolic behavior, not formally by
the deductive sciences which specify rules for the use of symbols in
logic and calculi, but empirically as a kind of event which takes
place in the same public domain as learning behavior. Sapir's gentle chiding about the lack of a science of symbolic behavior and the
need of such a science is more conspicuously true today than it was
thirty-five years ago.

I am well aware, of course, that the altogether praiseworthy objective of the behaviorist is to get beyond the old mentalist night-
mare in which interpersonal process is set forth in terms of my having "ideas," "thoughts," and "feelings," and giving them names
and so conveying them to you. If the word *meaning* refers to
such mental entities, researchers do well to have nothing to do with
it, for nothing has so effectively stifled the empirical investigation of
communication as this misbegotten offspring of Descartes, the
word-thing, the sound which I speak and which somehow carries
my idea over to you like a note in a bottle. Yet the question must
arise as to whether the alternatives lie only between a behavioristic
theory of meaning, the energy exchange bouncing back and forth
between speaker and hearer like a tennis ball, and the old miraculous mind reading by means of words. The phenomenon of *verstehen*, my understanding of what another person "means," has been
often called "subjective" by positive scientists and hence beyond the
competence of empirical science. But such a ruling places the
social scientist in the uncomfortable position of disqualifying his
own activity—in the psychiatrist's case, the activity of understanding his patient, writing papers, teaching courses.

Some Molar Traits of the
Communication Event

The fact is that the generic traits of symbolic behavior are not
"mental" at all. They are empirically ascertainable and have indeed

been observed often enough. Both Ruesch and Jaffe have noticed that interpersonal events are peculiarly dyadic in a sense not altogether applicable to the interaction of the organism with its environment. Ruesch speaks of the structure of the interpersonal relation as a two-person system; Jaffe calls it a dyad. I would lay even greater stress on this feature as a manifestation of a generic trait of symbolic behavior. One may say if one likes that the bee dance is a communication event occurring in a two-bee system, but one is multiplying entities and it is not particularly useful to say so anyhow. A bee responding to another bee can be considered quite adequately as an organism in transaction with an environment, quite as much so as a solitary polar bear responding to the sound of splitting ice. But it has proved anything but adequate to consider language in the same terms. A symbol is generically intersubjective. I can never discover that the object is called a chair unless you tell me so, and my inkling that it "is" a chair is qualitatively different from the bee's response to the bee dance of going to look for nectar.

Schachtel set forth another trait of symbolic behavior when he observed the genesis of an attitude among children which he called "autonomous object interest," an attitude which he was careful to distinguish from need-satisfactions and wish fulfillment. It is not difficult, I think, to demonstrate that this autonomous object interest is intimately associated with the genesis of object language in the second year of life and is in fact an enduring trait of all symbolic behavior.

Two observations by Martin Buber are also of the utmost relevance to the basic structure of symbolic behavior. One of the main theses of Buber's thought is his concept of *relation*, or the interhuman, which he holds to be beyond the reach of a behavioristic psychology. The other is the concept of *distance*. In contrast to the organism which exists wholly within its environment, man sets things at a distance. He is the creature through whose being (*Sein*), a phenomenon, "what is" (das *Seiende*), becomes detached from him and recognized for itself. Buber's observations are developed within the framework of a philosophical anthropology; the traits of distance and relation are expressed as modes peculiar to human existence rather than as directly observable features of human relations. Expressed thus, Buber's insights are perhaps somewhat uncongenial to many American social scientists with their strict empirical methodology—although it would be quite possible to defend the thesis that Buber's analysis of human existence and human relations is also empirical in the broad sense of the word. It may be true that these existential traits of distance and relation are not "mental," but they must strike the empirical scientist as vague in meaning and difficult to define operationally. Man is after all an organism, whatever else he is, and he does live in an environment. If he exists in uniquely human modes of being, such as distance and relation, it is not clear how these modes are grounded in or otherwise related to the present empirical knowledge of man. Precisely what does it mean to say that the human organism enters into the interhuman relation and sets things at a distance? Such theoretical grounding is, I believe, forthcoming from an empirical analysis of symbolic behavior. Indeed, it seems clear that Ruesch and Jaffe's more-than-one-person system, Schachtel's autonomous object interest, and Buber's distance and relation are neither random nor reducible characteristics of human behavior. They are rather among the prime and generic traits of the highly structured meaning-situation found in symbolic behavior. What is more important, these traits are ascertainable not by a philosophical anthropology—which source is itself enough to render them suspect in the eyes of the behavioral scientists—but by an empirical analysis of language events as they are found to occur in the genetic appearance of language in the encultured child, in blind deaf-mutes, and in the structure of everyday language exchanges.

The greatest danger of the narrow behavioristic framework within which American behavioral scientists almost instinctively conceive the interpersonal process is that peculiarly human phenomena, such as language, are held either reducible to response sequences which leave out symbols altogether, or else describable by analogy, which does not so much shed light on the subject as close the door. Thus it may be unexceptionable to compare genes and symbols as the permanent characters of their respective systems and to speak of "levels of organization," but such semantic shifts shed little or no light on intersubjective processes.* In an article about Buber, Leslie Farber wrote not long ago, "Having used only the single mode of scientific knowledge for the past hundred years or so, we are uneasily aware that this was the wrong mode—the wrong viewpoint, the wrong terminology, and the wrong kind of knowledge— ever to explain the human being." This is true enough, I believe. There is a danger, however, in setting philosophical anthropology over against empirical science in such a sharp dichotomy. It is apt to confirm the positive scientist in his determination to have nothing to do with the existentialist-phenomenological movement—and so further impoverishes his social behaviorism. At the same time it encourages from the opposite quarter all manner of irrational and antiscientific prejudice—in particular the ill-assorted crew of post-Cartesian mentalists who want to rescue "man" from "science" and restore him to the angelic order of mind and subjectivity. No, the present crisis of the social sciences need not polarize itself into an ideological issue between American positivists and European existentialists. Surely the better course is an allegiance to the empirical method—but not, let me carefully note, an allegiance to a theoretical commitment. The watchword of the empirical social scientist who confronts interpersonal phenomena should be, *Let us see what is going on*, and not, *Let us see how we can fit it into a stimulus-response transaction.*

The Structure of Symbolic Behavior

It would not, perhaps, be inaccurate to say that American psychology, as well as other behavioral sciences, has settled on an eclectic behaviorism in which the cruder features of Watsonian psychology

* I have in mind Paul Weiss's exasperation with behavioral scientists' perennial recourse to such terms as *levels of organization*. "We are struck with a lack of a practical, realistic, analytic approach that will go beyond the mere statement of the fact that we have hierarchical nature, that it does consist of a system of Chinese boxes one inside the other, that they are integrated, interrelated, coordinated and all these other terms."

have been refined by the work of Tolman, Skinner, Hull, Mowrer, Dollard and Miller, Sears, and Angyall. In this view, also put forward at the pragmatic level of semiotic, the organism, whether human or subhuman, is regarded as an open system living in an environment and adapting to that environment through its response to elements which are called signs. A sign is defined as an element in the environment which, through congenital or acquired patterns of behavior, directs the organism to something else, this something else being understood either as some other element or simply as biologically relevant behavior. Thus, the scent of deer directs the tiger to the deer; the scent of the tiger directs the deer to flight. A good representation of this relation is the semiotic triangle, shown in Figure 5.*

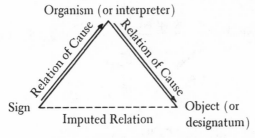

Figure 5. The Semiotic Triangle

The relations between signs and interpreters and between interpreters and objects are of the nature of space-time transactions between an organism and its environment and can be studied by a natural science. The relation between sign and object, shown in Figure 5 as dotted, has been called an imputed, as opposed to a real, relation. But this imputed relation is ambiguous. Does it mean that naming is folly and not the fit subject of a natural science, or does it mean that it is a formal relation and open to

* This schema, which is designed to apply alike to animal behavior and to human speech, follows, in the main, that of Morris with modifications by Ogden and Richards.

study only by a formal science? But naming does happen. People give names to things as surely as rats find their way through mazes.

The problem, it would seem, is how to give an account of symbolic behavior considered not in its formal aspects—as it would be considered by grammar, logic, and mathematics—but as a happening and, as such, open to a natural science.

Although the semiotic triangle is a useful model of stimulus-response arcs and of learning behavior, the fact is that symbolic behavior is irreducibly tetradic in structure, as shown in Figure 6.*

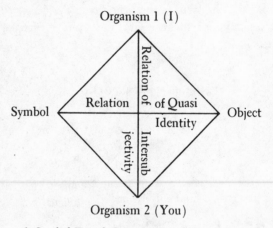

Figure 6. Symbol Tetrad: Generic Type of Symbolic Behavior

The second person is required as an element not merely in the genetic event of learning language but as the *indispensable and enduring condition of all symbolic behavior*. The very act of symbolic formulation, whether it be language, logic, art, or even thinking, is of its very nature a formulation for a *someone else*. Even Robinson Crusoe, writing in his journal after twenty years on the island, is nevertheless performing a through-and-through social and intersubjective act.†

* Cf. p. 259.

† And even Samuel Pepys. For, although he kept his journal for himself and in a private code, he was nevertheless formulating experience and so setting it at a distance for a someone else—himself.

The new ensemble of elements and relations which comes into being does not replace but rather overlays the organismic interaction. People still interact with each other behavioristically as much as do dogs and bees, but they also enter into intersubjective relations and cointend objects through the vehicle of symbols. It is possible, and indeed preferable, to describe symbolic behavior in an operational language which omits reference to mental contents or even to "meanings." "Ideas" are difficult to define operationally and even more difficult to bring into coherent relation with the observables of behavioral science. As for "meanings," the word is itself so ambiguous that there is more to be lost than gained from its use. It seems least objectionable to say that in the particular communication event under consideration, an organism intends such and such a designatum by means of such and such a symbol.

This approach still deals with elements and relations, just as does that of the neobehaviorist. A list of the elements and relations of the symbolic meaning-structure, and an example of their clinical application, follows.

The intersubjective community. Whenever behavioral scientists are confronted with a concrete language event, appropriate questions are: What is the community? What is the status of the intersubjective bond? Who is included and who is excluded? Is the community I-you-you or I-you–not you (as it is sometimes when one goes to a very high-toned lecture: we are listening and understanding, and we are quite aware that those out in the street are not)? The community may vary from a face-to-face confrontation of two people and the various colorations of the I-you bond, to the scattered and numerically unlimited community of mass communication in which one person communicates with others through various media. In the latter case, still other questions become pertinent. What is the effect of the interposition of the medium between speaker and hearer? When the President says on television, "I am counting on you right there in your living room to make a sacrifice," is the sentence received in the same way as it would be in a face-to-face encounter, or is it apt to constitute itself for the viewer as merely another item of "what one hears" on radio and television?

It should be emphasized that this empirical approach does not require the settling or even the raising of the question of the ontological status of the intersubjective relation. The latter is introduced as a postulate which is valid to the extent that it unites random observations and opens productive avenues of inquiry.

The object and the world. The notion of world here is not an epistemological construct, as it is in much of European phenomenology. I am not saying that the world is constituted by the *Dasein* or the transcendental ego. Nor do I say that a tree is exactly as it appears. I say only that if one makes an empirical study of sign-using animals and symbol-using animals, one can only conclude that the latter have a world and the former do not. Nor does such a notion require the entity "mind" in one and eliminate it in the other. It has only to do with the observable difference between sign behavior and symbolic behavior. A sign-using organism takes account only of those elements of its environment which are relevant biologically. A chick has been observed to take account of the shadow of a hen and the shadow of a hawk but not, I believe, of the shadow of a swallow. A two-year-old child, however, will not only ask for milk, as a good sign-using animal; he will also point to the swallow and ask what it is.

A sign-using organism can be said to take account of those segments of its environment toward which, through the rewards and punishments of the learning process, it has acquired the appropriate responses. It cannot be meaningfully described as "knowing" anything else. But a symbol-using organism has a world. Once it knows the name of trees—what trees "are"—it must know the name of houses. The world is simply the totality of that which is formulated through symbols. It is both spatial and temporal. Once a native knows there is an earth, he must know what is under the earth. Once he knows what happened yesterday, he must know what happened in the beginning. Hence his cosmological and etiological myths.* Chickens have no myths.

---

* Much of the formulating and objectifying function of the symbol has been set forth by Ernst Cassirer; see in particular vol. 1, *Language*. But the empirical insights are so submerged by the apparatus of German idealism that they are salvaged

Nor does the symbol refer to its object in the same mode as the sign does. True, one can use the word *mean* analogically and say that thunder means rain to the chicken and that the symbol *water* means water to Helen Keller. But the symbol does something the sign fails to do: It sets the object at a distance and in a public zone, where it is beheld intersubjectively by the community of symbol users. As Langer put it, say *James* to a dog, and as a good sign-using animal he will go look for James. Say *James* to you, and if you know a James, you will ask, "What about him?"

The genesis of symbolic behavior, considered both ontogenetically and phylogenetically, is an all-or-none change, involving a symbolic threshold. As Sapir observed, there are no primitive languages. Every known language is an essentially perfect means of expression and communication among those who use it. As Helen Keller put it, once she knew what water "was," she had to know what everything else was. The greatest difference between the environment (*Umwelt*) of a sign-using organism and the world (*Welt*) of the speaking organism is that there are gaps in the former but none in the latter.* The nonspeaking organism only notices what is relevant biologically; the speaking organism disposes of the entire horizon symbolically. Gaps that cannot be closed by perception and reason are closed by magic and myth. The primitive has names for edible and noxious plants; but he also has a name for all the others: "bush." He also "knows" what lies beyond the horizon, what is under the earth, and where he came from.

only with difficulty. Cassirer was concerned to extend the Kantian thesis to the area of culture and symbols and so to establish that it is through symbols that one not merely knows but constitutes the world. The task of the behavioral scientist is different. He confronts symbolic behavior from the same posture with which he studies sign behavior: as events in a public domain which he shares with other scientists. He sees people using words to name things and to assert states of affairs, just as he sees rats threading their way through mazes. He is concerned to explain what he sees by the use of mechanisms and models. I confess that this posture presupposes a species of philosophical realism.

* This notion of world and environment is close to the *Welt* and *Umwelt* of the Binswanger school. See Ludwig Binswanger, "The Existential Analysis School of Thought," in *Existence*. It is important to note, however, that this distinction is yielded by an empirical analysis of the language event and does not depend for its validity on the *Daseinanalytik* of Heidegger or on any other philosophical anthropology.

The distinction between *Welt* and *Umwelt* has been made before. Buber characterizes man as the creature who has a world and sets it at a distance, beyond the operation of his drives and needs. But, insightful as such an observation may be, it is of doubtful value to the behavioral sciences until it can be grounded in a coherent theory of symbolic behavior.

The being-in-the-world. Here again, my element is different from the *Dasein* of the existentialists, akin as the latter is to the transcendental subject of Kant and Husserl. It is no more than a working concept arrived at through the necessity of giving an account of the organism who participates in symbolic behavior. The organism who speaks has a world and consequently has the task of living in the world. It is simply inadequate to describe him in the organismic terms of adjustment, adaptation, needs, drives, reinforcement, inhibition, and so on. A psychiatric patient is, to be sure, an organism in an environment. He is also a creature who is informed by his culture. But he is something more. He is an organism who may not forgo the choice of how he is going to live in his world, for the forgoing is itself a kind of choice by default. It becomes pertinent to ask in what mode he inserts himself in the world. May has suggested that it sometimes seems more appropriate to ask a patient *Where are you?* rather than *How are you?* Certainly, becoming aware of the threshold of symbolic behavior makes one very curious about modes of existence: How does the person go about living in his world?

The intentional or quasi identity between the symbol and that which is symbolized. The mysterious "unreal but imputed" relation between the symbol and its designatum, the "wrong" identification of word and thing which the Polish semanticists condemn, never really fitted into a behavioristic theory of meaning. How did it come about that responding organisms imputed an unreal semantical relation between signs and things? How does an organism behave perversely by making a semantic identification at the "wrong" level of abstraction? What kind of organon is the unified science of signs when symbolic behavior is recognized as such by the formal sciences but disqualified by the natural sciences?

Once it becomes clear that what is to be studied is not sentence forms but particular language events, it also becomes clear that the subject of investigation in this instance is not the sentence itself but the mode in which it is asserted. The sentence can be studied only by a formal science such as grammar or logic, but a sentence event is open to a rich empirical phenomenology that is wholly unprovided by what passes currently as semantics. Nor can a neo-behavioristic psychology make sense of assertory behavior; it can only grasp a sequence of space-time events which it attempts to correlate by constant functions. But assertion—the giving of a name to a thing, *this is water*, or the declaring of a state of affairs, *the water is cold*—is not a sequence. It is a pairing or identification of word and thing, class and thing, thing and attribute, and so on. Stimulus and response events are studied by a quantitative science. But the quasi identification events of symbolic behavior can be grasped only by a qualitative phenomenology. This qualitative scale must take account not only of true-or-false-or-nonsense statements (water is cold, water is dry, water is upside down), but also of various modes of magic identification. It does not suffice, for example, to say that the assertion of a Bororo tribesman of Brazil, "I am a parakeet," is false or nonsense. Nor is it adequate to say that it is false scientifically but true mythically.* It is necessary to understand the particular mode of identification of a particular language-event.†

Sentences exhibiting the same syntactic and semantic structure may be asserted in wholly different modes of identification. For ex-

---

* It is characteristic of the current confusion of the behavioral sciences that theorists find themselves speaking of true myths and are even driven to the extremity of prescribing myth as such for the ills of contemporary society. (See, for example, Henry A. Murray, "A Mythology for Grownups.") The confusion can be traced, I believe, to the failure of behavioral theory to give an account of different modes of symbolic activity, in this case that of scientists and nonscientists. Thus when psychiatrists and clinical psychologists say that people nowadays need viable myths, they seem to be saying that scientists are different from people: scientists seek the truth and people have needs. Coherent theory would not, presumably, require such a generic distinction.

† The Bororo does not intend that he is literally a parakeet (he does not try to mate with other parakeets), yet he clearly intends it in a sense more magical than ordinary factual statements. See the "mystic identification" of L. Lévy-Bruhl in *How Natives Think*.

ample, the sentence "My son John has become a roentgenologist" has the logical form of the assertion of class membership, $a \in A$. It has this form regardless of the particular language event in which it is asserted. The sentence can be asserted in more than one mode, however. Thus, if a psychiatrist should hear his patient utter the above sentence, he may very well understand, knowing her as he does, that she is asserting a magic mode of class membership. Her son John has gone off to a scientific place where he has undergone a mystical transformation and emerged as a roentgenologist. Another patient may assert the same sentence and be quite clearly understood to mean that her son has acquired a skill which it is convenient to speak of as a class membership.*

The action sentence "John treats patients with X-rays" may also be asserted as a transparent vehicle intending a nonmagic action not utterly different from everyday actions of pushing, pulling, hitting, shooting, and so forth. Or it may be asserted magically: John makes a scientific pass with his paraphernalia and his ray, and the patient is cured.

The connotations of words themselves, apart from assertory behavior, undergo a characteristic semantic evolution which can be understood only by a science proper of symbolic behavior, for it is the particular word event which is studied and not the "semantic rule" by which it is applied to its designatum. The scale ranges from the almost miraculous discovering power of the word-vehicle as a metaphor in the hands of the poet, to its sclerosis through usage and familiarity until it becomes a semantic husk serving rather to conceal than to disclose what it designates. When Shakespeare compares winter trees with

> Bare ruined choirs where late the sweet birds sang †

the words come as fresh as creation from the symbolizer and serve to discover for the reader what he too saw but did not know he saw.

---

* Lévy-Bruhl's categories of "prelogical" thought are not, in my opinion, a genetic stage of psychic evolution but simply a mode of symbolic behavior to which a denizen of Western culture is as apt to fall prey as a Bororo.
† Sonnet 73.

But when, in everyday conversation, I tell you, "Last summer I went abroad and had some interesting experiences and saw some historical sites," the words act as biscuit cutters carving up memory into the weariest shapes of everyday usage.*

THE SYMBOLIC STRUCTURE OF A THERAPIST-PATIENT
COMMUNICATION EVENT

To determine how the generic structure of symbolic behavior is relevant to the therapist-patient relation as an instance thereof, I shall consider briefly a hypothetical language event.

Patient: "Here is a dream which may be of some interest to you. Since you are an analyst, I am sure you will agree it has psychiatric implications."

Therapist: "Sounds interesting."

Patient: "In this dream I was walking down a strange street. A sexy-looking woman standing behind a Dutch door beckoned to me. I hesitated for a second, then against my better judgment, I went into the house."

Therapist: "Horrendous! [Pronounced heartily with a *j*: horrenjus!]" †

In the study of a spoken language event, a written transcription is, of course, wholly unacceptable.‡ All phonetics and vocal modifiers are omitted. Even a tape recording is inadequate since it does

---

* Ernest Schachtel has described this "articulating and obscuring function" of language in "On Memory and Childhood Amnesia." He gives a good example of the sterility of the conventional phrase in which one distorts the ineffable content of memory—as when one reports having an "exciting time." He says, "No object perceived with the quality of freshness, newness, of something wonder-full, can be preserved and recalled by the conventional concept of that object as designated in its conventional name in language" (p. 9). It seems to me, however, that he is describing terms that have deteriorated in their semantic evolution rather than the entire spectrum of language itself. Symbols may conceal, distort, render commonplace, yes; but since people are not angelic intelligences, symbols are their only means of knowing anything at all.

† "Horrenjus" is borrowed from Norman A. McQuown's linguistic analysis of an interview reported by Otto A. Will and Robert A. Cohen, but the exchange is otherwise hypothetical and is offered not as clinical evidence but only illustratively, to exemplify some traits of symbolic structure.

‡ Reading is, it is true, an event of symbolic behavior, but it must be studied as such, as an event open to an appropriate phenomenology and not as a substitute for hearing.

not transmit gestures. In my comment on this exchange, moreover, I will say nothing of such strictly linguistic analyses as might be made of phonemes, morphemes, and grammar. Nor shall I say anything about the "content" of the exchange—for example, the dream and its "meaning"—important though this may be in the patient's dynamics. But if one does not consider the linguistics and content of the language event, what else remains to be said about it? What remains is nothing else but the particular structure of the symbolic behavior, of which the symbolic tetrad is the generic type (see Figure 2). The assumption that all that is going on is an interaction between organisms deprives the investigator of the means of taking account of the molar event of communication, leaving him only with the alternative of fitting as best he can the qualitative traits of interpersonal behavior into the Procrustean bed of a response psychology. But once the generic character of symbolic behavior is recognized, then the modes of intersubjectivity, "world," "being-in-a-world," and assertory identity are seen as particular expressions of the fundamental possibilities allowed by the structure of interpersonal process—just as drives, needs, reinforcement and extinction, stimulus, response, are the fundamental categories of organismic interaction.

The mode of assertory identity. It may very well be that some of the assertory behavior in this example is magical. The patient is an educated layman, the sort who takes pride in being well informed in scientific matters, especially psychiatry, and in his use of psychiatric jargon. He quite consciously uses "analyst" rather than "psychoanalyst." One often notices in psychiatric interviews a kind of pseudo reversal of the roles of scientist and layman. The patient often uses such phrases as "Oedipus complex" (he would never say "inferiority complex," since it passed long ago into everyday usage, passing, moreover, as a semantic husk of very questionable value), "sibling rivalry," "aggressions," and so forth, while the therapist is careful to steer clear of them, partly because he does not wish to use a technical phrase the patient would not understand, but perhaps even more because he is intuitively aware of the magic abuses to which expertise is peculiarly susceptible.* The patient in question may have, by reason of this very knowledgeability about psychiatry, fallen prey to a magic mode of identification. The clause *Since you are an analyst* very likely asserts a mystical transformation by which an ordinary human being is transfigured and informed by the resplendent scientific symbols "psychiatrist" and "psychoanalyst" and finally by the shorthand expression used among the elite, "analyst."

The world of the therapist and his being-in-the-world. Insofar as he is a scientist, the therapist has assumed the posture of objectivity. As a consequence of what might be called the Thalesian revolution, men have learned, beginning at about the time of the Ionian philosophers and the Vedantists of the epic period,† to strike a theoretical posture toward the world which would enable them to discover the underlying principles and causes by which particular things and events can be understood. The scientist is not in his world in the same way, as, say, a member of a cosmological culture like the Bororo tribesmen, nor as a wanderer between cultures like Abraham, nor even as his fellow culture members, the businessman and the streetcar conductor. Insofar as he practices his science, he stands, in Buber's phrase, "over against" his world as knower and manipulator of that which can be known and manipulated. The scientist may so be characterized without pejoration—indeed if he were in his world in any other way, he could hardly be a scientist. Yet as a psychiatrist, a "participant observer," he must also re-enter the world in some mode or other as a person who is friendly and sympathetic, or anyhow appears so, to his patient.

The single utterance of the therapist, "horrenjus," reveals a mode of the participant-observer stance, of necessity a kind of straddle in which the therapist stands outside and over against the

---

* What psychiatrist has not been disturbed by this penchant for "scientizing" concrete experience? When, for example, a patient reports that he has a "personality problem" at the office, the psychiatrist may pay proper respect to his patient's knowledgeability and objectivity, but he may also have good reason for wishing that he had said instead, "Oh God, how I hate my boss!"

† A time which Jaspers has called the axial period in world history.

world—including his patient—and yet enters into an interpersonal relation with his patient. He accomplishes the feat in this case through a kind of indulgent playfulness, tempered effectively, as McQuown comments, by his use of his pipe. The playful irony of "horrenjus!" pronounced with an exaggerated vaudeville-British propriety, expresses mock scandal at the patient's decision to approach the woman in his dream, a device which serves at once to neutralize the patient's anxiety and to extend to him a friendly hand: Come join me in a bit of good-natured deprecation of the Puritan streak in our culture. Yet, as sincerely warm as the therapist may feel toward his patient, there is hardly a second when his own objective placement in the world is not operative.* In fact, the very act which expresses his friendliness, the *horrenjus!* and the indulgent pipe-fondling behavior, also serves to set him gently but firmly apart as an elite-member, a tolerant Thalesian revolutionary who has made it his business to stand over against a sector of reality and study it according to the objective method.

The stance of the pure scientist is that of objectivity, a standing over against the world, the elements of which serve as specimens or instances of the various classes of objects and events which comprise his science. The behavior of the scientist, like any other mode of symbolic behavior, also implies a dimension of intersubjectivity; this is, of course, the community of other scientists engaged in the same specialty. Whether he is working with a colleague or alone, publishing or not publishing, the very nature of the scientific method with its moments of observation, concept formation, hypothesizing, verification, is a making public, a formulation for someone else.

But in the psychiatric interview the objective stance of the scientist with its attendant community of other scientists is overlaid by a second interpersonal relation, that of the therapist with his patient. This relation differs from that between the therapist and his col-

---

* Much of what the existential analysts call being-in-the-world is overlapped by the social scientist's concept of role taking—although the former also calls into question the authenticity of a self constructed only of roles. The notion of role taking, moreover, hardly does justice to the radical placement in the world required of anyone who has crossed the symbolic threshold.

leagues. The latter is a Thalesian community, which is set apart
from the everyday world by its esoteric knowledge of the underlying
principles of some world phenomena. The relation between the
therapist and his patient is, or at least might be, very much in the
world. It might be called a Samaritan-Jew dyad—one man in trouble and another man going out of his way to help him.

   The world of the patient and his being-in-the-world. This patient
is in his world in a way wholly different from that of his therapist,
yet it is a way which is heavily influenced by the presence of
science in the world. The patient, let me postulate, is the sort of
person who has also adopted the objective point of view but has
adopted it secondhand. He is convinced that the scientific world
view is the right way of looking at things, but since he is not a scientist and does not spend his time practicing the objective method,
his objective-mindedness raises some problems. Deprived of the
firsthand encounter with the subject matter which the scientist enjoys, he is even more apt than the scientist to fall prey to what
Whitehead called the "fallacy of misplaced concreteness" * and so
to bestow upon theory, or what he imagines to be theory, a superior
reality at the expense of the reality of the very world he lives in. His
problem is not, as is the scientist's, *What sense can I make of the
data before me?* but is instead, *How can I live in a world which I
have disposed of theoretically?* He is like the schoolgirl who, on
seeing the Grand Canyon for the first time, is unimpressed, either
because she has already "had" it in geology or because she has not
yet had it. Such a misplacement of the concrete is a serious matter
because, although one may dispose of the world through theory,
one is not thereby excused from the necessity of living in this same
world. This patient's mode of life is open to considerable anxiety
and he is apt to conceive of his predicament and its remedy in the
following terms: I am having trouble living in the world which I see
objectively; therefore I shall apply for relief to the very source of my

---

* Whitehead speaks here of the "great confusion" which the fallacy has brought to
pass in science and philosophy. In my opinion, it has caused greater confusion
among lay people and, what is worse, an impoverishment of the very world one lives
in.

world view, the scientist himself. His seduction by theory is such,
however, as to place him almost beyond the reach of the therapist.
Paradoxically, it is his veneration of psychiatry which all but dis-
qualifies him as a candidate for psychiatric treatment. For it is a
necessary condition of the therapist's method that he abstract to a
degree from the individuality of his patient and see him as an instance of, a "case of," such and such a malfunction.* But the patient is peculiarly prone to extrapolate a methodology into a way of
living. He is pleased when the dream he offers to the therapist turns
out to be a recognizable piece of pathology. He does not conceive a
higher existence for himself than to be "what one should be" according to psychiatry. But science cannot tell one how to live; it
can only abstract some traits from a number of people who do
manage to live well—he has read no doubt that one should have an
"integrated personality" or that one should be "creative" or "autonomous," and the like. But the patient who sets out to become
an integrated personality has embarked on a very peculiar enterprise. An almost intractable misunderstanding is apt to arise between therapist and patient. It is of this order: The therapist offers
the assistance of the method and technique of his science and
hopes that the patient can make use of it to become the individual
he is capable of becoming. But the patient in his anonymity labors
under the chronic misapprehension that he is trying to become
"one of those"—that is, an integrated personality. The patient as
good as asks: Am I doing it right now? Am I not now an individual
in my own right?

The intersubjective community. The character of the community
in this example may be inferred from the foregoing. The community is a special instance of the I-you dyad in which the inclusion of
the patient implies a significant exclusion. The exclusion is signifi-

---

* As Sullivan pointed out, psychiatry, insofar as it is a science, must have to do
with the general and not the individual. "Let me say that insofar as you are interested in your unique individuality, in contradistinction to the interpersonal activities
which you or someone else can observe, to that extent you are interested in the really private mode in which you live—in which I have no interest whatever. The fact
is that for any scientific inquiry, in the sense that psychiatry should be, we cannot be
concerned with that which is inviolably private."

cant because of its function in therapy. Although the encounter is that of a sick man supplicating a healer, a special status is conferred upon the patient by virtue of the technique itself. I may be sick and I may have come to a doctor for help, the patient is saying, but this is no ordinary therapy in which all I have to do is hold still while the doctor works on me; this is analysis. And a good bit of the exchange between therapist and patient consists of the patient's acceptance of the therapist's invitation to come see it all from where he sits, as a tolerant pipe-fondling Thalesian, to share in the analyst's understanding of symptoms, social behavior, culture—an understanding obtained by an elite technique to which to a degree the patient can, by reason of his own gifts, also aspire. Although he may have failed and so needs help, he enjoys a privileged status vis-à-vis the people out there in the street. They don't know what we know. They don't even know about themselves what we know about them. Thus the we-community of scientists—I, the therapist, and you, the patient but also now the surrogate scientist—can become a useful therapeutic instrument by means of which the patient's low self-esteem is offset by Thalesian insights into himself and the society he lives in.

The interpersonal process is a multilevel one. Some estimation of its immense complexity is made possible by realizing that there occurs at one level the interaction between organisms which the behaviorist speaks of. Conversation is still a space-time journey of energy exchanges between organisms in all its molecular complexity. But this interaction is overlaid by the molar structure of symbolic behavior. Symbolic behavior is in turn as many-tissued as there are participants in the language event and as there are media of communication. The world and the being-in-the-world of the therapist collide with the world and the being-in-the-world of the patient. The possibilities of communication failure are unlimited. Yet it is not sufficient to say that one man says something and another man hears and understands or misunderstands, agrees or disagrees, rejoices or is saddened. It is also necessary to ask and try to answer such questions as: In what mode does the listener receive the assertion of the speaker? In what mode does he affirm it? In what way does his own mode of being-in-the-world color and specify everything he hears?

Perhaps what needs most to be emphasized is the intimate relation between the phenomenological structure of intersubjectivity and being-in-the-world, on the one hand, and the empirical event of symbolic behavior, on the other. The existential modes of human living do not take place in an epistemological seventh heaven wholly removed from the world of organisms and things. Rather do they follow upon and, in fact, can be derived only from this very intercourse: one man encountering another man, speaking a word, and through it and between them discovering the world and himself.

10

CULTURE: THE ANTINOMY
OF THE SCIENTIFIC METHOD

THE SCIENTIFIC METHOD issues in statements about the world. Whether one is a realist, pragmatist, operationalist, or materialist, one can hardly doubt that the various moments of the scientific enterprise—induction, hypothesis, deduction, theory, law—are all assertions of sorts.* Even observation and verification are in the final analysis not the physiological happenings in which the retina and brain of the scientist receive the image of pointer readings—a dog might do the same. They are rather the symbolic assertory acts by which one specifies that the perception, pointer on numbered line, is a significant reading.

It shall also be my contention, following Ernst Cassirer, that the main elements of cultural activity are in their most characteristic moments also assertory in nature. The central acts of language, of

---

* Some contemporary philosophers have denied that hypotheses are propositions, since, unlike direct observations, they express a generalization and their meaning is always indirect. As Braithwaite observes, however, "such a limitation is inconvenient, since hypotheses as well as propositions in the limited sense obey the laws of propositional logic, are capable of truth and falsity, are objects of belief or other cognitive attitudes, and are expressed by indicative sentences; they thus satisfy all the usual criteria for being a proposition."

The argument which follows prescinds from an explicit philosophy of science. It does not matter for the argument what one believes the ontological character of the scientific statement to be, as long as one admits it to be a statement. Even if one holds with many positivists that a hypothesis is an arbitrary convention in a calculus which is to be interpreted as an applied deductive system and as not having a meaning apart from its place in such a calculus, what is significant is that the hypothesis and the deductions which follow are acknowledged to be assertions.

worship, of myth-making, of storytelling, of art, as well as of science, are assertions.

What I shall call attention to first is a remarkable difference between the sort of reality the scientific method is and the sort of reality it understands its data to be. To be specific: The most characteristic product of the scientific method is the scientific law. Perhaps the ideal form of the scientific law, the formulation to which all sciences aspire, is the constant function, the assertion of an invariant relation between variable quantities. In physics, the function takes the form of the functional equation, $E = f(C)$, in which variable C (cause) issues in dependent variable E (effect) in a determinate ratio f. This formula is, of course, an assertion. It asserts that such a function does in fact obtain between the variables. What takes place in the phenomenon under investigation, however, is not an assertion. It is a sequence of space-time events, an energy exchange. Thus we have two different kinds of activities here: (1) a space-time event in which state A issues in state B; (2) a judgment which asserts that such is indeed the case. Thomas Aquinas called attention to the qualitative difference between the events which take place in the world and the act by which an intellect grasps these events.*

Secondly, I wish to investigate the state of affairs which comes about when the scientific method is applied to this very activity of which it is itself a mode: the assertory phenomena of culture. I think it will be possible to show that when the method is used, with the best possible intentions, to construe assertory behavior, it falls into an antinomy. Examples will be given from ethnology, from semiotic, from current philosophies of science, to illustrate the kind of antinomy into which the method is driven when it seeks to explain as functions those activities of man which are not primarily physiological or psychological but assertory: language, art, religion, myth, science—in short, culture.

Finally, a suggestion will be made toward the end of a more

---

* "But when the intellect begins to judge about the thing it has apprehended, then its judgment is something proper to itself—not something found outside in the thing."

radical science of man than the present discipline known as cultural anthropology or ethnology, which, it will have been my hope to show, is essentially a nonradical science.

THE DIFFERENCE BETWEEN A
SYMBOLIC ASSERTION AND A
SPACE-TIME EVENT

If one examines the characteristic moments of the scientific method, one will discover that they are basically assertions. Even if one happens to be an operationalist and maintains that the business of science is defining the physical operations by which concepts are arrived at and properties defined, the fact remains that the *terminus ad quem* of the operationalist method is the scientific formula or assertion. Indeed, the operationalist cannot even express his operationalism without using assertions.

The three characteristic assertions of the scientific method are:

(1) The Naming or Classificatory Assertion. This form of the assertion is a pointing at and a naming, or, in semiotical language, an indexical sign plus a symbol.

This is grass is such an assertion. The assertion could be made simply by pointing at the grass and uttering aloud the symbol *grass*. So also is the scientific classification: Certain plants which bear functional similarities toward each other because of a common phylogenetic origin we agree to designate by the symbol *Gramineae*. The latter is a scientific and definitory abstraction. But the former is also an abstraction, though of a much more primitive or "concrete" sort.* Both statements assert that that something over there is one of these.† The simplest act of naming and the under-

---

* This gross classification by naming would correspond roughly with Lotze's "first universal," a primitive form of objectivization prior to logical abstraction. Ernst Cassirer, *Philosophy of the Symbolic Forms.*

† We are not concerned here with the logical form of the copula. Let us admit with Peano that the "is" here means "is a member of." It is only necessary to understand that whatever the form of predication, the word "is" also asserts that the predicate holds, that this particular grass plant does in fact belong to the family Gramineae.

standing of the act by another is the assertion and grasping of the assertion that there is a family of plants with bladelike leaves and hollow jointed stems and that that one there is one of them. The two types of classification overlap but do not coincide. The primitive classification *This is grass* may include grassy-looking plants which are not related phylogenetically to the family Graminae. The scientific classification *Graminae*, on the other hand, includes bamboo, which to the layman is not at all "grassy."

(2) The Basic Sentence. This sentence asserts a scientific observation or "fact." It can be verified by the observation or experiment of another.*

Water boils at 100 degrees centigrade at 760 mm atmospheric pressure.
The human heart has four major chambers.
The Trobriand Islanders are matrilineal.

The form is *S* is *P*, in which *S* is the subject designated by the naming sentence above, *P* is the predicate, property or quality, "is" is the verb which specifies the nature of the relation between *S* and *P* and also asserts that it holds.†

(3) A scientific law.

Bodies attract each other in direct proportion to the product of their masses and in inverse proportion to the square of the distance between them.

* Cf. Cassirer's distinction between the scientific statements of quantum physics, between "statements of the first order" relating to definite space-time points, and physical law of the form, "if *x* then *y*."

† Here again we are not concerned with the controversies over the predicate form: (1) whether the subject-predicate form is a "relation of monadic degree"; (2) whether the subject-predicate form is the expression of a universal ontological state or only a linguistic form imposed by the Indo-European language family. Whorf holds that some languages convey meanings without predicates. For example, a flash of light occurs which we would report as "A light flashed." The Hopi language reports the flash with the single verb *rehpi*: "flash (occurred)." "There is no division into subject and predicate, not even a suffix like the Latin -t in *tona-t*, 'it thunders.' " But surely the burden of proof rests with Whorf to show that in saying *rehpi*, the Hopi is not saying a one word pointing-at-and-naming sentence like the American child who points at the earth and says "Grass."

In either case, however, whether the predicate is a "relation of monadic degree" or whether it is a Hopi grammatical form, something is being asserted.

>The glomerular filtrate of urine is a function of plasma osmotic pressure and blood pressure.

>Primitive tenues (k, t, p) become aspirates in Low German (e.g., English) and mediae in High German. (Grimm's Law)

Such generalizations are of the form $E = f(C)$, in which C represents a numerical value or a space-time configuration, E a subsequent value or configuration, f a determinate ratio of energy exchange, and "is" or "$=$" an assertion of identity between the two.

Each of these typically scientific statements is an assertion of sorts concerning space-time events. Even Grimm's Law, which is about words, is not about the assertions of words but about the changes of consonantal sounds. Yet none of these statements is itself a space-time event. We can, if we like, study the energy exchanges which take place in a blind deaf-mute when he makes the discovery that *this is grass*. It was theoretically possible to do the same thing when Einstein conceived the relativity principle. We can observe the overt behavior of a physicist as he goes about setting up his apparatus and making measurements. But even if we had an exact knowledge of the colloidal brain events which occur in each case, these events can never be coterminous with the assertions *This is grass* and $E = mc^2$. It is possible to say this, not because of our present knowledge of brain events, but because no space-time event, however intricate, no chemical or colloidal interaction, no configuration of field forces, can issue in an assertory event. As Cassirer put it, there is a gap between the responses of animals and the propositions of men which no amount of biological theorizing can bridge.

We can also make a chemical analysis of a written word or an acoustic analysis of a spoken word; we can study the science of phonetics, which traces regularities in the changes of speech sounds. But neither science will have anything to say, does not wish to have anything to say, about the assertion which these symbols convey.

In the first type of statement, the naming sentence, we may determine from an empirical standpoint that symbolization is qualitatively different from a sign-response sequence and that denotation is not a space-time relation but a semantical one.*

In the next two types of assertions, S is P and $E = f(C)$, we have two different kinds of identity asserted, one intentional and the other real.

S is P asserts what a thing is by dividing the thing from its property or definition and reuniting it in the sentence. This assertion of identity is not real but intentional.†

$E = f(C)$ asserts a real identity. It asserts that a numerical value or a physical configuration E is nothing more or less than the numerical value or physical configuration C which has undergone a determinate energy transformation or mathematical function f. The force of gravity is precisely identical with the product of the masses involved multiplied by a constant G.‡

---

* As Susanne Langer says, we may, if we like, interpret language as a sequence of events entailing signs, sounds in the air, vibration of ear drums, nerve excitation, brain events, responses, and so on. All this does happen. But something has been left out and it is the most important thing of all. It is that the symbol symbolizes something. There is a qualitative difference between a dog's understanding of the sound *ball* as a stimulus to search for the ball, and a man's understanding of the sound to "mean" ball, one of those round things.

I use the word "sign" as synonymous with C. W. Morris's "signal," to mean an element in the environment directing the organism to something else. It is thus a segment of a space-time sequence, sign-organism-response-referent.

But a symbol is an element in an assertion, in which something is symbolized, in which two elements are paired, the symbol and that which is symbolized.

† H. D. Veatch: "Indeed I think it can be shown that all of the three main logical instruments of knowledge—concepts, propositions, and arguments—are really nothing but just such relations of identity. For instance, a concept or universal (an *unum versus alia*) such as 'tree' is simply a relation of identity between a 'what' and possible individual trees, and likewise with an affirmative proposition. . . . Indeed, to say that S is P is not to assert that S is included in P, or is a number of P, or is equal to P, or is an argument of the function P; instead it involves nothing more or less than the identification of the predicate concept (the 'what') with the subject (the 'it')."

‡ It is revealing that those philosophers who hold that knowledge is altogether an affair of electrocolloidal brain events must also deny that there are such things as assertions. Thus, Russell says that the word "is" in the sentence A *is yellow* means nothing, that a logical language will express the same meaning by saying *yellow* (A).

Russell can leave out the "is" if he likes. But the fact remains that when we see the logician's symbols, *yellow* (A), we must know whether he has put them on the blackboard as an exercise in logical possibility, or whether he means that such is indeed the case, that A is in truth yellow.

Similarly, a scientist must make a distinction between real and possible pointer

I shall refer in what follows to all linguistic assertions by the form *S* is *P*, not because I am presupposing a realistic metaphysic, but because it is a convenient way to designate a sentence.

To summarize: Science characteristically issues in assertions. But that which science asserts is not itself an assertion but a space-time event. Science asserts that matter is in interaction, that there are energy exchanges, that organisms respond to an environment, etc. But the assertion itself is a pairing of elements, a relation which is not a space-time event but a kind of identity asserted by an assertor.

CULTURE AS A SUBJECT OF THE
SCIENTIFIC METHOD

What happens when the functional method of the sciences is applied to cultural phenomena? Does culture lend itself to such an understanding? If there are difficulties in the cultural sciences, are the difficulties due to the complexity of the material, as is often alleged, or are the difficulties inherently methodological?

Let us keep in mind what the scientific method does and what culture is. The scientific method seeks to arrive at regularities of two sorts, those which separate according to differences and those which unite according to functional similarities, the classificatory and the functional. Cassirer describes the totality of scientific knowledge as a complex of overlapping functions. Biologists who claim that biological laws like the law of allometry and Mendel's rules are different from mechanical laws nevertheless insist on the unity of scientific knowledge.* Franz Boas was frank to set forth the ultimate objective of anthropology as the understanding of cul-

readings. His assistant, whose job it is to call off readings, may fall into a daydream and utter aloud all the numbers on the dial, "2.1, 2.2, 2.3," etc. But the scientist must still know which of these is actually the reading at the moment.

Some further symbolic notation is required to signify the difference. Perhaps we could subdivide Russell's *yellow* (A):

yellow (A) (?)   yellow (A) (!)

* F. Mainx: ". . . the experience of inorganic and that of organic science join together to give a unitary and consistent picture of the world, derived from the fundamental unity of method."

ture as a dynamic and lawful process.* The steadfast conviction behind the scientific method, whatever its subject matter, is that "every detailed occurrence can be correlated with its antecedents in a perfectly definite manner exemplifying general principles."

Culture, in its most characteristic moments, is not a catalogue of artifacts or responses to an environment but is rather the ensemble of all the modes of assertory activity. Culture has been defined as all human inheritance, material as well as spiritual. As such it would include hoes, baskets, manuscripts, and monuments, as well as the living language and art of the current culture. If we consider culture in a broader, yet more exact sense—the sense in which Cassirer considered it—we will see it as the totality of the different ways in which the human spirit construes the world and asserts its knowledge and belief. These are the "symbolic forms": language, myth, art, religion, science. Cassirer's contribution has been described as the first philosophy of culture. The major symbolic forms of Cassirer's long work, *The Philosophy of the Symbolic Forms*, provide a convenient frame of reference for the assertory phenomena of culture and I shall use them as such and without endorsing the Kantian mold in which they are cast.

If we examine Cassirer's symbolic forms, we shall discover that each is, in its moment of actualization, an assertion. The major cultural forms which Cassirer treats in his long work—and the phenomena which we shall examine from the perspective of the scien-

---

* Although anthropologists differ greatly in their philosophical allegiances, it is my contention that the two main schools, the functionalists and the superorganicists, share a common theoretical posture toward their subject matter. A functionalist like Malinowski may understand culture more or less biologically, as "an instrumental reality, an apparatus for the satisfaction of fundamental needs, that is, organic survival, environmental adaptation, and continuity in the biological sense." A superorganicist like Kroeber or White or Sorokin may understand culture as an autonomous reality which is "participated in and produced by organic individuals."

In both cases, however, man himself, his personality, is understood as a function of an underlying reality, in the one case, a function of his encounter and response to his environment, in the other, as a function of the culture in which he particpates. In neither case is culture understood as the creation of man which stands over against man as the means by which he can develop the potentialities of his nature—or the means by which he can fall prey to anonymity. For a searching critique of modern anthropology from the point of view of a realistic humanism, see David Bidney's *Theoretical Anthropology* (New York, 1953).

tific method—are myth, language, and science. Now an ethnologist can list any number of items which are the proper subject matter of his science and which are not assertions. A linguist may indeed spend his entire life compiling a dictionary of Kwakiutl without ever dealing with an assertion as such, as the phenomenon under investigation. But the fact remains that language, when it is spoken, is a tissue of assertions. Religion is not a museum of cult objects but a living tissue of beliefs, professions, avowals. The central act of myth and religion is the act of belief or worship. There is no such thing as an isolated word in speech; it is only to be found in dictionaries. The heart of science is not the paraphernalia of the laboratory; it is the method, the hunch, the theory, the formula. The art work is not the paint on the canvas or the print on the page; it is the moment of creation by the artist and the moment of understanding by the viewer.

But suppose this is true, suppose that cultural activity is mainly assertory activity. Does it follow that culture is placed beyond the reach of objective knowledge in general and the scientific method in particular? Certainly an assertion is a real event in the world albeit not a space-time event; it is also a natural, not a supernatural, event. People make assertions and we observe them do so. We can hear a man speak, read a formula, understand a painting. Then, if these various assertions are real happenings, phenomena in the world, is there any reason why they should be exempt from the searching gaze of science? Clearly not. And specifically, the functional method we have described should be used as long as it is useful. It has been so applied to culture and with great energy and resourcefulness.

The question which must be raised is not whether the scientific method should or should not be applied to culture. The question is rather whether its application has not already issued in an antinomy which compromises the usefulness of the method. If this is the case, two further questions must be asked. What is the source of the antinomy? And, how may the method be modified so that it may yield valid and fruitful conclusions when it is applied to culture?

THE ANTINOMIES OF THE
SCIENTIFIC METHOD IN ITS
GRASP OF CULTURE

Kant believed that when "pure reason" ventures beyond the manifold of experience, it falls into an antinomy. That is to say, equally
valid trains of argument lead to contradictory conclusions. Now,
apart from the truth or falsity of Kant's argument, the fact is that
practicing scientists and scientifically minded laymen care very little either for metaphysical reasoning or for Kant's a priori assault
upon it. As Marcel has said, the spirit of the age is basically "on-
tophobic," perhaps disastrously so. The scientist can hardly be indifferent, however, if it can be shown that the scientific method itself falls into a characteristic antinomy whenever it confronts a
certain sector of reality. Such an antinomy can be demonstrated, I
think, not by syllogistic argument but from the testimony of the
empirical scientists themselves, when the scientific method tries to
grasp the assertory phenomena of culture.

It is hardly necessary to add that my purpose in calling attention
to the crisis of the cultural sciences is not to out-Kant Kant, not
further to indict reason, but on the contrary to advance the cause of
a radical anthropology, a science of man which will take account of
all human realities, not merely space-time events.

The Antinomy of Myth

Examples of mythic assertions, S is P.

Marduk split Tiamat like a shellfish with two parts
Half of her he set up and ceiled it as the sky.

(Enuma Elis)

The Brahmin was his [the world's] mouth, his arms were made the
Rajanya [warrior], his two thighs the Vaisya [trader and agriculturalist],
from his feet the Sudra [servile class] was born.

(Rg Veda)

Maui, our ancestor, trapped the wandering sun and made it follow a
regular course.

(Maori myth)

(1) What the scientist thinks of the assertion S is P when the assertion is proposed to him as a true-or-false claim:

The myth, S is P, is false. To say that the world was made by the Babylonian city-god Marduk from the body of Tiamat is absurd. There is not a shred of evidence to support such an assertion, and there is a great deal of evidence to the contrary.

(2) What the scientist thinks of the assertion S is P when the assertion is itself a phenomenon under investigation by the scientific method, to be ordered with other phenomena in the general corpus of scientific knowledge:

A myth believed is true (Schelling). All societies have their myths; myths are therefore necessary for the function of a society (Malinowski, McIver). Myth serves the function of seeing man through periods of peril and crisis (James, Malinowski). One of the troubles with modern society is the mythic impoverishment of the man of facts due to his rejection of old beliefs and the loss of archetypes. The answer is a "new mythology" (Langer). Recovery of mythic archetypes is necessary for mental health (Jung).

When myth is studied as an empirical phenomenon, it is evaluated not according as it is true or false or nonsensical but according to the degree to which it serves a social or cultural function. Thus a "genuine" culture (and a genuine myth) is a culture which is viable, satisfying the spiritual and emotional needs of the culture member; a "spurious" culture fails to do so (Sapir). It is a mistake to use rigid scientific standards and say that a myth is false; a myth may be poetically and symbolically "true" according as it satisfies the symbolic needs of world envisagement (Langer, Cassirer).

(3) Comment. The antinomy is manifest in the very usage of the word *myth* by modern ethnologists. As Bidney has pointed out, it is, to begin with, a value-charged term: myth means a belief which is not true. Then myth is used *neutrally* as a data-element along with other data-elements, canoes, baskets, dwellings. Bidney goes on to say, "The greatest myth of the twentieth century is the identification of all cultural ideology with myth in the name of social science."

One serious consequence of this initial antinomy is a canceling of the social prescriptions of the scientist for the ills of the day. It becomes necessary for the scientist to recommend to culture or patient that which he, the scientist, has labeled false at the outset. But the fallacy of the prescription is that a myth can hardly be believed if it is believed to be false. The motto of the scientist when he is prescribing myth as a data-element necessary for mental and cultural health is: It may not be true but you had better believe it.

Another consequence is the compromise of the scientist's own position in the face of the onslaught of the contemporary myths of fascism and Communism. If the scientist believes theoretically in the indispensability of myth for an integrated culture, it becomes difficult for him to make a coherent objection to the Nazi or Soviet ethos. The upshot is the anomalous situation, so familiar in academic circles today, of the professor who in the field and classroom recognizes only functional relationships and refuses to recognize norms, and who in private and public life is a passionate defender of the freedom and rights and sacredness of the individual.

The source of the antinomy is the arbitrary decree of the scientist that only functional relationships shall be certified among his "data" and that even ideological beliefs and assertions shall be evaluated not according to the true-or-false claim of the assertion but according to its function in the culture. The decree requires that a belief be labeled as a myth and at the same time certified as valid as a cultural function. Only two kinds of judgments about beliefs are forthcoming: false in fact and bad in function (Sapir's "spurious" myth), false in fact and good in function (Sapir's "genuine" myth). Thus the old-style rationalist attitude toward religion is reversed. The eighteenth-century rationalist accepted the true-or-false claim of religious belief—and usually argued against it. The modern culturologist denies the claim and accepts only a functional criterion in judging its validity. Thus C. G. Jung "accepts" the Catholic dogma of the Assumption because it validates the anima archetype, while at the same time he denies its claim to literal truth. Jung's approach, once the total competence of the functional method is accepted, seems reasonable. I am not interested in the truth or falsity of religion, says Jung, but only in the structure and function of the human psyche. Yet such a neutrality is warranted only if the neutrality is consistent. It is not consistent when ideological belief is assigned first to the category of myth, then made to do duty as a neutral term in an objective culturology.

The Antinomy of Language

Examples of the linguistic assertion S is P.

Dr. Itard writes in *The Savage of Aveyron* that he tried to teach Victor the wild boy the word for milk, *lait*, as a sign of a biological need, by withholding the milk and uttering the word in its absence. This failed: After the milk was given to Victor, however, and the word *lait* uttered by chance, to Dr. Itard's astonishment, Victor understood at once that *lait* was the name of the milk.

> What is this?
> Milk.
> What color is it?
> White.
> Did you drink some?
> This morning I drank some milk.
>
> tl 'imshya 'isita 'itlma
> (He invites people to a feast)
>   (A sentence in the Nootka language)

(1) What the scientist thinks of the assertion S is P when the assertion is proposed to him as a true-or-false-or-nonsense claim:

I receive your statement S is P as a true-or-false-or-nonsense claim. I shall accept it as more or less true or false or as nonsense according to my criteria of verification.

If you wish to call this white liquid *milk*, then I will agree to the semantic rule by which the symbol "milk" shall henceforth be applied to this white liquid.

If you say that milk is a liquid, or that milk is a gas, or that milk is upside down, I shall accept your statement as asserting a state of affairs which is open to verification and otherwise is nonsense.

(2) What the scientist thinks of the assertion S is P when the assertion is itself a phenomenon under investigation, to be ordered

with other phenomena in the general corpus of scientific knowledge:

An interchange of language is not the uttering and receiving of
sentences which assert or deny a state of affairs in the world; it is
rather a space-time sequence of stimuli and responses which are
meaningful only in the sociobiological sense of learned behavior. A
language symbol and the understanding of it are not qualitatively
different from the signal and response of animal behavior (Morris,
Mead). "In its *biophysical* aspect language consists of sound-
producing movements and of the resultant sound waves and of the
vibration of the hearer's eardrums. The *biosocial* aspect of language
consists in the fact that the persons in a community have been
trained to produce these sounds in certain situations and to respond
to them by appropriate actions" (Bloomfield). Human meaning is
a context of stimulus and response (Ogden and Richards). Only
causal sequential relations between signs and organisms are real;
denotative relationships are not real but semantical (Ogden and
Richards, Chase). The relation of identification between word and
thing, subject and predicate is "wrong" (Korzybski). Human meaning and mind itself is a product of responses and responses to
responses (Mead). A symbol and the idea associated with it cannot
possibly refer to a real state of affairs in the world; if it did, it could
only be a copy; a realistic metaphysic must always end in skepticism
(Cassirer).

In summary, the sentence you speak is not, after all, a true-or-
false-or-nonsense claim referring to a state of affairs in the world. It
is instead a biological signal mediating an adjustment between organisms and the organisms' response to an environment. It is impossible for me to take your meaning intersubjectively; I can only
respond to your behavior.

(3) Comment. The source of the antinomy and the central phenomenon of language is a relationship which the scientific method
cannot construe by its functional schema and hence must disqualify as "wrong." It is the peculiar relationship of denotation between
name and thing and the relationship of identity between subject
and predicate.

The antinomy is found in its most characteristic form in the cur-

rent discipline of "semiotic," which attempts to bring together pragmatics, syntax, and semantics into the unity of a single science.
Semiotic is basically incoherent because it tries to unite the corpus
of natural science (organic and inorganic matter in functional interaction) with the corpus of semantics and syntax (naming and asserting and calculus formation by rule) without showing how one
discipline is related to the other.

Thus semanticists find themselves in the position of protesting as
objective scientists against the very subject matter of their science,
the relation of denotation. The science of semantics is the study of
the rules by which symbols are assigned to their designata. Yet the
science of responding organisms (behavioristics) does not explain
how organisms can "assign" names to things in the first place. The
relation of denotation is said to be only a "semantical relation," but
its status is never settled from the point of view of the scientific
method beyond saying that it is not a "real" relation. One simply
speaks in one breath of organisms responding to an environment
and in the next of organisms assigning names and making propositions about the world (Reichenbach).

The central act of language, both of naming-classificatory sentences and predicate sentences, is an intentional act of identity. It is
essentially a *pairing* of elements which amounts to an is-saying. In
a naming sentence, *This is grass*, a symbol and a thing are paired
and the pairing is the means by which the namer intends that this
green blade is one of a group. The basic sentence *Grass is green* is
an identification brought about by a dividing and a composing, a
union of the thing with what the thing is. The identity in either
case is not real—no one believes that word is the grass or that the
grass is the same as its color—but intentional. The identity is the
instrument with which the knowing subject affirms the object to be
what it is.

The stumbling block to a scientific philosophy of language is the
pairing of elements in the assertory act. The scientific method can
only grasp elements ordered in a functional or dependent relation,
the causal order of the function $E = f(C)$.* The assertory act can-

* I use the word "causal" without prejudice. It means whatever the reader would
have it mean in the context: either efficient causality or a probability function.

not be grasped in a scientist-data framework in which the scientist practices an activity which he disallows in the data. A scientist will accept the statement S is P as a proposition open to verification or disproof. He pays attention to sentences and for himself accepts them as stating a possible fact about the world. When he hears this sound in the air, "A gas expands in direct proportion to temperature increases," he receives the sound as an intending instrument, an assertion open to verification. But if one asked the scientist to study the sound-sentence not as an assertion to be proved or disproved, not as a phonetic phenomenon subject to Grimm's law of consonantal change, *but as an assertory phenomenon to be grasped as such by his method,* the scientist cannot reply coherently. *The functional method of the sciences cannot construe the assertory act of language.* The only alternative open to the positivist philosopher of language is to accept the peculiar assertory relation of language as a "semantical phenomenon" but to disqualify it as a real "scientific" phenomenon. The upshot is not merely an incoherent exposition of language but a contradictory one, an antinomy.

The Antinomy of Science

Examples of the scientific assertion S is P:

The square of the time of revolution of any planet is proportional to the cube of the mean distance from the sun.
$T^2 = KD^3$

(Kepler's third law of planetary orbits)

The force of attraction between two bodies is in direct proportion to the product of the masses of the two bodies and varies inversely as the square of the distance between them.
$F = GM_1M_2/d^2$

(Newton's law of gravitation)

The inertia of a system necessarily depends on its energy content . . . inert mass is simply latent energy.
$E = mc^2$

(Einstein)

In isolated historical systems tribal organization precedes the beginnings of the state.

(Zilsel: a "temporal historico-sociological law")

(1) What the scientist thinks of the assertion S is P when the assertion is proposed to him as a true-or-false-or-nonsense claim:

The scientific assertion, observation, correlation, hypothesis, theory, deduction, law, is accepted as a true-or-false, or at least as a more or less probable, claim. The claim is assumed to refer to a state of affairs other than the claim and the scientist, and to be open to techniques of verification, pointer readings, and so on. The scientific method presupposes that there is something to be known, that a degree of knowledge is possible, that this knowledge can be expressed as assertions and reliably transmitted from teller to hearer.

(2) What the scientist thinks of the assertion S is P when the assertion is itself a phenomenon under investigation to be ordered with other phenomena in the general corpus of scientific knowledge:

What does the scientist think of science as a phenomenon, not, what does he do as a scientist as he practices his science, assembles his data, sets up a controlled experiment, makes pointer readings, puzzles over discrepancies, gets a hunch, tries a new hypothesis, etc.—but what does he think of science as a happening in the world which takes its place along with other happenings?

If he is to understand science as a phenomenon to be ordered to other phenomena in a general functional scheme, he is obliged to disqualify the major assumptions which he has made in the practice of his science: that valid scientific knowledge is possible and that it can be transmitted from teller to hearer by means of assertions.

The dilemma of the modern philosopher of science has these two horns. It appears to him that he may pursue only one of two alternatives without betraying the rigor of the scientific method. Yet in each case the consequence is an antinomy in which his explanation of science as an activity stands in contradiction to his assumptions about science if he is a practicing scientist.

First, he may proceed according to the realistic assumptions of science, that here we are with a real happening between us which we must try to understand—and study science as a phenomenon which happens to real organisms in a world, just as metabolism and bee dances and dog salivation are real happenings. It seems reasonable to approach the organisms who are scientists with the same objectivity with which he approaches organisms who are searching for food or organisms who are making a myth. Thus he is obliged to understand science as an *instrumentality*, as either a mode of biological behavior or of cultural behavior and meaningful only as gauged by biological or cultural needs. Thus Dewey sought to understand science and knowledge as but one of many social instrumentalities whose validity and adequacy are measured in terms of the degree to which they make possible an adjustment between the individual organism on the one hand and the social and physical environment on the other. A kindred view of science as a phenomenon-to-be-explained is that of dialectical materialism, which sees research not as an enterprise freely undertaken and specified by the subject to be known but as itself determined by the economic organization and needs of society. In each case, instrumentalism and dialectical materialism, the theorist appears to be following the legitimate procedure of the scientific method; he is looking upon science as a phenomenon to be explained by a functional principle. In one case the principle is sociobiological, in the other dialectical.

Second, the theorist may elect to remain altogether on the cogito side of the mind-body split. He may view the problem simply as a semantico-logical one, stipulating a natural law as a "syntactical rule," a free convention for the manipulation of symbols, refusing to deal with the problems of knowledge and induction and intersubjectivity (Carnap).* Or he may adopt the operationalism of Bridgman, who is frank to admit the consequence of solipsism: ". . . it is obvious that I can never get outside myself . . . there is no such thing as a public consciousness . . . in the last analysis science is only my private science." In this case, the antinomy is overt: a practicing scientist who reports his findings in journals and

* Another member of the Viennese circle is highly critical of Carnap's logicizing of natural laws. Moritz Schlick writes: "It [the natural law] is then not a natural law any more at all; it is not even a proposition, but merely a rule for the manipulation of signs. This whole reinterpretation appears trivial and useless. Any such interpretation which blurs such fundamental distinctions is extremely dangerous."

his theories in books—and who denies the possibility of a public realm of intersubjectivity. A kindred approach is a neo-Kantian one, which seeks scientific validity entirely within the forms and categories of consciousness: "The validity of the physical concept does not rest upon its content of *real elements of existence*, such as can be directly pointed out, but upon the strictness of *connection*, which makes it possible" (Cassirer).

(3) Comment. Einstein once wrote, "If you want to find out anything from the theoretical physicists about the methods they use, I advise you to stick closely to one principle: don't listen to their words, fix your attention on their deeds."

Whitehead once remarked that it was a matter for astonishment that while scientists have succeeded in learning a great deal about the world in the past two hundred years, philosophers of science seem equally determined to deny that such knowledge is possible.

Both men allude to the antinomy which the functional method of the sciences encounters when it tries to grasp itself as a phenomenon among other phenomena in the world. The antinomy has been noticed often enough but it is usually attributed to the bad faith or bad philosophizing of the theorist. It seems to be a case, however, of too much good faith rather than too little—that is, an uncritical acceptance of the scientific method of physics as a total organon of reality. The antinomy has come to pass precisely because of the faithfulness and rigor with which the theorist tries to grasp the scientific enterprise in particular, assertory activity in general, by his superb instrument, the functional method of the sciences.

The ineluctable reality upon which the scientific method founders and splits into an antinomy is nothing else than the central act of science, "sciencing," the assertions of science. From the primitive observation to the most exact mathematical deduction, science is a tissue of assertions. It is ironical but perhaps not unfitting that science, undertaken as a total organon of reality, should break down not at the microcosmic or macrocosmic limits of the universe but in the attempt to grasp itself. Heisenberg's uncertainty relations seem to be a material difficulty resulting from an interfer-

ence of measuring instrument with particle to be measured.* But
the antinomy into which the scientific method falls in treating assertory behavior is a formal methodological impasse. It lies beyond
the power of the functional method to grasp the scientific, the
mythic, the linguistic assertion as such. It will succeed in grasping
itself according to its mode—as a functional space-time linkage—
but in so doing it must overlook its most important characteristic,
that science is an assertory phenomenon, a real phenomenon but
not a causal space-time event. Science may seek to understand itself as a social instrumentality or as an intracultural activity, and to
a degree no doubt correctly so; but it must remain silent in the face
of the true-or-false claim, *S* is *P*, considered as such.

Here, as in the other antinomies, it is the assertory act itself
which is refractory to the scientific method. Since an assertion—
mythic, linguistic, mathematical—is an immaterial act in virtue of
which two elements are paired or identified, and since the scientific
method requires that elements be ordered *serially*, according to
dependent functional ratios, the two are not commensurate. The
corpus of scientific knowledge ascending in a continuum from
inorganic energy exchanges to organic responses is not in principle
coterminous with assertory behavior. To speak of culture as an
"emergent" or a "superorganic level" is only to erect a semantical
bridge across the abyss, when the need is to explore the abyss, not
to ignore it.

Different as are the various scientific philosophies mentioned
above, they share one conviction about the subject matter of
science and it is this conviction which gives rise to the antinomy. It
is the antirealist and antimetaphysical dogma that there is no lawful
reality to be known apart from the activity of the knower. This tenet
is usually expressed in an exaggerated language: "Knowledge conceived in the fashion of an infallible grasp of final truths without

---

* Heisenberg's uncertainty relations have been hailed by some enemies of science
as proof of the freedom or irrationality or whatnot of the ultimate particles of matter.
As Nagel observes, however, "a more sober and prima facie plausible account of the
uncertainty relations is that they express relatively large but unaccountable modifications in certain features of subatomic elements, resulting from an interaction between these elements and the instruments of measurement."

the mediation of overt organic activity is not something which modern science supplies." What should be pointed out, however, is that it is not the claim to "infallible knowledge" which gives scandal to positivist philosophers of science; it is the claim to any valid knowledge whatsoever, however modest the claim of the knower. A realist would be the first to admit, would in fact insist upon, "the mediation of overt organic activity" in the knowing act. But this is not the real point at issue. The issue is the validity of knowledge and the providing for this validity in one's scientific world view. The difficulty is that knowledge entails assertions and assertions are beyond the grasp of the functional method.*

THE SOURCE OF THE ANTINOMY

The general source of the antinomy is not to be found, as is sometimes alleged, in the nature of the subject, man, the culture member who practices science but needs myths. Such an anthropology is in the last analysis incoherent because it requires two sorts of men, scientists who observe and tell the truth, culture members who respond and have mythic needs.

---

* It would be possible to develop the same antinomy in other "symbolic forms"— art, history, religion.

For example, a contrast could be drawn between the pragmatic theories of art as a "play activity" or the behavioristic theory of art as a traffic in emotions, on the one hand, and the seriousness of the artistic enterprise and the revelatory nature of the art experience, on the other.

In history, a contrast could be drawn between the basically particular and historical character of the scientific observation, on the one hand, and the general character of the ultimate scientific expression, the scientific law, and the inability of the scientific method to grasp singulars except insofar as they exemplify general principles.

As for religion, although it is listed by Cassirer as a separate "symbolic form," the very nature of the method used cancels the difference between religion and myth, since it refuses on a priori grounds to grant cognitive content to religion, and so ranks religion as a "higher form" of myth. Once the scientific method is elevated to a supreme all-construing world view, it becomes impossible to consider a more radical science, the science of being. Thus, when Cassirer is confronted with the assertion of pure existence which Moses received from God as His Name, I am Who Am, he is obliged to see it as a piece of semantical magic, a "mythical predication of being."

It seemed more expedient, however, to develop the antinomy by using the same three "symbolic forms" used by Cassirer in his major work: myth, language, and science.

The source is rather to be found in the structure and limitations of the scientific method itself. For the antinomy comes about at that very moment when that sort of activity of which the scientific method is a mode, assertory activity, enters the scientific situation, not as the customary activity of the scientist, but as a phenomenon under investigation.

The basic structure of the scientific situation is an intersubjective confrontation of a world event and its construing by a symbolic assertion. The general structure of any symbolic cognition is tetradic, as diagrammed in Figure 7, as contrasted with the triadic structure of significatory meaning (sign-organism-thing).

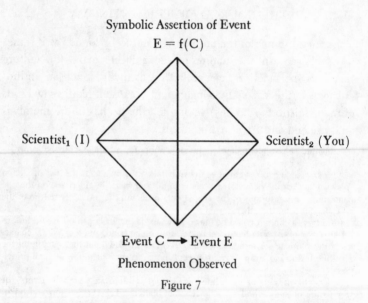

Figure 7

What should be noticed is that there is a difference between the sort of thing we, Scientist$_1$ and Scientist$_2$, understand the world to be (a nexus of secondary causes, event $C \rightarrow$ event E), and the assertion by which we express this understanding ($E = f(C)$). One is a dynamic succession of energy states, the other is an assertion, an immaterial act by which two *entia rationis* are brought into a relation of intentional identity. Both these elements, world event and symbolic assertion, are provided for in the scientific method but it is a topical provision such that a symbolic assertion, S is P, $E = f(C)$, is admitted as the sort of activity which takes place between scientists but is not admitted as a phenomenon under observation. A scientific assertion is received only as a true-or-false claim, which is then proved or disproved by examining the world event to which it refers. *The symbolic assertion cannot itself be examined as a world event unless it be construed as such, as a material event of energy exchanges, in which case its assertory character must be denied.*

At the subcultural, subassertory level of phenomena (physics, chemistry, biology), no antinomy occurs because the distinction between world event and intersubjective assertion is not violated. Physics lends itself without exception to the nonradical discipline in which you and I construe the world as a series of events expressible by assertions which are generically different from the events they assert.

At the cultural level, however, a further task is required of the method. It is required that an assertion be accepted not only as a true-or-false claim between scientists, to be proved or disproved, but as a phenomenon under investigation, to be ordered to other phenomena in the corpus of scientific knowledge. It is required that the assertions S is P and $E = f(C)$, be fitted into the scheme of world events, event $C \rightarrow$ event E.

This is an impossible requirement however. An assertion is a real event but it is not a space-time event. The attempt must have one of two consequences: (1) The cultural assertion S is P (myth, language, science) is actually construed as a world event and its assertory character denied. (2) The cultural assertion S is P is accepted as an assertion, but not as a world event, as rather a true-or-false claim about world events.

The final result is an antinomy with scientists interpreting the same event in a contradictory fashion, as a world event and denying its assertory character, as an assertory event, a true-or-false claim, but refusing to examine it as such.

TOWARD A RADICAL ANTHROPOLOGY

When Socrates met Phaedrus on the banks of the Ilissus, the latter asked him if this was not the spot where, according to the myth, Boreas carried off fair Orithyia. Socrates replied that it was; when asked whether he believed it, he replied that he did not. Questioned further, he refused to speculate about the symbolic meaning of the myth, as the Sophists and Rhetoricians did when they theorized that the myth was in a sense true because she might have been blown off the cliff, and Boreas being the north wind, etc. "But I have no leisure at all for such pastimes, and the reason, my dear friend, is that as yet I cannot, as the Delphic precept has it, know myself. So it seems absurd to me that as long as I am in ignorance of myself, I should concern myself about such extraneous matters."

Socrates might well have made the same objection to modern culturology. Cassirer, who quotes the above incident with approval, then goes on to do just what Socrates declines to do: search for meaning in the symbolic forms of myth. Indeed, Cassirer explicitly rejects the Delphic motto and so rules out the possibility of a radical anthropology. In Cassirer's view, it is hopeless to attempt to fathom the human source of the symbolic forms of culture. "Philosophy has no choice but to reverse the *direction* of inquiry. Instead of taking the road back (to the nature of man), it must attempt to continue forward. If all culture is manifested in the creation of specific image-worlds, of specific symbolic forms, the aim of philosophy is not to go behind these creations, but rather to understand and elucidate their basic formative principle."

As David Bidney has said, anthropology is divided into two main disciplines, physical anthropology, "which takes up such problems as the evolution and comparative anatomy of races . . ." and ethnology, which, "on the other hand, is said to be the study of human customs, institutions, artifacts, and products of mental exercise. The science of culture as practised is the study of these impersonal, superorganic, historical products of society and the 'laws' of their development."

Put more bluntly, modern anthropology deals with man as a physical organism and with the products of man as a culture member, but not with man himself in his distinctive activity as a culture member. Ethnology has only recently gotten around to the study of man as personality affecting culture and being affected by culture.* Modern anthropology has been everything except an anthropology.

How may we deal scientifically with man considered precisely in those activities which distinguish him as a culture member? It is a perfectly legitimate scientific pursuit to study the material elements of culture as objective phenomena: the tools, the products of tools, the sounds of language, hunting, warfare, food gathering, the behavior of chiefs and shamans. It is perfectly legitimate to classify and study objectively languages, religions, societies. It is perfectly legitimate to write a sympathetic study of an island culture viewed from within as a way of life, an aesthetic pattern of existence. It is perfectly legitimate to write straight cultural history. But may we not also require of anthropology, the science of man, some assessment of that creature himself who makes culture possible?

The question which cannot be put off forever is not what is the nature of culture and what are the laws of culture but what is the ontological nature of the creature who makes the assertions of culture? How may we apply the scientific method in all its rigor and fruitfulness to man considered as a creature of culture? If one refuses to answer this question, one can hardly be called an anthropologist, perhaps anthropometrist or ethnographer, but not the scientist whose business it is to know man as such. A biologist, after all, is not afraid to speak about organisms.

The answer, I think, is not to be found in a limitation or compromise of the scientific method but rather in making it a more radically useful instrument. To return to the tetradic structure of the scientific enterprise: a radical science must be willing to admit as eligible phenomena all real events, not merely space-time link-

* D. Bidney: "The thesis I am concerned to establish is that the postulate of an ontological human nature is a prerequisite of both individual and social psychology."

ages. It must deal with assertory behavior as such; it cannot disqualify as a datum the very phenomenon of which it is itself a mode.

Such a requirement stems not from an "extra-scientific" position but from the exigency of the scientific method itself. The method must be able to give an account of its own elements and structure.

The functional method of the sciences is a nonradical method of knowing because, while it recognizes only functional linkages, it presupposes other kinds of reality, the intersubjectivity of scientists and their assertions, neither of which are space-time linkages and neither of which can be grasped by the functional method. Therefore, when the functional method is elevated to a total organon of reality and other cognitive claims denied, the consequence must be an antinomy, for a nonradical instrument is being required to construe the more radical reality which it presupposes but does not understand.

In order that progress be made toward a more radical science, it is necessary to take into account the framework within which the scientific method is mounted. In the case of anthropology, for example, it is necessary to realize that the "properties" of its subject, man, are of a more radical order of being than the operation of the functional method. Indeed, it is one of these "properties," the assertory act of symbolization, which makes the scientific method possible. The assertory behavior of man, whether true or false, mythic or scientific, is on the same ontological plane as the intersubjective enterprise of scientists. It is in the last analysis absurd to explain this activity entirely *within* the intersubjective framework, as not itself an intersubjective assertion but a space-time linkage grasped by an assertion. The attempt to account for cultural phenomena, language, myth, science, art, as events which are ontologically "below" the activity of the theorist can only fall into an antinomy.

A radical anthropology must take account of ontological levels more radical than the scope of the functional method. Its subject, man, is not merely an organism, a social unit, a culture member (though he is all of these), but also he who, even as the scientist, makes assertions, is oriented not merely on a biological scale of need-satisfactions (though he is so oriented) but on a polar scale of truth-falsity, right-wrong, authenticity-inauthenticity, as well. A radical anthropology must be a normative science as well as a classificatory and functional science. This normative character, moreover, is not to be understood in the usual sense of "cultural values" lately acquired and relatively assessed but rather as constituting in the most radical sense the very mode of existence of the asserting creature of culture. The culture member is he who lives normatively.

Anthropology must be willing to accept not only functional criteria: what social and biological purpose is served by this or that cultural element; or aesthetic criteria: whether or not a cultural element conforms to the prevailing cultural pattern and contributes to "cultural integration," but a normative criterion as well. It must not be afraid to deal with the fact that a man may flourish by one scale and languish by another—that he may be a good organism and an integrated culture member and at the same time live a trivial and anonymous life. As Bidney has expressed it, "In evaluating a given culture, the essential problems are how it is integrated and for what is it integrated, not is it integrated."

It is not enough to study a culture element with only the objective of discovering its immanent role in a culture. It is also necessary to judge it according to whether it does or does not contribute to the development of the potentialities of human nature. This does not imply ethnocentrism; it does imply a recognition of a common human nature with the attendant possibilities of development and deterioration. It is not enough, for example, to study the function of the Kula among Trobriand Islanders, the complex system of exchanging beads and shell bracelets (though Malinowski's study is magnificent and one sympathizes with his attack on those who refuse to enter into the inner spirit of a culture). One cannot defer indefinitely a normative decision about the Kula—would or would not the islanders be better occupied doing something else? A chemist or a biologist is not faced with a normative variable in his data; the behavior of an organism or a compound always coincides with its potentiality and the opportunities for realization; it is no more nor less. But a man may fall short of the potentialities offered by his culture—and he may transcend them.

Our objection to cultural relativism need not be mounted on religious grounds and certainly not on the ground of ethnocentricity. It is sufficient here to note the interior contradictions which such a view entails and its manifestly antiscientific consequences. For if one takes seriously the position of the cultural relativist, that there is no reality but a cultural reality, that "even the facts of the physical world are discerned through an enculturative screen so that the perception of time, distance, weight, size, and other 'realities' are mediated by the conventions of a given group"—if we take this seriously, we can only conclude that science itself, even ethnology, is nonsense, since it is at best only a reflection of the culture within which it is undertaken.

In sum, it is high time for ethnologists and other social scientists to forgo the luxury of a bisected reality, a world split between observers and data, those who know and those who behave and are "encultured." Scientists of man must accept as their "datum" that strange creature who, like themselves, is given to making assertions about the world and, like themselves, now drawing near, now falling short of the truth. It is high time for social scientists in general to take seriously the chief article of faith upon which their method is based: that there is a metascientific, metacultural reality, an order of being apart from the scientific and cultural symbols with which it is grasped and expressed. The need for a more radically scientific method derives not merely from metaphysical and religious argument but also from the antinomy into which a nonradical science falls in dealing with man.

11

SEMIOTIC AND A THEORY

OF KNOWLEDGE

A STUDENT OF current philosophies of science must sooner or later become aware of a curious state of affairs. If he is accustomed to the discipline and unity of a particular science, he may reasonably expect that a philosophy of science will in turn confer a larger unity on the elements of the scientific enterprise, not merely the various data of the sciences, but also the conclusions and the activities of the scientists themselves. This is not, however, what he will find. What he is more apt to encounter in the various symposia and encyclopedias of unified science is an inveterate division of subject matters. Some may be written entirely in one language and some entirely in the other; some may be a mixture of both; but neither seems to have much to do with the other. The two approaches are (1) the nomothetic method with which he is familiar, arising from the "inexpugnable belief," as Whitehead put it, "that every detailed occurrence can be correlated with its antecedents in a perfectly definite manner exemplifying general principles"; and (2) the quite different program which Russell, after completing the *Principia Mathematica*, staked out for philosophy as its sole concern—the logical analysis of empirical propositions established by perception and science.

To take the most ambitious and interesting example of a "metascience," semiotic, the science of signs—interesting because, unlike pure symbolic logic, it tries to unite logical analysis with the explanatory enterprise of science, and because, whatever its shortcomings, it has at least hit upon the fruitful notion of man as the sign-using animal—here too one encounters the same division of subject matters with no visible means of getting from one to the other, despite the many assurances that semiotic confers unity. If one expects a larger epistemological unity in which the relation of logical analysis to the scientific explanation of natural events is to be made clear, he will be disappointed. He will get logical analysis and he will get scientific theorizing, but he will not learn what one has to do with the other.* There are studies on the biology of sign function, and here one recognizes a basic continuity with the manifold of natural phenomena. When one speaks of animal A responding to buzzer B by salivation in expectation of food F, one is speaking a language familiar to psychologist, physiologist, and physicist alike, the language of spatio-temporal events which lend themselves to causal hypothesis. Stimulus-and-response events occur among natural existents and are mediated by physical structures and a causal nexus which is recognized as valid for organic and inorganic matter.† Thus, whatever the limitations of a biological science of signs in man and animals,‡ one readily recognizes its validity as far as it goes. But then one suddenly finds oneself in the charged atmosphere of the Polish semanticists with their scoldings at the human *abuse* of signs. At one moment one is studying sign behavior as a natural science, in which "interpreters" behave ac-

---

* C. W. Morris: "Languages are developed and used by living beings operating in a world of objects, and show the influence of both the users and the objects. If, as symbolic logic maintains, there are linguistic forms whose validity is not dependent upon nonlinguistic objects, then their validity must be dependent upon the rules of the language in question." Characteristically, semioticists do not find it remarkable that sign-using animals should have developed symbolic logic "whose validity is not dependent on non-linguistic objects." It is therefore not worth investigating how this could have come about but only necessary to note that it has and to define this unusual activity as the "syntactical dimension" of semiotic.

† Nor should one be confused by the encyclopedists' disavowals of determinism in favor of the probability approach, which is supposed to resolve the nomothetic-ideographic dichotomy of object-science and history. For, as becomes abundantly clear, the laws of probability are relied upon quite as heavily as strict causality. As Nagel insists, although laws connecting micro-states may be statistical in character, that does not mean that laws connecting macro-states are not strictly deterministic.

‡ For example, the methodological negation of mental entities and the inability to take account of Gestalt qualities.

cording to lawful empirical regularities, and in the next moment as a quasi-ethical science, in which "interpreters" disobey semantical rules and in general behave stupidly and perversely. There will also be articles dealing exclusively with syntactical rules in logic and mathematics, with the arbitrary formation of calculi, with the principles of logical implication. Or one may read statements by the same semioticist that (1) the basic terms of semiotic are all formulable in terms applicable to behavior as it occurs in an environment, and (2) semiotic can be presented as a deductive system with undefined terms and primitive sentences which allow the deduction of other sentences as theorems.

The fact is that a man engaged in the business of building a logical calculus is doing a very different sort of thing from an animal (or man) responding to a sign, and it is a difference which is not conjured away by ignoring it or by leaping nimbly from *res extensa* to *res cogitans* as though there were no epistemological abyss in between. I cannot say it as well as Professor Crockett: "I do not know whether one should try to describe the universe or whether one should play games with marks arranged according to certain rules; but I do know that one should decide which of these vastly different kinds of activities one is engaged in and inform the reader accordingly."

It is not my intention to make a case against either of the two major components of semiotic, symbolic logic, and behavioristics—the shortcomings of each are well known by now. Rather it is my hope to show that a true "semiotic," far from being the *coup de grâce* of metaphysics, may prove of immense value, inasmuch as it validates and illumines a classical metaphysical relation—*and this at an empirical level*.

I think it will be possible to show (1) that the "unified science" of semiotic is a spurious unity conferred by a deliberate equivocation of the word *sign* to designate two generically different meaning situations (the sign relation and the symbol relation) and (2) that an open "semiotical" analysis of symbolization—that is, one undertaken without theoretical presuppositions—will encounter and shed light upon two metaphysical relations: the first, the cognitive relation of identity by which a concept, a "formal sign," comes to contain within itself *in alio esse* the thing signified; the second, the relation of intersubjectivity, one of the favorite themes of modern existentialists. It may well turn out that the semioticist has good reason to ignore the symbol relation in view of his dictum that sign analysis replaces metaphysics, since an impartial analysis of symbolization can only bring one face to face with the very thing which the semioticist has been at all pains to avoid—a metaphysical issue.

Let us not be too hasty in surrendering the symbol to the symbolic logician or, as is sometimes done, to the mythist.* It is possible that a purely empirical inquiry into the symbol function, an inquiry free of the dogmatic limitations of positivism, may provide fresh access to a philosophy of being.

SYNTAX AND SCIENCE

Semiotic, the science of signs, is an attempt to bring together into the formal unity of a single science three separate disciplines: (1) the semantical rules by which symbols are applied to their designata, (2) the logical analysis of the relations of symbols as they appear in sentences, and (3) the natural science of behavioristics (to use Neurath's terminology), in which organisms are studied in their relation to the environment as it is mediated by signs. It was soon discovered, as Sellars points out, that the limitation of scientific empiricism to logical syntax is suicidal; and so the semantical and biological study of signs was added under the guidance of C. W. Morris. According to Morris, these three disciplines may be regarded as three "dimensions" of the same science, the semantical dimension of semiotic, the syntactical dimension, and the

---

* J. F. Anderson: "This is the last word of symbolism; it is the last word because symbolism moves in the order of univocal concepts, concepts which are merely given an 'analogical' reference by the mind; and through univocal concepts one can never acquire any proper and formal knowledge of reality as such, because reality as such is analogical. Follow the *via symbolica* as far as you like; follow it as far as it goes; it will never lead beyond agnosticism, either in metaphysics or theology."

pragmatic dimension.* This division is held to be analogous to the division of biology into anatomy, ecology, and physiology; a symbolic logician, a semanticist, and a behaviorist are said to be emphasizing different aspects of the same science. Physiology requires anatomy, and ecology requires both; all three conform admirably to the biologist's conception of organism as a system reacting to its environment according to its needs of maintaining its internal milieu and reproducing itself. Physiology is complemented by anatomy; one flows into the other without a hitch. But how does syntactical analysis flow into behavioristics? One may make a syntactical analysis of the sentences written down by a behaviorist, or one may study the sign responses of a symbolic logician; but in what larger scheme may the two be brought into some kind of order? We find symposia written from either point of view, from the physicalist's, who starts with matter and its interactions and tries to derive mind therefrom, or from the symbolic logician's, who conceives the task to be the syntactical investigation of the language of science. Far from the one flowing naturally into the other, the fact is that one has very little use for the other. It takes the encyclopedist to bring them together.

It is well known that logical empiricism is without a theory of knowledge since it restricts itself to an abstract theory of the logic of language. It is equally well known—and perhaps one is a consequence of the other—that the history of logical empiricism is the history of wide fluctuations on the mind-body axis. Examples of the extremes are the solipsism of Mach, Wittgenstein, and the early

* "It will be convenient to have special terms to designate certain of the relations of signs to signs, to objects, and to interpreters. 'Implicates' will be restricted to Dsyn, 'designates' and 'denotes' to Dsem and 'expresses' to Dp. The word 'table' implicates (but does not designate) 'furniture with a horizontal top on which things may be placed,' designates a certain kind of object, denotes the objects to which it is applicable, and expresses its interpreter."

Note the ambiguity of the term "expresses its interpreter." "Implicates," "designates," and "denotes" are purely semantical-syntactical terms with no biological analogue. But what are we to take "expresses" to mean? Is it to be taken in the biological sense of a sign "announcing" its significatum to its interpreter or in the symbolic sense of "expressing a meaning"?

Carnap of *Der logische Aufbau* and the physicalism of the American behaviorists and the later Carnap. But even in the more modern attempts at unity, one is aware of the tendency to construe the field exclusively from the logical or the physicalist point of view—and indeed, how can it be otherwise when the problem of knowing is ruled out of court? A semioticist can easily take the position that the only genuine problem, as Carnap claimed, is one of logical analysis; that is, the question of the formal relations among the concepts that describe the data of first-person experience, the concepts of physics, and those of behaviorist psychology. Or one can begin at the other end with the causal relations between signs and interpreters and derive mind and consciousness with never a thought for syntactical analysis. Anatomy is indispensable to physiology, but syntax can get along very well without neurology. Neither symbolic logicians nor behaviorists are constrained to make contact with each other, and it is perhaps proper that they do not. But it is the semioticists who have brought them willy-nilly together to form the new organon. It is not unreasonable, therefore, to expect that this metascience will provide a larger order. Perhaps, then, it is the semanticists who fill the gap. For semantics professes to deal with both the words of the logicians and the natural objects of the scientist.

We are destined to disappointment. Semantics, it turns out, abstracts from the user of language and analyzes only the expressions and their designata. Like syntax it operates from the logical pole in that it is chiefly concerned with formation of "rules" for the application of symbols to things. Korzybski, we discover, is not interested in how it is that words get applied to things, in the extraordinary act of naming, but only in our perverse tendency to use words incorrectly, and in making a "structural differential" so that one may use words with the full knowledge of the level of abstraction to which they apply. Or if we turn to Tarski's classic paper on the semantic conception of truth with high hopes that at last we have come to the heart of the matter, we will find as the thesis of the article the following criterion of "material adequacy": *X is true if, and only if, p is true,* which when interpreted yields: "*Snow is* *white" is true if, and only if, snow is white.* I do not wish to deny the usefulness of Tarski's criterion within the limits he has set; I only wish to point out that Tarski by his own emphatic asseveration is not concerned with the problem of knowing.*

If, in order to bring the twain together by the semiotic method, we strain forward to the furthest limits of behaviorism and backward to the earliest take-off point of semantics, we will find that the gap between them is narrow but exceeding deep. Logical syntax begins *with* the "protocol statement," the simplest naming sentence; semantics is exclusively concerned with its rules of designation. In regard to the logical syntax of the language of science, Carnap wrote: "Science is a system of statements based on direct experience and controlled by experimental verification. . . . Verification is based on *protocol statements.*" Protocol statements are "statements needing no justification and serving as the foundations for all the remaining statements of science."

Behavioristics, even taken at its own estimation, brings us to a point considerably short of the relation of denotation and the protocol sentence. It deals with the sign behavior of animals and man according to the method of natural science—that of discerning empirical regularities and later attributing them to a causal function, $a = f(b)$. An organism's response to a stimulus is resolvable into a sequential series of commotions mediated by structures, beginning with an air vibration and ending with an efferent nerve discharge into a glandular end-organ.†

---

* For example, in answer to the charge that his "Snow is white" sentence seems to imply a naïve realism when it lays down the condition "if and only if snow is white," he writes: ". . . the semantic definition of truth implies nothing regarding the conditions under which a sentence like (1) *snow is white* can be asserted. It implies only that, whenever we assert or reject this sentence, we must be ready to assert or reject the correlated sentence (2): the sentence 'snow is white' is true.

"Thus we may accept the semantic conception of truth without giving up any epistemological attitude we may have had; we may remain naïve realists, critical realists, or idealists—whatever we were before. The semantic conception of truth is completely neutral toward all these issues."

† Nor does the Gestaltist, for that matter, take us an inch closer to the mysterious act of naming. By his concept of field forces and perceptual wholes, he can make sense of molar phenomena which escape the behaviorist. He can arrive at certain traits of configuration which apply alike to chickens and humans (see for example

An object-science of behavior can only make sense of language by trying to derive it from some refinement of sign response. As Susanne Langer has pointed out, when the naming act is construed in these terms, when the situation in which you give something a name and it is the same for you as it is for me, when this peculiar relation of denotation is construed in terms of stimulus response, one has the feeling that it leaves out the most important thing of all. What is left out, what an object-science cannot get hold of by an intrinsic limitation of method is nothing less than the relation of denotation—*a name above all denotes something*. If you say "James" to a dog whose master bears that name, the dog will interpret the sound as a sign and *look* for James. Say it to a person who knows someone called thus, and he will ask, "What about James?" That simple question is forever beyond the dog; signification is the only meaning a name can have for him.

The upshot is, even if we go no further than Mrs. Langer, who is otherwise in sympathy with the positivism of the semioticists, that in semiotic symbol analysis and the science of sign behavior are brought willy-nilly together into a unity which has no other justification than that both have something to do with "sign." No larger sanction can be forthcoming because of the dictum that sign analysis replaces metaphysics. To say to a semioticist that he is confusing the logical with the real is unacceptable to him because of the "metaphysical" presuppositions involved. One might nevertheless expect that, within the limits of the semiotical method, some attempt might be made to achieve the continuity so highly prized by semioticists since the time of Peirce.* Failing this, one cannot help wondering whether to do so, to explore the gap between prag-

---

the Jastrow illusion in Koffka's *Gestalt Psychology*). But neither the behaviorist nor the Gestaltist has anything to say, indeed does not wish to have anything to say, about the naming act. The very methodology of an object-science precludes its consideration of an object-sentence as such, perhaps for no other reason than that the object-science takes place within the very intersubjective nexus which attends language. (Cf. Marcel: "Without doubt the intersubjective nexus cannot in any way be asserted; it can only be acknowledged. . . . I should readily agree that it is the mysterious root of language."

* Continuity "is the absence of ultimate parts in that which is divisible." It is "nothing but perfect generality of a law of relationship."

matics and symbol analysis, will not run squarely into an "extrasemiotical" relation—not as a "metaphysical presupposition" or a "naïve realism" but as an issue which is precisely arrived at by the semiotical method itself.

SIGN AND SYMBOL

Semiotic uses as its basic frame of reference the meaning triad of Charles Peirce (Figure 8). Its three components are sign, interpretant, and object. The "interpretant" in man is equivalent to "thought" or "idea" or, in modern semiotical usage, to "takings-account-of." The interpretant therefore implies an organism in which the interpretant occurs, the interpreter. The virtue of the triadic conception of the meaning relation is that it is conformable with the biological notion of stimulus-response, in which the sign is equivalent to a stimulus, the conditioned response to the interpretant, and the designatum to the object of the response.

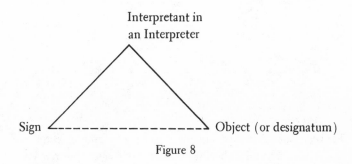

Figure 8

The triad can be looked at in either its biological (pragmatical) or its logical dimension. That is to say, it can be conceived either as a causal relation obtaining between natural existents and mediated by neural structures, sound waves, and so on; or it can be viewed syntactically-semantically. Thus, in the biological dimension, the buzzer (sign) has no direct relation to the object (food); whereas in the semantical dimension the word (sign) has the direct relation of designation with the object, precisely insofar as it is specified by a semantical rule to designate the object. Syntactics has to do with the logical relation which one sign bears to another.

The semioticists, however, when they speak of the meaning relation as it is taken to occur among natural existents whether human or subhuman, regardless of whether they are speaking of the pragmatical or semantical dimension, always assume that it is a causal sequential event.* They are careful to use *response* instead of *conception* or *thought* or *idea*.† Even in Ogden and Richards's variation of Peirce's triad, in which the terms "symbol" and "thought" (or "reference") and "referent" are used, it is stated that "between a thought and a symbol causal relations hold."

We may therefore express the basic semiotic relation in terms of the simple biological triad (represented in Figure 9).

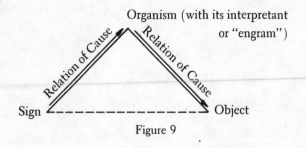

Figure 9

Between the sign and organism, organism and object, "real" causal relations hold. The line between sign and object is dotted because no real relation holds but only an imputed relation, the semantical relation of designation. A major doctrine of the semanticists is that most of the difficulties which thought encounters

---

* I use the word "causal" unprejudicially, to mean whatever the reader would take it to mean in the context. It does not matter for the argument whether one interprets this cause as efficient causality or as a probability function.

† C. W. Morris: ". . . terms gain relations among themselves according to the relations of the *responses* of which the sign vehicles are a part, and these modes of usage are the pragmatical background of the formation and transformation rules."

come about through the imputation of a real relation where only a semantical one exists.

One knows at once what Ogden and Richards mean by *real* even though latter-day semioticists would avoid the term. Signification occurs as a material happening among natural existents, from the sound of the buzzer to an electrocolloidal change in the dog's brain to glandular secretion. There is, however, no such "real" relation between sign and object.*

Two considerations arise in connection with the semiotical theory of meaning. The first is simply this: If the semioticists insist on giving a biological account of the meaning relation as it is taken to occur among natural existents (human organisms, words, things), what account are they prepared to give in these terms of the imputed and logical relations which occur in semantics and syntax? If the semantical relation between sign and designatum is not "real," then what is its status? Is its status settled by the nominal device of calling it an "imputed" relation? Is it simply "wrong" as one might gather from the semanticists? The answer is not forthcoming. One simply speaks in one breath of concepts as "responses" and in the next of the logical relations between concepts. This treatment is, as we have seen, ambiguous. Either it can mean that the semantical-syntactical relation stands in so obvious a continuity with sign behavior that nothing more need be said about it; or it may mean that of course it is "mental" and has nothing to do with sign behavior and that it goes without saying that the Cartesian dualism of *res extensa* and *res cogitans* prevails. In any case, it is unsatisfactory to be required to shift attention without further ado from the great corpus of natural science to an "unreal but imputed" relation. It would not seem unreasonable to ask what one is to make of this queer relation in terms of a "unified science."

The second consideration, and one which on investigation leads

---

* It is irrelevant that in the case of thunder announcing rain, the thunder happens to have a real connection with the rain process. The same relation of signification could be made to take place in a deaf organism by using a blue light to announce rain. Thus, to use Saint Augustine's nomenclature, whether the sign is natural or conventional, the mode of response is the same.

to such unexpected consequences, has been raised, not by a hostile critic of semiosis, but by an erstwhile symbolic logician. There is something wrong, writes Susanne Langer, about regarding the word symbol as a sign and a conception as a response. Since the notion of meaning as signification in the narrow sense, as a response, "misses the most important feature of the material," *what is this feature and what are its epistemological consequences?* *

What is this most important feature which is left out by a causal rendering of meaning? It is, of course, the relation of denotation as opposed to signification. To give something a name, at first sight the most commonplace of events, is in reality a most mysterious act, one which is quite unprecedented in animal behavior and imponderable in its consequences. The semioticists are obliged by method to render symbol as a kind of sign. Morris defines a symbol as a sign produced by its interpreter which acts as a substitute for some other sign with which it is synonymous. Thus, in a dog, hunger cramps can take the place of the buzzer in the control of the dog's behavior: "Hunger cramps might themselves come to be a sign (that is, a symbol) of food at the customary place." Although we may sympathize with Morris's purpose, not to disqualify "mind," but simply to advance semiotic as a science, the fact remains that this is an extraordinary use of the word *symbol*— certainly it has nothing to do with denotation. It is the relation of denotation, as Mrs. Langer points out, which has been completely overlooked. The question is this: Can denotation be derived by a refinement of behavioral reaction, or is it something altogether different? Can any elaboration of response issue in naming? Why is it, we begin to wonder, the semioticists refuse to deal with symbolization, excepting only as it is governed by semantical rules?

That symbolization is radically and generically different from signification is confirmable in various ways. There is the sudden discovery of the symbol in the history of deaf-mutes, such as the well-

---

* If we hoped that Mrs. Langer would follow up the epistemological consequences of this most important insight into the noncausal character of symbolic meaning, we shall be disappointed. She drops it quickly, restates her allegiance to positivism, and goes on to the aesthetic symbol as the form of feeling.

known incident in which Helen Keller, who had "understood" words but only as signs awoke to the extraordinary circumstance that the word *water* meant, denoted, the substance water.* There are the genetic studies of normal children, as for example the observation of Schachtel, who speaks of the "autonomous object interest" of young children as being altogether different from the earlier need-gratification interest.† Symbolization can be approached genetically, as the proper subject of an empirical psychology, or it can be set forth phenomenologically, as a meaning structure with certain irreducible terms and relations.

Let us first take notice of the gross elements of the symbol meaning situation and later of the interrelations which exist between them.

THE SECOND ORGANISM AND
THE RELATION OF INTERSUBJECTIVITY

What happens, then, when a sign becomes a symbol; when a sound, a vocable, which had served as a stimulus in the causal nexus of organism-in-an-environment, is suddenly discovered to *mean* something in the sense of denoting it?

It will be recalled that the relation of signification is a triadic one of sign-organism-object (Figure 9). This schema holds true for any significatory meaning situation. It is true of a dog responding to a buzzer by salivation; it is true of a polar bear responding to the sound of splitting ice; it is true of a man responding to a telephone

---

* For example, she had understood the word *water* (spelled into her hand) but only as a sign to which she must respond by fetching the mug, drinking the water, and so on. The significance of her discovery that this *is* water may be judged from the fact that having discovered what water *was*, she then wanted to know what everything else *was*. (Cf. also the experiences of Marie Huertin, Lywine Lachance, and the well-authenticated account of Victor, the wild boy of Aveyron, who discovered the symbol *despite* every attempt of his positivist teacher to present it as a sign of a want.)

† "These considerations cast some doubt on the adequacy of Freud's theory of the origin and nature of thought . . . According to Freud thought has only one ancestor, the attempt at hallucinatory need-satisfaction . . . I believe that thought has two ancestors instead of one—namely, motivating needs, *and* a distinctively human capacity, the relatively autonomous capacity for object interest."

bell; * it is true of little Helen Keller responding to the word *water* by fetching water. The essential requirement of signification is that there be an organism in an environment capable of learning by effecting an electrocolloidal change in the central nervous system and as a consequence responding to a stimulus in a biologically adaptive fashion.†

It is important to realize that whereas signification often occurs between two or more organisms, it is not essential that it should, and that generically the sort of response is the same whether one or more organisms are involved. The action of a dog in responding intelligently to the bark or feint of another dog—Mead's "conversation of gesture"—is generically the same sort of meaning relation as that in which a solitary polar bear responds to the sound of splitting ice. It is the *environment* to which the organism responds in a biologically adaptive fashion, and the mode of response is the same whether the environment consist of other organisms or of inorganic nature.

Only a moment's reflection is needed to realize that the minimal requirement of symbolization is quite different. By the very nature of symbolic meaning, there must be *two* "organisms" in the meaning relation, one who gives the name and one for whom the name becomes meaningful. The very essence of symbolization is an entering into a *mutuality* toward that which is symbolized. The very condition of my conceiving the object before me under the auspices of a symbol is that you name it for me or I name it for you. The act of symbolization requires another besides the hearer; it

* It is also true of a human responding to the shout "Fire!" in a crowded theater (Mead's example in *Mind, Self and Society*). Here, characteristically, the semioticist confuses symbol and sign by citing human significatory responses as illustrative of human meaning in general. One may indeed *respond* to a word and in this respect our understanding is similar to Helen's understanding of signs prior to her discovery of the symbol and, in fact, generically the same as a dog's response to a spoken command. But it is an altogether different situation when a father tells his child that this *is* fire, and the child awakes to the fact that by this odd little sound of *fire* his father means this leaping flame.

† It does not matter for the present purpose that some intelligent responses are acquired by conditioning and that others are congenital dispositions of the organism. The learned response of the dog to the buzzer and the innate response of the chick to the sight of grain are both explicable in physico-causal terms as an event in an electrocolloidal system.

requires a namer. Without the presence of another, symbolization cannot conceivably occur because there is no one from whom the word can be received as meaningful. *The irreducible condition of every act of symbolization is the rendering intelligible; that is to say, the formulation of experience for a real or an implied someone else.*

The presence of the two organisms is not merely a genetic requirement, a *sine qua non* of symbolization; it is rather its enduring condition, its indispensable climate. Every act of symbolization, a naming, forming an hypothesis, creating a line of poetry, perhaps even thinking, implies *another* as a co-conceiver,* a co-celebrant of the thing which is symbolized. Symbolization is an exercise in intersubjectivity.

A new and indefeasible relation has come into being between the two organisms in virtue of which they are related not merely as one organism responding to another but as namer and hearer, an I and a Thou. Mead's two dogs quarreling over a bone exist in a conversation of gesture, a sequential order of gesture and countergesture. But a namer and a hearer of the name exist in a mutuality of understanding toward that which is symbolized. Here the terminology of object science falls short. One must use such words as mutuality or intersubjectivity, however unsatisfactory they may be. But whatever we choose to call it, the fact remains that there has occurred a sudden cointending of the object under the auspices of the symbol, a relation which of its very nature cannot be construed in causal language.†

---

* If there is a natural wisdom in etymologies, perhaps this is a case of it—for *conceive*, one suddenly realizes, means "to take *with*."

† George Mead, the great social behaviorist, clearly perceived that language and mind are essentially social phenomena. We owe a great deal to his prescience that the interpersonal milieu is of cardinal importance in the genesis of mind, even though he felt compelled to render this relation exclusively in behavioristic terms for fear of "metaphysical" consequences (it is clear that by "metaphysical" he meant anything airy and elusive). It is typical of his integrity, however, that even with his commitment to behaviorism, he did not shrink from mental phenomena and consciousness, and in fact attempted to derive consciousness from social interaction.

Having realized that language is an interpersonal phenomenon, however, he set himself the impossible task of deriving the symbol from a stimulus-response sequence. For since it was an article of faith with him that the explanatory science of behavioristics is the only hope of approaching mind, he could not do otherwise than render symbolization as a response. As a consequence, he is obliged to define a sym-

Is it possible, then, that an unprejudiced semiotic may throw some light on the interpersonal relation, the I-Thou of Buber, the intersubjectivity of Marcel? As things stand now, the empirical mind can make very little of this entity "intersubjectivity," and the behaviorist nothing at all. Like other existential themes, it seems very much in the air. Yet an empirical approach to the genesis of symbolization is bound to reveal it as a very real, if mysterious, relation. Perhaps the contribution of a new semiotic will be that intersubjectivity is by no means a reducible, or an imaginary, phenomenon but is a very real and pervasive bond and one mediated by a sensible symbol and a sensible object which is symbolized.*

We may therefore revise the sign triad as the symbol tetrad (see Fig. 9A).

The "organisms" no longer exist exclusively in a causal nexus but are united by a new and noncausal bond, the relation of intersubjectivity.

But a new relation has also arisen between the object and its symbol. What is the nature of the "imputed relation of identity"?

THE INTENTIONAL RELATION OF IDENTITY

Mead said that a vocal gesture (sign) becomes a symbol when the individual responds to his own stimulus in the same way as other

bol as the kind of sign which "calls out" the same response from the speaker as from the hearer. This definition drives him into the absurdity of saying that a word can only mean the same thing for you and me if it provokes the same response from you and me. Thus, if I ask you to get up and fetch the visitor a chair, it must follow that I also arouse in myself the same tendency to get up and fetch the chair. Clearly, as Mrs. Langer noticed, something is wrong here.

Is it possible, we wonder, that Mead was right in his emphasis of the social bond but mistaken in construing it behavioristically?

* Hocking writes of intersubjectivity as a direct unmediated bond from which mind and language arise: ". . . without the direct experiential knowledge of 'We are,' the very ideas of 'sign,' 'language,' 'other mind,' itself could not arise."

Yet one might wonder whether it is not the other way around—whether the relation "We are" does not arise through a mutual intending of the object through its symbol, the word which you give me and I can say too. It would perhaps be more characteristic of angelic intelligences to experience such an immediate intuitive knowledge rather than a knowledge mediated by sensible signs and objects.

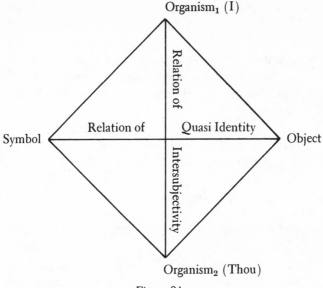

Organism₁ (I)

Relation of

Relation of   Quasi Identity

Symbol   Object

Intersubjectivity

Organism₂ (Thou)

Figure 9A

people respond. Yet one cannot fail to realize that something is amiss in construing as a response Helen Keller's revelation that this *is* water. And certainly it misses the peculiar representative function of language to declare that, when I ask you to do something, I also arouse in myself the same tendency to do it.

What, then, is changed in the semiotic relation by Helen Keller's inkling that this *is* water? Physically, the elements are the same as before. There is Helen; there is Miss Sullivan; there is the water flowing over one hand, and there is the word spelled out in the other. Yet something of very great moment has occurred. Not only does she have the sense of a revelation, so that all at once the whole world is open to her, not only does she experience a very great happiness, a joy which is quite different from her previous need-satisfactions (see Schachtel's "autonomous object interest" above), but immediately after discovering what the water *is*, she must then know what everything else *is*.

The critical question may now be raised. In discovering the

peculiar denotative function of the symbol, has Helen only succeeded in opening Pandora's box of all our semantical ills of "identification," or has she hit upon the indispensable condition of our
knowing anything at all, perhaps even of consciousness itself? * Is
her joy a "hallucinatory need-satisfaction," an atavism of primitive
word-magic; or is it a purely cognitive joy oriented toward being
and its validation through the symbol?

It comes down to the mysterious naming act, this *is water* (the
word spelled out in her hand). Here, of course, is where the trouble
starts. For clearly, as the semanticists never tire of telling us, the
word is *not* water. You cannot eat the word *oyster*, Chase assures
us; but then not even the most superstitious totemistic tribesman
would try to.† Yet the semanticists themselves are the best witnesses of the emergence of an extraordinary relation—which they
deplore as the major calamity of the human race—the relation of
an imputed identity between word and thing. Undoubtedly the
semanticists have performed a service in calling attention to the
human penchant for word magic, for reifying meanings by simply
applying words to them. Gabriel Marcel frequently speaks of the
same tendency of "simulacrum" formation, by which meanings
become hardened and impenetrable to thought. Yet one wonders if
it might not be more useful to investigate this imputed identity for
what part it might play in human knowing, rather than simply
deplore it—which is after all an odd pursuit for a "scientific empiricist."

To awake to the remarkable circumstance that something has a
name is neither a response nor an imputed real identity. No one
believes that the name is really the thing, nor does the sentence
This is water mean this. Then what is the relation? It might clarify
matters to eliminate the mysterious copula, leaving the sentence

---

* Cf. her comment on presymbolic thought: ". . . if a wordless sensation may
be called a thought."
   † In regard to primitive identification, Oliver Leroy writes: "The logic of a Hui-
chol (who mystically identifies stag with wheat) would be deficient only on the day
when he would prepare a wheat porridge while he thought he was making a stag
stew." Yet in some sense, the symbol is identified with the thing, a sense, moreover,
which is open to superstitious abuse.

This: water. Or even more simply, eliminate the word *this*, leaving a pointing at and a naming (in semiotic language, an indexical sign plus a symbol). In its essence the making and the receiving of the naming act consist in a coupling, an apposing of two real entities, the uttered name and the object. It is this *pairing* which is unique and unprecedented in the causal nexus of significatory meaning. But what is the nature of this pairing? The two terms, it is clear, are related in some sense of identification, yet not a real identity. To express it in modern semiotical language, the water is conceived through the vehicle of the symbol. In Scholastic language, the symbol has the peculiar property of containing within itself *in alio esse*, in another mode of existence, that which is symbolized.*
Helen knows the water *through* and by means of the symbol.

The word is that by which the thing is conceived or known. It is, in Scholastic language, an intention. The Scholastics speak of concepts as "formal signs," intentions whose peculiar property it is, not to appear as an object, but to disappear before the object. But here we are not dealing with concepts or mental entities. We are dealing with natural existents, the object and the vocable, the sound which actually trembles in the air. It is this latter which is in some sense intentionally identified with the thing. Or rather the thing is intended by the symbol. Perhaps much of the confusion which has arisen over the "identification" of the symbol with its designatum could have been avoided by an appreciation of the phenomenological (and Scholastic) notion of intentionality and by distinguishing real identity from the intentional relation of identity.

An interesting question arises in connection with the intentional function of the symbol. Is it possible that the symbol is a primitive precursor of the concept or "formal sign" of the Scholastics? The latter contains its object in an intentional mode of existence, *in alio esse*. *But so in an extraordinary fashion does the sensuous symbol.* In cases of false onomatopoeia, the symbol is transformed inten-

* John of St. Thomas: *Quid est illud in signato conjunctum signo, et praesens in signo praeter ipsum signum et entitatem ejus? Respondetur esse ipsummet signatum in alio esse.* "What may be that element of the signified which is joined to the sign and present in it as distinct from the sign itself? I answer: No other element than the very signified itself in another mode of existence."

tionally to imitate the thing symbolized (for example, *crash*, *glass*, *limber*, *furry*, *slice*, and so on). The word *glass* bears no resemblance to the thing glass. Yet it actually seems to transmit a quality of brittleness, glossiness, and so on. The fact is that a symbolic transformation has occurred whereby the drab little vocable has been articulated by its meaning.*

The semanticists supply a valuable clue by their protestations. Confronted by a pencil, Korzybski says, it is absolutely false to say that this is a pencil; to say that it is can only lead to delusional states. Say whatever you like *about* the pencil, but do not say that it is a pencil. "Whatever you say the object is, well, it is not." The pencil is itself unspeakable. True; but insofar as it remains unspeakable—that is, unvalidated by you and me through a symbol—it is also inconceivable. Clearly the semanticists are confusing an epistemological condition with a true identity.

How does it happen, Cassirer asked, that a finite and particular sensory content can be made into the vehicle of a general spiritual "meaning"? And we know his answer. It is the Kantian variant that it is not reality which is known but the symbolic forms through which reality is conceived. Yet the empirical approach belies this. An empirical semiotic deals with natural existents and takes for granted a lawful reality about which something can be truly known. Even a strict behaviorist operates publicly in a community of other knowers and data to be known; he performs experiments on real data and publishes papers which he expects other scientists to understand. What account, after all, can Cassirer or any other idealist give of intersubjectivity? If it was, according to Kant, a "scandal of philosophy" in his day that no satisfactory solution could be found to the problem of intersubjectivity, is it any less a scandal now? But

* "The natural sound element has been taken up into and practically disappears from our consciousness in its significant symbolic connotation. In other words the natural sounds have been completely transmuted into conventional sound symbols."
One can establish this transformation to his own satisfaction by a simple experiment. Repeat the word "glass" many times; all at once it will lose its symbolic guise, its "glassiness," and become the poor drab vocable that it really is. Yet it is from its original poverty that its high symbolic potentiality derives. It is for this reason, as Mrs. Langer says, that a vocable is very good symbolic material, and a peach very poor.

a broad semiotical approach can only bring one into the territory of epistemological realism. Since we do not know being directly, Wilhelmsen writes, we must sidle up to it; and at the symbol-object level, we can only do this by laying something of comparable ontological status alongside.

> Existence is attained immediately in the judgment; but judgments necessarily entail the use of phantasms, and, except in direct judgments of existing material things, the phantasms employed are symbolic. The philosopher must go through phantasm to reach being.

Perhaps it would be truer, genetically speaking, to say that the primitive act of symbolization, occurring as it does prior to conception and phantasm, consists in the application, not of the phantasm, but of the sensuous symbol to the existing thing. A being is affirmed as being what it is through its denotation by symbol.* Is it not possible that what I primarily want in asking *what* something is is not an explanation but a validation and affirmation of the thing itself as it is—a validation which can only be accomplished by laying something else alongside: the symbol?

We might therefore reverse Korzybski's dictum: It is *only* if you say what the object *is* that you can know anything about it at all.

The symbol meaning relation may be defined as not merely an intentional but as a cointentional relation of identity. The thing is intended through its symbol which you say and I can repeat, and it is only through this quasi identification that it can be conceived at all. Thus it is, I believe, that an empirical and semiotical approach to meaning illumines and confirms in an unexpected manner the realist doctrine of the union of the knower and the thing known. The metaphysical implications of semiotic are clear enough. Knowing is not a causal sequence but an immaterial union. It is a union, however, which is mediated through material entities, the

---

* Marcel observes that when I ask what is this strange flower, I am more satisfied to be given a nondescriptive name than a scientific classification. "But now we find the real paradox—the first unscientific answer (it is a lupin, it is an orchid) which consisted in giving the *name* of the flower, although it had practically no rational basis, yet satisfied the demand in me which the interpretation by reduction tends . . . to frustrate."

symbol and its object. Nor is it a private phenomenon—rather is it an exercise in intersubjectivity in which the Thou serves as an indispensable colleague. Both the relation of intersubjectivity and the intentional relation of identity are real yet immaterial bonds.

To render human cognition physico-causally can only end in the hopeless ambiguity of current semioticists who must speak in two tongues with no lexicon to translate, the language of the scientist who deals with signs as natural existents and the language of the formal logician who deals with the syntactical relations between signs.

The intentional relation of identity is not only the basic relation of logical forms, as Professor Veatch has pointed out; it is also the basic relation of symbolization. No wonder, then, that the symbolic logician has no use for it—for once the intentional character of knowing is recognized, "so far from being independent of metaphysics or first philosophy, [it] necessarily presupposes it."

12

SYMBOL, CONSCIOUSNESS, AND INTERSUBJECTIVITY

THERE ARE two interesting things about current approaches to consciousness as a subject of inquiry. One is that the two major approaches, the explanatory-psychological and the phenomenological, go their separate ways, contributing nothing to each other. They do not tend to converge upon or supplement each other as do, say, atomic theory and electromagnetic theory. One can either look upon consciousness as a public thing or event in the world like any other public thing or event and as such open to explanatory inquiry; or one can regard it as an absolutely privileged realm, that by which I know anything at all—including explanatory psychology. As exemplars of these two approaches, I shall refer in the sequel to the work of George H. Mead and Edmund Husserl. The other interesting thing is that both approaches encounter the same perennial difficulty, albeit each encounters it in its own characteristic way. This difficulty is the taking account of intersubjectivity, that meeting of minds by which two selves take each other's meaning with reference to the same object beheld in common. As Schutz has pointed out, intersubjectivity is simply presupposed as the unclarified foundation of the explanatory-empirical sciences. A social behaviorist writes hundreds of papers setting forth the thesis that mind and consciousness are an affair of responses to signs or responses to responses; yet he unquestionably expects his colleagues to do more than respond to his paper; he also expects them to understand it, to take his meaning. As regards phenomenology, on the other hand, philosophers as different as James Collins and Jean-Paul Sartre have noticed that the chief difficulty which Husserl (not to mention Hegel and Heidegger) encounters is the allowing for the existence of other selves.

It is the purpose of this essay to suggest that these two chronic difficulties which have beset the study of consciousness have come about in part at least from a failure to appreciate the extraordinary role of the symbol, especially the language symbol, in man's orientation to the world. I am frank to confess a prejudice in favor of Mead's approach to consciousness as a phenomenon arising from the social matrix through language. It seems to me that the psychological approach possesses the saving virtue that it tends to be self-corrective, whereas in transcendental phenomenology everything is risked on a single methodological cast at the very outset, the famous *epoché*. But I wish to suggest first that positive psychology, in its allegiance to the sign-response as the basic schema of psychogenesis, has failed or refused to grasp the peculiar role of the language symbol. I would further suggest that an appreciation of this role will (1) confirm in an unexpected way Mead's thesis of the social origin of consciousness, (2) reveal intersubjectivity as one of the prime relations of the symbol meaning-structure, (3) provide access to a phenomenology of consciousness, not as a transcendental idealism, but as a mode of being emerging from the interrelations of real organisms in the world.

SYMBOL AND INTERSUBJECTIVITY

I do not think it would be too far from the truth to say that the phenomenologist, having ruled out intersubjectivity in his reduction, has the greatest difficulty in reinstating it thereafter; and that the positive psychologist simply takes intersubjectivity for granted. It is one thing to be aware, as the phenomenologists are aware, that a fundamental connection with the other self must be seized, in Sartre's words, at the very heart of consciousness. Whether such a connection is allowed by the rigor of the phenomenological reduction is something else again. It is also one thing to be aware, as

Mead was aware, of the social origin of consciousness. Whether this connection between consciousness and the social matrix can be demonstrated in terms of a sign-response psychology is something else again. But there is this difference: If Mead's social behaviorism is too narrow a theoretical base, it can be broadened without losing the posture from which Mead theorized, that of an observer confronting data which he can make some sense of and of which he can speak to other observers. For this reason I shall be chiefly concerned with the general approach of George Mead.

The most conspicuous divergence between Husserl's and Mead's approaches to consciousness is the opting of one for the individual cogito character of consciousness and of the other for its intrinsically social character. In the phenomenological reduction all belief in existents and in one's theoretical attitude toward existents is suspended. What remains over as a residuum, as the subject matter of an apodictic science? Only consciousness itself, "a self-contained system of being, into which nothing can penetrate and from which nothing can escape; which cannot experience causality from anything nor exert causality upon anything. . . ." Mead, on the other hand, is quite as emphatic in regarding mind and consciousness as developing within the social process, "within the empirical matrix of social interactions." Let us suppose for the moment that Mead is right—I have not the space here to go into a critical comparison of Mead and Husserl on this point: I only wish to offer a suggestion from the objective-empirical point of view—let us suppose that we may study consciousness as we study anything else, and that, moreover, "it is absurd to look at the mind from the standpoint of the individual organism." Let us also suppose that Mead, along with many others, is probably right in focusing upon language as a key to the mysteries of mind. "Out of language arises the field of the mind." The question which must be asked is whether this seminal insight is confirmed by Mead's behaviorism or whether Mead did not in fact fall short of his goal precisely because of his rigid commitment to the sign-response sequence and his consequent failure to grasp the denotative function of the language symbol. Mead, along with most other American psychogeneticists, has felt obliged to construe the symbol as a variety of sign, and symbolic meaning as a refinement of sign-response. Mead saw no other alternative and was frank to declare that, once you abandon social or biological response, there only remains "transcendentalism."

It would perhaps not be too gross a simplification to observe that the phenomenologist starts with consciousness but never gets back to organisms and signs, and that the positive psychologist starts with organisms and signs but never arrives at consciousness. Mead's problem, once he had limited himself to the response as the ground of consciousness, was to derive a set of conditions under which a stimulus evokes the same response from the organism who utters it as it does from the organism who hears it. This is accomplished through role-taking, when the speaking organism comes to respond to its own signs in the same way as the hearing organism. Consciousness is the response of the organism to its own responses. We cannot fail to be aware of the forced character of Mead's response psychology in coping with human meaning when, for example, he is obliged to say that, when I ask you to get up and fetch the visitor a chair, I also arouse in myself the same tendency to get up and fetch the chair. This strained interpretation is fair warning, as Mrs. Langer has pointed out, that the most important feature of the material is being left out.

What is missing, of course, is the relation of denotation. It may be correct in a sense to say that a word "calls forth a response," "announces an idea," and so on. But more important, it names something.

Now of course there is nothing new in this. Semioticists take due notice of the relation of denotation in semantics, which is that dimension of semiotic which has to do with the *rules* by which a symbol is said to denote its denotatum. What concerns us, however, is what one is to make of this relation from an objective-empirical point of view, rather than a logical one, as something which is actually taking place in the "data" before us, as assuredly it is taking place. To put the problem concretely: Given the phenomenon in which the normal child or the blind deaf-mute discovers that this stuff "is" *water*, what we wish to know (and what Mead always wished to know) is not the semantic "rule" by which Helen and

Miss Sullivan agree to call the stuff *water*—this is a convention, not an explanation—what we wish to know is *what happens.* Certainly, whether we approve or disapprove, something very momentous has taken place when a sign which had been received as a signal—go fetch the water—is suddenly understood to "mean" the water, to denote something. Then what is it that happens? Semioticists dodge the issue by parceling out sign function to "behavioristics" and symbolic denotation to "semantics," leaving the gap in limbo. Morris, for example, refuses to consider the symbol as anything other than a sign in behavioristics, allowing its denotative function only in semantics. Mead's objective, however, was to bring all entities, mind, consciousness, sign, symbol, under the single gaze of the objective-empirical method. If, therefore, there is such a thing as denotation, naming, and if it does assuredly take place in the public realm we are studying, then what exactly happens and what relevance does this happening have for the phenomena of intersubjectivity and consciousness? How does it illumine these realities which no refinement of signification seems to get hold of? What would happen if instead of trying to get rid of denotation by calling it semantics, or by reducing it to a response sequence, we examined it as a real event among organisms?

I wish to call attention, without pretending to have determined their entire role in the act of consciousness, to two characteristics of the symbol meaning-relation, *as they are empirically ascertainable,* which distinguish it from the sign relation and which have the utmost relevance for the topics under consideration.

The first is a unique relation between the "organisms" involved in the symbolic meaning-structure, a relation which can only come about through a radical change in the relations which obtain in the sign-response. Signification is essentially and irreducibly a triadic meaning-relation, whereas symbolization is essentially and irreducibly a tetradic relation. The three terms of the sign-response are related physico-causally.* The schema, sign—organism—significatum, has so persistently recommended itself as the ground of

---

* I use the word "causal" without prejudice, to mean whatever the reader would have it mean in the context. It does not matter for the argument whether it is read as efficient causality or as a probability function.

meaning, human and subhuman, because it deals with physical structures and with causal relations and energy exchanges between these structures. Thus, no matter whether we are considering a solitary polar bear responding to the sound of splitting ice, or a bee responding to the honey dance of another bee, or a human responding to the cry of *Fire!* in a theater, each case is understandable as a sequential stimulus-response action acquired or inherited according to the exigencies of biological adaptation: sign → sound waves → sensory end-organ → afferent nerve impulse → cortical pattern → efferent nerve impulse → motor (or glandular) activity with reference to significatum. Whether we are trying to understand the behavior of a solitary organism in an inorganic environment (polar bear) or a society of organisms (bee hive), the behavior in each case is understood as a response of an organism to its environment. In one case the environment is inorganic (splitting ice), in the other case organic (other bees). But the central concept in both cases is that of an organism-in-an-environment responding and adapting through the mediation of signs.

The symbol meaning-relation is radically and generically different. It is a tetradic relation in which the presence of the *two* organisms is not merely required as an irreducible minimum but in which the two are themselves co-related in an unprecedented fashion. Denotation, the act of naming, requires the *two*, namer and hearer. My calling this thing a chair is another way of saying that it "is" a chair for you and me. (Mead's "conversation of gestures" between two boxers or two dogs would seem also to require the two. However, the boxer or the dog responding to his opponent's gestures is not generically different from the polar bear responding to splitting ice.) It is inconceivable that a human being raised apart from other humans should ever discover symbolization. For there is no way I can know this "is" a chair unless you tell me so. But not only are the two a genetic requirement of symbolization—as the presence of two is a genetic requirement of fertilization—*it is its enduring condition*. Even Robinson Crusoe writing in his journal after twenty years alone on his island is performing a through-and-through social act. Every symbolic formulation, whether it be language, art, or even thought, requires a real or posited *someone else* for whom the symbol is intended as meaningful. Denotation is an exercise in intersubjectivity. The two are suddenly no longer related as organisms in a nexus of interaction but as a namer and hearer of a name, an I and a Thou, co-conceivers and co-celebrants of the object beheld under the auspices of a common symbol.

It is something of a fool's errand to attempt to derive intersubjectivity by theorizing about interactions among organisms, responses to responses. Physico-causal theory is formed entirely *within* the intersubjective milieu and cannot of its very nature transcend it. A physical function, $a = f(b)$, is a saying of one scientist to another, an I to a Thou, that such and such a quantifiable relation obtains among the data before them. It does not say anything about the behavior of the scientists themselves because they are practicing intersubjectivity in their uttering and understanding of their causal function. They are co-knowers and co-affirmers of the function $a = f(b)$, but their co-knowing and co-affirming cannot itself be grasped by this particular instrument which they have devised between them. If we wish to study the knowers themselves, the I-Thou relation, we must use some other instrument, speak some other language, perhaps an ontological one rather than a physico-causal.*

Symbolization can only occur by a radical shift in the elements of the old meaning structure of sign-organism-significatum. I do not know whether it is more proper or fruitful to speak of this new state of affairs as a social emergent or as a mode of being, but in any case there has come into existence a relation which transcends the physico-causal relations obtaining among data. This relation is intersubjectivity. It is a reality which can no longer be understood

* Cf. Marcel's "Intersubjective nexus": ". . . It is a metaphysic of *we are* as opposed to a metaphysic of *I think*. . . . But it is apparent by definition that what I may call the intersubjective nexus cannot be given to me, since I am myself in some way involved in it. It may not perhaps be inaccurate to say that this nexus is in fact the necessary condition for anything being given me. . . . Without doubt the intersubjective nexus cannot in any way be asserted; it can only be acknowledged . . . the affirmation should possess a special character, that of being the root of every expressible affirmation. *I should readily agree that it is the mysterious root of language.*" (Italics mine.)

in the instrumental terms of biological adaptation.* The "organisms" implicated are no longer oriented pragmatically toward their
environment but ontologically as its co-knowers and co-celebrants.
Intersubjectivity may not be construed as an interaction. It requires
instead a suitable phenomenology which takes due notice of its
most characteristic property, a polarity of authenticity-unauthen-
ticity. Here a normative terminology is unavoidable. One must take
account of the authentic I-Thou relation and the deteriorated I-It of
Buber. The problem is how such a phenomenology may be related
to the great corpus of objective-empirical science. I believe that an
impartial empirical analysis of the extraordinary act of symbolization will bridge the gap between the behavioristics of Mead and the
existentialia of Marcel.

SYMBOL AND CONSCIOUSNESS

The selective and intentional character of consciousness has been
stressed by empiricists and phenomenologists alike. The conscious
act is always intentional: One is never simply conscious, but conscious of this or that. Consciousness is, in fact, defined by the phenomenologist as noematic intentionality in general.† But quite as
essential to the act of consciousness is its symbolic character. Every
conscious perception is of the nature of a recognition, a pairing,
which is to say that the object is recognized as being what it is. To
amend the phenomenologist: It is not enough to say that one is
conscious of something; one is also conscious of something as being

* When the two-year-old child discovers one day that the sound *ball* is no longer
a direction, look for ball or fetch ball, but "is" the ball for him and me, he experiences a sudden access of recognition and joy which is something quite different from
all previous need-satisfactions. (Cf. Ernest Schachtel: "According to Freud thought
has only one ancestor, the attempt at hallucinatory need-satisfaction. . . . I believe
that thought has two ancestors instead of one—namely, motivating needs *and* a distinctively human capacity the relatively autonomous capacity for object interest.")

† It is a curious fact that intentionality, one of the favorite theses of the phenomenologist, is least congenial to the solipsistic character of transcendental phenomenology. As Collins has observed, the one thing Husserl fails to explain is the intentional character of consciousness. What is intended?

something. There is a difference between the apprehension of a gestalt (a chicken perceives the Jastrow effect as well as a human) and the grasping of it under its symbolic vehicle.* As I gaze about the room, I am aware of a series of almost effortless acts of *matching*: seeing an object and then knowing it for what it is. If my eye falls upon an unfamiliar something, I am immediately aware that one term of the match is missing. I ask what it is—an exceedingly mysterious question. Marcel has observed that when I see an unfamiliar flower and ask what it is, I am more satisfied to be given a name than a scientific classification, even though the name may mean nothing to me. May this satisfaction be dismissed as a residue of name-magic, or is there a radical epistemological need of a something of comparable ontological weight (the sensuous symbol) to lay alongside the object in order that the latter be known? It is the pairing in the act of perception which must not be overlooked. It is a relation, moreover, which goes far deeper than the attaching of a label to something already known, as the semanticists suggest. Rather is it the pairing or formulation itself, as Cassirer has said, which comprises the act of knowing.† Each conscious recognition may be regarded as an approximation, a cast of one thing toward another toward the end of a fit. Thus, if I see an object at some distance and do not quite recognize it, I may see it, actually see it, as a succession of different things, each rejected by the criterion of fit as I come closer, until one is positively certified. A patch of sunlight in a field I may actually see as a rabbit—a seeing which goes much further than the guess that it may be a rabbit; no, the perceptual gestalt is so construed, actually stamped by the essence of rabbitness: I could have sworn it was a rabbit. On coming closer, the sunlight pattern changes enough so that the rabbit-cast is disal-

---

* Roy Wood Sellars used "denote" more or less interchangeably with "perceive" and "intend": ". . . we should need to distinguish between the intuition of a sensory appearance, which alone is given, and the denotative selection of a thing-object which is believed in and characterized."

† Cassirer thus stands at the opposite pole from the semanticists. So far from it being a case of a thing being known and a label later attached by a semantic rule, it is the symbolic formulation itself which is the act of knowing. The "real" object tends to vanish into Kant's noumenon.

lowed. The rabbit vanishes and I make another cast: It is a paper bag. And so on.* But most significant of all, even the last, the "correct" recognition is quite as mediate an apprehension as the incorrect ones; it is also a cast, a pairing, an approximation. And let us note in passing that even though it is correct, even though it is borne out by all indices, it may operate quite as effectively to conceal as to discover. When I recognize a strange bird as a sparrow, I tend to dispose of the bird under its appropriate formulation: It is only a sparrow (cf. Marcel's "simulacrum").

Awareness is thus not only intentional in character; it is also symbolic. The phenomenologist tells only half the story. I am not only conscious of something; I am conscious of it as being what it is for you and me. If there is a wisdom in etymologies, the word consciousness is surely a case in point; for consciousness, one suddenly realizes, means a knowing-with! In truth it could not be otherwise. The act of consciousness is the intending of the object as being what it is for both of us under the auspices of the symbol.

It does not, of course, solve the problem of consciousness to say that it is an exercise in intersubjectivity. I only wish to suggest that the conviction of the phenomenologists that intersubjectivity must somehow be constituted at the very heart of consciousness, a consummation devoutly to be desired but evidently not forthcoming under the phenomenological reduction, is illuminated and confirmed by the empirical method, a method which takes account of natural existences, organisms and symbols and objects, and real relations in the world. But I would also suggest that a recognition of the denotative function of the symbol, as a real property, yields the intersubjectivity which is not forthcoming from Mead's sign-response psychology. Consciousness and intersubjectivity are seen to be inextricably related; they are in fact aspects of the same new orientation toward the world, the symbolic orientation.

* Is not symbolization, the pairing of sensuous symbol with an impression, a kind of judgment and abstraction? In even its most primitive form, a pointing at and naming, it is a saying that that over there is "one of these." It is an abstraction, however, which is a far cry from the conventional notion of concept formation by which two given representations are combined. We must, as Cassirer says, take a step further back. This will take us to Lotze's "first universal," the primitive abstraction by which impressions are first raised to symbolizations.

This empirical insight into the intersubjective constitution of consciousness suggests an important corrective for the transcendental reduction. Is the phenomenologist's stronghold of the absolute priority of the individual consciousness so invulnerable after all? Is there in fact such a thing as the "purified transcendental consciousness" or is it a chimera from the very outset? Is it a construct masquerading as an empirical reality? If my every act of consciousness, not merely genetically speaking my first act of consciousness, but each succeeding act, is a through-and-through social participation, then it is a contradiction in terms to speak of an aboriginal ego-consciousness. There may be such a thing as an isolated ego-consciousness, but far from being the apodictic take-off point of a presuppositionless science, it would seem to correspond to Buber's term of deterioration, the decay of the I-Thou relation into the objectivization of the I-It. It would appear that the transcendental phenomenologist is seizing upon a social emergent, consciousness, abstracting it from its social matrix, and erecting a philosophy upon this pseudo-private derivative. But the organism does not so begin. The *I think* is only made possible by a prior mutuality: *we name.*

Sartre's even more radical revision of the transcendental consciousness falls that much shorter of the mark. Declaring that the Cartesian *cogito* is insufficiently radical, that it is a derived condition of consciousness in which consciousness intends itself as an object, Sartre probes back to the "prereflective *cogito.*" This fundamental reality is a nonposited, nonobjectified, prereflective consciousness. But is there such a thing? Or is it not the very nature of the search that the most radical backtracking into consciousness cannot carry us beyond what Marcel calls the "intersubjective milieu," by which he means the prime and irreducible character of intersubjectivity?

Mead's major thesis was that the individual transcendental consciousness is a myth, that mind and consciousness are indefeasibly social realities. This thesis, it seems to me, is not borne out by Mead's behavioristics, however refined, but is dramatically confirmed as soon as the peculiar character of the symbolic orientation is recognized.

Sartre would amend the Cartesian and Husserlian formula for the originary act of consciousness,

I am conscious of this chair,

to read,

There is consciousness of this chair,

both of which single out the individual consciousness itself as the prime reality. An empirical study of the emergence of symbolization from the biological elements of signification suggests the further revision of Sartre:

This "is" a chair for you and me,

which co-celebration of the chair under the auspices of the symbol is itself the constituent act of consciousness.

13

SYMBOL AS HERMENEUTIC

IN EXISTENTIALISM

IF IT IS TRUE that both Anglo-American empiricism and European existentialism contain valid insights, then in respect of the failure to make a unifying effort toward giving an account of all realities, the former is surely the worse offender. For the existentialists do take note of empirical science, if only to demote it to some such category as problem *Seiendes*, or passionate abstract. But the empiricists are notably indifferent toward existentialism. In the empirical mind, existential categories are apt to be dismissed as "emotional" manifestations, that is, as dramatic expressions of a particular historical circumstance, or—what is worse—as exhortatory, and deserving the same attention as any other pulpiteering. Such notions as dread, *Dasein*, boredom, and the dichotomies authenticity–unauthenticity, freedom–falling-prey-to, aesthetic–ethical, will inevitably appear as *reducibles*—if they have any meaning at all. Whatever significance they have will be assumed to yield itself in their objective correlates.

That empiricism has not found a fruitful method of dealing with these distinctively human realities is no mere normative judgment but may be inferred from the confusion of the social sciences themselves. If there is an unresolved dualism of questioner-and-nature in the professed monism of the empiricist, its difficulties do not become apparent as long as the questions are asked of nature. The canons of induction-deduction hold good: data, induction, hypothesis, deduction, test, verification, prediction, planning. But as soon as the data come to comprise not the physical world or subhuman biology but other questioners, other existents, the empirical method finds itself in certain notorious difficulties (1) The imperialism of the social sciences. As long as there is one datum man and several disciplines, each professing a different irreducible—i.e., cultural unit, libido, social monad, genetic trait—there is bound to result a deordination of the sciences of man with each claiming total competence and each privately persuaded that the other is pursuing a chimera. (2) The transcending of the questioner by his own data. Sociological material resists fixed inductions. A familiar example is the transposition of a biological method, the human subject conceived as an organism with an inventory of "needs," with "cultural needs" as well as caloric needs. But the delineation of a "cultural need" tends to bring about the transcendence of this need by the very fact of its delineation. (3) The practice of smuggling in existential activities in a deterministic discipline. In psychoanalysis, for example, which in Freud's words derives all mental processes from an interplay of forces, the crucial act of therapy is the exercise by the patient of a *choice*, that is, the assumption of a burden of effort in overcoming resistances. (4) The uncritical taking for granted or the equally uncritical ignoring of consciousness and intersubjectivity. Behaviorism ignores both, but what account can behaviorism give of the behavior of the questioner himself? The sociologist and anthropologist practice intersubjectivity; that is, they are not content merely to observe the externals of cultural traits— they try to understand the meaning of them. But what account are they prepared to give of this intersubjectivity? If Kant called it a "scandal of philosophy" that intersubjectivity had found no solution in the thought of his day, it is no less a scandal now.

Perhaps the difficulties arise not through an innate limitation of empiricism—an experiential and heterodox empiricism which, according to Hocking, would include the method of Gabriel Marcel—but because of what Dawson calls the religious presuppositions of a naturalist social science. The doctrinal precondition of this particular kind of "theological" sociology is that (1) the sociology is of the same order of determinism as physical science, (2) man is a fixed social unit, an integer, and can be regarded as a receptacle of quantifiable needs. Having laid down such a substratum, the social scientist deprives himself of the means of taking notice of existentialia in his data, let alone of giving an account of them.

But the existentialists suffer in their own way from the same deordination of the ways of knowing as the empiricists. In the Anglo-American view, existential insights appear to be "in the air"—either manifestly reducible or insufficiently grounded by causal strata. The confusion among the existentialist only confirms these suspicions. To some (Kierkegaard) the existentialia are psychological, to others (Heidegger) ontological, that is, they are the constituent traits of *Dasein*. Phenomenological bracketing is taken by the empiricist to be a confession of causal rootlessness.

The need of the empirical sciences of man is of an insight, a proper empirical finding, that will *introduce* an order of reality, a reality of existential traits, which latter, if they cannot be reduced to supposedly prime elements or verified by measurement, can at least be validated experientially and hierarchically grounded in a genuinely empirical framework.

The need of existentialism—in the empirical view at least—is a deliverance from Kantian subjectivity, whether it be Sartrean or Jasperian. As Collins puts it, the task is to take account of Kierkegaard without surrendering to Kant. This is to be achieved, as far as the sciences of man are concerned, not by a precipitous search for a regional ontology, such as the ontologizing of the existentialia of the *Dasein*, but by an "open" experiential empiricism which tacitly posits the world. After all, scientific method has never had much use for the Kantian Copernican revolution. But in the empirical view, the ordination of the sciences, if it is to be accomplished at all, must be accomplished from "below," that is, from an empirically valid substratum.

The necessary bridge from traditional empiricism to existential insights may have already been supplied—unwittingly, and from the empirical side of the gulf—by the study of that particular human

activity in which empiricism intersects, so to speak, with existentialism—language. It is the discovery of the symbolic transformation as the unique and universal human response.

Its crucial importance lies in its recognition as belonging to an
order radically different from the purely behaviorist or causal theory
of meaning. As Susanne Langer points out, any attempt to reduce
the symbol function to a signal process will leave out precisely that
which is unique in the symbolic relationship. A symbol is the
vehicle for the conception of an object and not a term in a reflex
schema which directs the organism to a referent.

The inadequacy of doctrinal empiricism and the deliverance of
the symbolic transformation are perhaps best illustrated by beginning with the emblem of positivist semiotic, Ogden and Richards's
triangle symbol-reference-referent. This relation is alleged to be a
refinement of the signal-significatum relation and is to be conceived in a strictly causal context. Meaning is a stimulus-response
sequence in which reference follows symbol in the same way as dog
salivation follows the buzzer signal. As Charles Morris puts it, a
symbol is nothing more than a signal produced by the interpretent
which acts as a substitute for some other sign with which it is
synonymous. Thus in the absence of food, when the buzzer
sounds, hunger cramps may come to be a "symbol" for food.

What is omitted in this schema is the obvious but nonetheless
extraordinary characteristic of symbolization—that the symbol *denotes* something. It is the *name* of something. It is the vehicle by
which we are able to speak and perhaps to think about something.
The relationship between symbol and conception is generically and
irreducibly different from the purely causal order of signal-significatum.

It is the very indispensability of the role which symbolization
plays in cognition which prevents our seeing its unprecedented
character. The most graphic warrant for its uniqueness and for the
qualitative difference between the signal world and the symbol
world is the unwitting testimony of blind deaf-mutes like Helen
Keller and Laura Bridgeman.

Of the many consequences of the insight into the uniqueness of the symbolic function, there are two or three which are particularly relevant to our purpose.

Once it dawns upon one, whether deaf-mute or not, that *this is water*, then the first question is *What is that*, and so on, toward the end that *everything is something*. There has come into existence an all-construing mode of cognition in which everything must be formulated symbolically and known intentionally *as* something. There is a need for formulation of such a degree that that which is not fixed and formulated by the symbol is the source of a disability before the thing which, depending upon the formidability of the thing, can range from a simple insentience—not "knowing" the thing because it has not been named for one—to acute anxiety before a pressing something which is unformulated.

Besides the symbol, the conception, and the thing, there are two other terms which are quite as essential in the act of symbolization. There is the "I," the consciousness which is confronted by the thing and which generates the symbol by which the conception is articulated. But there is also the "you." *Symbolization is of its very essence an intersubjectivity.* If there were only one person in the world, symbolization could not conceivably occur (but signification could); for my discovery of water as something derives from your telling me so, that this is water for you too. The act of symbolization is an affirmation: Yes, this is water! My excitement derives from the discovery that it is there for you and me and that it is the same thing for you and me. Every act of symbolization thereafter, whether it be language, art, science, or even thought, must occur either in the presence of a real you or an ideal you for whom the symbol is intended as meaningful. *Symbolization presupposes a triad of existents: I, the object, you.* Hocking suggests that the symbol arises from the direct experiential knowledge that "We are." But surely it is that the "We are" follows upon and is mediated by the symbolization, the joint affirmation that *this is water*.

What has this to do with existentialism?

We will pass over the epistemological consequences of symbolic knowing, the possession of the thing by the symbol rather than adaptation by signal—a knowing which is indeed existential in the broad sense of knowing something by being something—and go at once to the more typical existentialia. The recognition of the uniquely human use of the symbol will provide insights into the favorite concepts of existentialism—serving by no means as a key to their reducibility but as an hermeneutic toward the grounding and ordering of human realities in a hierarchical but nonetheless empirically valid scheme. The act of symbolization is to be conceived as a threshold beyond which new entities come into being, not by fiat, but precisely as they are enabled by the symbol.

(1) The symbolic predicament of Self. (a) The Self, the object, and the thou.

A study of the aboriginal symbol relation will be seen to be highly relevant for the existentialia, in particular as it illuminates and rectifies existential theories about the nature of consciousness.

Sartre, for example, ontologizes the primary transphenomenal consciousness as the being-for-itself, and the transphenomenal object as being-in-itself. The prime reality of human consciousness is accordingly not the Cartesian *cogito* but a pure impersonal awareness, the "prereflective *cognito.*" Such an entity is probably fictitious, however, since consciousness is of its nature intersubjective. The originary act of consciousness is the joint affirmation that the object is there for you and me. The formula for the "prereflective *cogito*" is properly not the Cartesian

   I am conscious of this chair

nor the Sartrean

   There is consciousness of this chair

both of which *presuppose* consciousness but

   This *is* a chair for you and me

which joint act of designation and affirmation by symbol *is itself* the constituent act of consciousness.

The symbolic corrective is that both the empiricists and the existentialists (excepting Marcel) are wrong in positing an autonomous consciousness, whether a series of conscious "states" or a solitary subjective existent. The decisive stroke against the myth of the autonomous Kantian subject is the intersubjective constitution of consciousness. There is a mutuality between the I and the Thou and the object which is in itself prime and irreducible. Once, in theorizing, this relation is ruptured, it cannot be recovered thereafter—witness the failure of both Sartre and the empiricists to give an account of intersubjectivity.

Thus the two term subject-object division of the world, as the situation in which one finds oneself, is not the original predicament of consciousness but rather a decadent "unauthentic" state, a falling away from an earlier communion.

(b) The self and the symbolized other. The world of the Nought and the world of the Other. Being-for-itself and Being-in-itself. Self as Nought.

It is of the nature of the symbol-mongering consciousness to delineate and transform all sensory data into intentional symbolic forms. The whole objectizing act of the mind is to render all things *darstellbar*, not "proper" but presentable, that is, formulable. The world before me is divided and configured into a great assembly of autonomous and resplendent forms. The naming judgment, This is a chair, That flower is a lupin—an identification which, as Marcel says, satisfies a peculiar need which has nothing to do with the definatory uses of the name—this naming act is both existential and figurative. It affirms that this *is* something, but in so rescuing the object from the flux of becoming, it pays the price of setting it forth as a static and isolated entity—a picture-book entity. But at any rate it is the requirement of consciousness that everything *be* something and willy-nilly everything *is* something—*with one tremendous exception!* The one thing in the world which by its very nature is not susceptible of a stable symbolic transformation is *myself!* I, who symbolize the world in order to know it, am destined to remain forever unknown to myself. The self, that which symbolizes, will, if it perverts its native project of being conscious of something else and tries to grasp itself as a something, either fail and remain as the unformulable, a nothingness (Sartre), the aching

wound of self (Marcel)—or it will fall prey to miserable unauthentic transformations (the impersonations of Marcel and Sartre, and
in primitive life, the totemic transformation: In the importunate
need for construing all things, the self in its terrible inscrutability is
as capable of being one thing as another; I can as well "be" a
parakeet as an alligator—anything at all is more tolerable than the
vacuum which I am). As Marcel puts it: *It may be of my essence to
be able to be not what I am.*

The motto of the symbolic (and existential) predicament is: This
is a chair for you and me, that is a tree, everything is something,
you are what you are, but *what am I?*

In the situation-in-which-we-find-ourselves, two zones can be
delineated, the zone of the nought and zone of the other. The
nought of the self is not confined to the enclosure of the knower,
but is expansile. The zone of the nought is coextensive with the
domain of my property, in which there is a simultaneous exercise
of my sovereignty of having and the exclusion of the other's having.
Yet what paradoxically characterizes the zone of having is the progressive annihilation of forms, an emptying out and a rendering
nought by the very act of having. In the "passive unauthentic self
which has fallen prey to things," new things enter into the zone of
the nought and are devoured. There is a real consumption of
goods. A new product, an automobile, resplendent in its autonomous form (and endowed, we shall see later, with certain
magic properties by virtue of the mystery and remotion of its manu-
facture) is loved for the sake of its form—what characterizes an
idolatrous desire for a new car is not the need of a means of getting
from one place to another but a prime desire to *have* the car itself.
If I can have that car, my life will be different, for my nothingness
will be informed by the having of it. But possession turns out to be
a gradual neutralization. Once it enters the zone of my nought, the
car is emptied out and, instead of informing me, only participates
in my nothingness. There is a dynamic quest for resplendent
forms—in two separate moments: the assumption of identities (impersonations), and the consumption of goods (in order to be informed by them).

(2) The ambiguity of the Thou. The Thou is at once the source of my consciousness, the companion and co-celebrant of my discovery of being—and the sole threat to my unauthentic constitution of myself.

The Thou is different from the other forms around me in that, while it can be objectized and relegated to the order of the stable configuration, it tends under certain conditions (the stare) to escape symbolization and to recover its unique and indispensable role in the sustaining and validating of my consciousness. When Sartre instances the stare of another as the supreme aggression, he is uncovering but one of two extreme alternatives. The look is of the order of pure intersubjectivity without the mediation of the symbol, and if it can be hatred in the exposure of my impersonation, it can also be love in the communion of selves. The unique importunacy of the look of another, the guardianship which one exercises over one's own look, and the urgent need to deal with the look of another, derive from a tacit recognition of the absolute character of the alternatives—a look can only be an aggression or a communion, nothing else. It is not formulable. In the exchange of stares everything is at stake. *L'enfer c'est autrui.* But so is heaven. My vulnerability before the look derives from the aboriginal triadic communion of consciousness. The Thou is the knower, the namer, the co-inspector with me of the common thing and the authority for its name. Whatever devious constitution of self I have been able to arrive at, whatever my "self-system," my impersonation, it melts away before the steady gaze of another.

Sartre is surely mistaken in analyzing the source of my shame at being caught out in an unworthy performance by the look of another. It is the other's objectizing me, he says, that makes me ashamed. I had been aware of myself as not strictly coinciding with what I am. But when he looks at me, "I am sitting like that ink pot on the table . . . my original fall is the existence of the other, and shame is, in the same way as pride, the *becoming aware of myself as a nature.*" But surely it is the other way around. What is revealed, as it seems to me, in the discovering look of another, is literally my *unspeakableness* (unformulability). To be taken for a nature, an ink pot, would be the purest happiness. No. I am exposed—as what? not as a something—as *nothing*, as that which unlike everything else in the world cannot be rendered *darstellbar*.

Who is the Thou that gazes at me? Whoever he may be and despite the importunacy of his gaze and the need at any cost to come to terms with it. I know one thing about him—he is an existent. However successfully I may have been able to objectize him, when he looks at me, his being escapes through his eyes. As Marcel says, it is of the nature of the other that he *exists*.

The Sartrean elevation of nothingness as the prime reality of the human existent, the awarding of priority to existence over essence, is perhaps a confusion of the psychological and the ontological orders, a mistaking of human being for the predicament of consciousness. When Matthieu stops in the middle of Pont Neuf and discovers his freedom in his nothingness—"Within me there is nothing, not even a wisp of smoke; there is no within. There is nothing. I am free"—he is after all only hypostasizing the unformulability of self. The telltale sign is his elation, his sense of having at last discovered his identity. He is something after all—Nothing! And in so doing, is he not committing the same impersonation which Sartre so severely condemns in others? If the structure of consciousness is intentional, to be of its essence directed toward the other, a being-towards, then the ontologizing of this self-unformulability as Nought is as perverse as any other impersonation—really a kind of inferior totemism.

Yet even Sartrean existentialism can only be edifying to the empirical mind. For whatever the sins of bad faith of an existentialism which *postulates* atheism, it has been able to recover that which the empiricist in his obsessive quest for reducibility and quantification has lost—the uniqueness of human being.

Prescinding entirely from final ontological constructions as befits an empirical science, and approaching existential realities solely in the light of an empirical finding—the uniquely human symbolic transformation—a science of man can only prove true to itself by seeing the human existent for what, at its minimum reach, it really is—not a quantifiable integer, a receptable of biological needs and so susceptible to fixed inductions, but a transcending reality, and hence a reality which can be studied, not by an uncritical transposition of the method of physical science, but by a broad and untrammelled empiricism, a sensitivity and a neutrality before structures which will neither rule out nor preconceive causal connections for reason of doctrinal requirement.

14

SYMBOL AS NEED

AFTER READING *Feeling and Form*, Susanne Langer's extraordinary work on aesthetics, one inevitably goes back to her earlier book *Philosophy in a New Key*, of which according to the author the former is the companion volume—not just to get one's bearings in the general semiotic on which the aesthetic is based, but in all curiosity to trace out the origins of what is surely an ambiguity in the thought of the recent study. *Feeling and Form* is written with all the power and contagious excitement of first-class mind exercising a valuable new insight. In brief, it is an application to art of her general thesis that the peculiarly human response is that of symbolic transformation. The communication of meaning, positivists to the contrary, is not limited to the discursive symbol, word, and proposition; the art symbol conveys its own appropriate meaning, a meaning inaccessible to the discursive form. In each medium, the virtual space of the painting, the virtual life of the poem, the virtual time of music, the form which is created represents, *symbolizes*—not just the thousand and one subject matters of the various arts but rather the *feelings*, the *felt life* of the artist and so of the observer. Music symbolizes passage, "the form of growth and attenuation, flowing and stowing, conflict and resolution," the pattern in time of sentience. (Here it is worth pointing out that the "feelings" that Mrs. Langer talks about are not at all feelings in the modern sense of the word, that is, "emotions," amorphous affect, but rather the *form* of sentience, a notion which it would be interesting to compare with the Thomist concept of the tendential forms of orexis.)

Not the least remarkable thing in a remarkable book is how very close at times she comes to a Scholastic view of art, and that in a theorist with an otherwise encyclopedic grasp of her subject, there is not a single reference to Maritain or any other Scholastic source (not that *this* is surprising from the author of *Philosophy in a New Key*). This resemblance may be noted without in the least suggesting that her theory should be judged by a Scholastic standard of aesthetics, if indeed there is any such thing, or that she is approaching analogously "what the Schoolmen knew all along"—for the fact is that her contribution is in the highest degree original and potent in its unifying effect, and if any one thing is certain it is that she owes not the slightest debt to a Scholastic source. As we shall see, she has the most compelling of all reasons—one's own philosophical presuppositions—for steering as far clear of Scholasticism as ever she can, and so it is all the more remarkable that from such a heroically disinterested source there should come forth

> The making of the symbol is the musician's entire problem, as it is, indeed, every artist's.

That, whereas language is the discursive symbol, the word symbolizing the concept,

> Art is the creation of forms symbolic of human feelings.

> That is why [because it gives the forms of imagination] it has the force of a revelation and inspires a feeling of deep intellectual satisfaction, though it elicits no consciousness of intellectual work (reasoning).

And in protest against Croce's equating "intellectual" and "discursive":

> But by contemplating intuition as direct experience, not mediated, not correlated to anything public, we cannot record or systematize them, let alone construct a "science" of intuitive knowledge which will be the true analogue of logic.

Compare with Maritain

> The sphere of Making is the sphere of Art.

> Art is above all intellectual.

Beauty is essentially the object of *intelligence,* for what *knows* in the full meaning of the word is the mind.

. . . it is mind and sense combined, the intellectualized sense which gives rise to aesthetic joy in the heart.

. . . the splendor or radiance of form glittering in the beautiful thing is not presented to the mind by a concept or an idea but precisely by a sensible object, intuitively apprehended.

The capital error in Benedetto Croce's neo-Hegelian aesthetics . . . is the failure to perceive that artistic contemplation, however *intuitive* it may be, is none the less above all intellectual. Aesthetics ought to be intellectual and intuitivist at the same time.

Maritain is more explicit about the dual role of the art symbol in his latest work than in *Art and Scholasticism.*

Be it painting or poem, this work is made object—in it alone does poetic intuition come to objectivization. And it must always preserve its own consistence and value as *object.* But at the same time it is a sign— both a *direct* sign of secrets perceived in things, of some irrecusable truth of nature of adventure caught in the great universe, and a *reversed sign* of the subjective universe of the poet, of his substantial *Self* obscurely revealed.

A text from Thomas Aquinas is interesting in this connection:

Therefore beauty consists in proper proportion because the sense derives pleasure from things properly proportioned *as being similar to itself* for sense also is a kind of reason (*logos tis*) like every cognitive virtue and as knowledge comes about through assimilation and similtude is concerned with form, the beautiful strictly pertains to the concept of a formal cause.

It is apparently Saint Thomas and not Mrs. Langer or Cassirer who had the first inkling of the mysterious analogy between the form of beauty and the pattern of the inner life.

It is not intended here to make out a case but only to draw attention to a rather remarkable example of two thinkers converging on the same truths from opposed positions and—unlike experimental science—each arriving and remaining unaware of the other. For although the idioms are different—to read one after the other, it is necessary to make a conscious shift of media, like changing

languages—they are both saying the same things: (1) that art is a
making and appreciation is a *knowing*, intellectual but peculiarly
distinct from discursive knowing, and that delight is secondary and
logically subsequent to the knowing; (2) that the art symbol represents both thing and self. It is a formidable construction indeed that
is arrived at from exactly opposite directions, from a logical empiricism in one and a theistic realism in the other—though perhaps
it must be allowed that in order of achievement, in her breaking
away from the restrictive *a prioris* of pragmatism and psycholo-
gism, the experiential aesthetics of Dewey, and the "minute stimuli"
aesthetics of Richards, and in respect of the powerful and *explicit*
delineation of a uniquely human faculty, it is Mrs. Langer who has
come the longer way.

Since, however, her naturalism is apparently as stoutly avowed as
ever, and since at the same time her debt to Cassirer and idealism
is freely acknowledged, we turn or return to *Philosophy in a New
Key* to discover how she has come to this pass, from logical positivism (she wrote a textbook on the subject) to a near-realistic aesthetic by way of idealism—and kept her old allegiance, or
whether, in truth, she has. What we must evaluate are the consequences of her insight, what she calls her "heresy," for an empirical science of man. Has she exposed a fatal weakness in an exclusively empirical semiotic and anthropology, deliberately in the
former and perhaps inadvertently in the latter? Is her heresy, in
short, an apostasy?

It is part of the stock in trade of *Philosophy in a New Key*—one of
the unquestioned assumptions-behind-the-questions which, as Mrs.
Langer says, are the most interesting thing about any philosophy—that the development of thought is linear. The history of philosophy could be written as the periodic sloughing of worn-out
world views in favor of new generative ideas, of new ways of conceiving the world (she does not distinguish science and philosophy).
The contrary notion, that truly generative ideas might be centripe-
tal in action, that is, that they might progressively illuminate and
specify a perennial humanist philosophy, is not allowed in court.
Thus the Cartesian *cogito* can *only* be seen as one in a series of

generative ideas because by the very nature of things there can be no criteriology to discriminate and measure, on the one hand, the unquestioned service of Descartes in clearing the decks of a corrupt Scholasticism, or on the other, the disastrous effects of the mind-matter split. She is committed to the uniform and irreversible action of her "generative ideas." The worth of an idea is measured by the enthusiasm it generates; there is no good and bad to it. And so the later difficulties of Cartesianism must be ascribed to just the inevitable exhaustion of a great concept rather than the reaping of noxious tares planted in the beginning.

The naturalist orthodoxy of *Philosophy in a New Key* is well known, indeed repeatedly avowed (could the wheel have come full turn?—one can't help thinking of the protestations of Christian orthodoxy by Hobbes and Locke), but what is not recognized as widely is the thorough wrecking job done on behaviorist theories of meaning.

The new key in philosophy—and a truly exciting idea it is—is the universal symbolific function of the human mind. The failure of behaviorism to give an adequate account of meaning has been pointed out before (Urban, Barfield). Charles Morris has tried to justify a purely behaviorist semiotic on a methodological basis, declaring that his purpose is simply to advance semiotic as a science, and that there can be no science where there is no observable behavior. This conclusion might be warranted if it were true, as he assumes, that the symbolific function in the human is of the same order as the signal function in the animal. The fact is, however, as Mrs. Langer so admirably sets forth, that it is radically different, and any science which assumes that the symbolic transformation is but a genetic extension of the function of signification must omit precisely that which is peculiar to human semiotic.

For once and for all, we hope, Mrs. Langer has made clear the generic difference between sign and symbol, between the subject-sign-object triad and the subject-symbol-conception-object tetrad. Signs announce their objects. Thunder announces rain. The bell announces food to Pavlov's dog. When I say James to a dog, he *looks* for James; when I say James to you, you say, "What about him?"—you *think* about James. A symbol is the vehicle for the conception of an object and as such is a distinctively human product.

This distinction of sign function and symbol function, she admits, is in direct contravention of the old biogenetic motto: *Nihil est in homine quod non prius in amoeba erat.* Heretofore the symbol function had been hailed by the psychogeneticists as a useful variation of the sign function, enabling man the better to adapt to his environment—and likened, we all remember, to the telephone exchange with its trick of sidetracking and storing messages. That it does not so operate is sufficiently attested by the positivists themselves (Ogden and Richards, Korzybski, Chase, Ritchie, *et al.*) who somewhat anachronistically complain about man's abuse of language and scold him for his perversities. All in all, the anthropologists and geneticists have had a bad time of it in their attempts to fit man's manifold follies into a plausible evolutionary scheme. It is as if he had not proven worthy of a decent evolutionary past.

Although Mrs. Langer credits several sources for the discovery of the new idea—namely, physical science, logical positivism, mathematics, Freudian analysis, German idealism—it would appear from her subsequent thought that the empirical and logical disciplines have actually had very little to do with the truly generative force of the idea, that is, the transformational character of the symbol function. Such arbitrary designations, for example, as let x equal an unknown, let a equal a variable, let p equal a proposition, are indeed symbol formations in the sense that x and a and p are convenient substitute counters for unwieldy concepts and so can be used in calculations. But this simple proxy relation would seem to have little bearing on the far more seminal and revolutionary concept of symbol as vehicle for meaning, the sensory form which is in itself the medium for organizing and re-presenting meaning.

It is the idealists and notably Ernst Cassirer who must be credited with the clearest explication of the peculiar nature of the symbol; and it is Mrs. Langer's distinction to have rescued it from the toils of idealism. After a shrewd look at the metaphysical antecedents of the insight, she saw clearly that there is no reason why it must remain as the end product of speculation on a world spirit and whatnot, that in fact it only achieved its true vitality when seen as detached: as a finding, a human activity, and the beginning rather than the end of a science. (It is curious that Cassirer in his youth foundered on the same rock as the naturalists: the difficulty of reconciling human stupidity with a monist view of reality. But instead of throwing up his hands at folly, he began to study it as a significant human activity and it was in this pursuit—in the act of boarding a streetcar, he relates—that the great idea came to him that by the symbol man conceives the world.)

Cassirer asks the question, How can a sensory content become the vehicle of meaning? and answers in effect that it cannot, unless it, the symbol, the word, the rite, the art form, itself *constitutes* the meaning. (And here, as much as in Hegel, or for that matter, as in naturalist anthropology, there is excluded in the assumption any criterion of truth or value except an evolutionary one—in this case the extent to which the symbol is elaborated: Thus the Mass is indeed a "higher" form than a native dog dance, but only in the sense that it is more highly developed.) According to Cassirer, the only alternative to an idealist theory of meaning is a skeptical one, and to Urban the particular skepticism of the causal sign theories. As Richards puts it: We can never expect to know what things are but only how they hang together.

How indeed *can* a sensible, a vocable, an odd little series of squeaks and grunts, *mean* anything, represent anything? Therein surely lies the mystery of language. The word *buttermilk* and the word *William* (if I know a William) mean, represent, the objects referred to in a wholly different sense than thunder means rain, and different too from the etymological intention of the word. There is an articulation of word to thing so powerful that word can still be taken for thing (i.e., the false onomatopoeia of words like *fuzzy, scream, limber, slice*). Is not a profound avenue of thought opened up by the realization that the sound I make can become for me the thing I see? Marcel has said that when I ask, "What is that flower?" I am not satisfied merely to be given a definition. I am only sa-

tisfied to be told, "That flower is a lupin," even though the word
lupin may convey nothing to me.

> But now we find the real paradox—the first unscientific answer,
> which consisted in giving the name of the flower, although it had prac-
> tically no rational basis, yet satisfied the demand in me which the in-
> terpretation by reduction tends on the contrary to frustrate.

Can this satisfaction be dismissed as just a prelogical remnant of
the superstition of identifying words with things, or is this "superstition" in fact the very condition of our knowledge (and our ignorance)? When I am told as a child that this flower is a lupin, when
you name something for me and I confirm it by saying it too—what
I know now is not only that the flower *is* something but that it is
something for you and me. Our common existence is validated. It
is the foundation of what Marcel calls the metaphysics of *we are* instead of *I think*.

What then is this extraordinary faculty, if as Mrs. Langer believes, it is neither a refinement of an animal function nor an idealist *logos* which constitutes the world? It is, according to Mrs.
Langer, a *basically human need*.

> This basic need, which is certainly obvious only in man, is the need
> of symbolization.

Symbolization is the essential act of the mind, whether it be in art,
in language, in rite, in dreams, in logic, and as such cannot be
grasped by conventional biological concepts. It is an "elementary
need" of the new cerebral cortex. There is no other way, it appears,
of accounting for the "impractical" uses of language and the "perversity of ritual."

Now something is wrong here.

In what sense does Mrs. Langer speak of a "need"? Everyone
agrees that in the genetic or naturalist schema the responses of an
organism to the environment are adaptive and are specified by the
needs of the organism. These needs are variously characterized as
sex, hunger, defense, etc., but are all reducible to the service of
two basic biological requirements: maintenance of the internal mi-

lieu and parturition. Moreover, a response can be evaluated simply by the degree of success with which it fulfills the need. Now how can the *basic human need of symbolization* be subsumed under these valid biological categories? Can it be subsumed at all, except nominally: by calling it a "need," a need of symbolization as there is a need of food? One represents things by symbols simply because one needs to do so. But a need in the biological sense is always but one term in a functional schema, thus, for example: need: sex, manifesting as drive: sexual activity, serving the function: propagation of species. Simply to call the symbolic transformation a need and let it go at that is to set up an autonomous faculty which serves its own ends, the equivalent of saying that bees store honey because there is in bees a need of storing honey.

This is an intolerable disjunction, intolerable from any reasoned point of view, whether it be materialism, idealism, or realism. On the one hand, Mrs. Langer has seen that the naturalist theory of meaning, however admirable may be its effort to account for all meaning under the one rubric of causal relation between organism and environment, leaves out precisely what she has hit upon as the very essence of meaning—on the other, she senses that there is no reason at all to drag in the whole apparatus of idealism with its denial of subsistent reality.

If the language symbol is not just a sign in an adaptive schema, and if it does not itself constitute reality but rather represents something, *then what does it represent?*

It is regrettably at this point that she drops the whole epistemological problem, so charged with implications, and turns to aesthetics. There she sets forth to perfection the truly distinctive character of the symbol: that it neither signifies another meaning nor constitutes meaning anew, but that it re-presents something. And so she can speak of the truth and falsity of the art symbol, according as it does or does not succeed in representing its subject.

If, by the same token, it ever be admitted in the field of cognition that the symbolic transformation is not an end in itself, a "need," but a means, a means of *knowing*, even as is the art symbol—then the consequences are serious indeed. For it will be knowledge, not in the sense of possessing "facts" but in the Thomist and existential sense of identification of the knower with the object known. Is it not possible that this startling semantic insight, that by the word I *have* the thing, fix it, and rescue it from the flux of Becoming around me, might not confirm and illuminate the mysterious Thomist notion of the interior word, of knowing something by becoming something? that the "basic need of symbolization" is nothing more or less than the first ascent in the hierarchy of knowledge, the eminently "natural" and so all the more astonishing instrument by which I transform the sensory content and appropriate it for the stuff of my ideas, and that therefore the activity of knowing cannot be evaluated according to the "degree to which it fills a biological need," nor according to the "degree to which the symbol is articulated," but by nothing short of Truth itself?

It must remain to be seen how valuable a hermeneutic of knowledge Mrs. Langer's new key will prove to be. We may admire the intrepidity with which she sets forth without regard for philosophical labels or consequences, while at the same time reserving the right to examine these latter, especially in view of her professions of allegiance. It is not impossible that the consequences of this particular "generative idea" may surprise even its gifted delineator.

15

A THEORY OF LANGUAGE

A Martian View of Linguistic Theory,
Plus the Discovery That an Explanatory Theory
Does Not Presently Exist, Plus the Offering
of a Crude Explanatory Model on the Theory
That Something Is Better than Nothing

ALTHOUGH THE WRITER of this paper is not, strictly speaking, a Martian, his distance from and innocence of standard linguistic disciplines is, if not extraterrestial, at least extralinguistic. Accordingly, this paper can commend itself to readers more by reason of its ignorance than its knowledge. What virtues it may have are mainly those of its perspective. I do not presume to compare myself to the boy who noticed that the king was naked nor linguists to the king's subjects. Yet innocence—and distance—may have its uses. Just as a view of the earth from space may reveal patterns in forested areas and deserts which might be missed by the most expert foresters and geographers—because they are too close—so it is that what follows is what might be seen from a Martian perspective, that is to say, a perspective worlds removed from the several admirable disciplines of linguistics.

Imagine, anyhow, a Martian astronaut of average intelligence and an average scientific education. He lands on earth with the assignment of making a brief survey of the status of earth sciences. After taking cram courses in physical, chemical, and biological sciences, he reads up all he can on theoretical linguistics. Upon his return to Mars, and after thinking things over, he fancies he can see a thing or two which might be useful to earth linguists—by virtue of his perspective. It is somewhat as if he had been in orbit a hundred years ago when Sir Richard Burton and Captain Speke were thrashing around East Africa in search of the Nile's source. From his altitude the astronaut can beam down instructions to the explorers: "No no no! You're too far west! Head due east and in fifty miles you'll strike a large body of fresh water. Proceed north along shore until . . ."

What the Martian sees in the case of earth linguistics is a, to him at least, remarkable bifurcation of theoretical effort of such a nature that the central phenomenon is straddled and, as he sees it, largely missed—as if Speke were on one side of Lake Victoria and Burton on the other. There is, on the one hand, a triumphant tradition in modern linguistics taking several forms and variously named, "descriptive," "structural," "transformational," associated with people like Bloomfield, Harris, Chomsky—varied theoretical approaches, to be sure, yet sharing one important trait in common: that of approaching the phenomenon of language through a formal analysis of the corpora of languages, an analysis which abstracts both from the people who speak the language and the things they talk about. Semantics or the relation between words and things, the Martian notices, is mentioned now and then but is treated by and large like a bastard at a family reunion. Kinship is admitted, yes—after all words are often used to mean things—but the visitor does not exactly fit into the family. He, the Martian, recalls, for example, Bloomfield's model where "experience" is stuck onto an otherwise neat hierarchy of phonemes, morphemes, and such, somewhat like a sore thumb; or the transformation model (Chomsky) which specifies a "central syntactic component" to which a somewhat mysterious "interpretive semantic component" is added as a kind of afterthought.

This is one branch of the bifurcation then, the structural-descriptive-generative analysis of language as a corpus. The other branch is not so much a working science as it is a shared belief, a faith that human language must surely be of such-and-such an order. Until a few years ago it was set down, again with all the fervor of an article of faith, that human language must not be different in kind from communication in other species. Proposals to the contrary were taken as a rejection of the entire scientific tradition of the West (Hockett). The traditional model was of course that of the behaviorists and learning theorists with one or another refinement, for example, Bloomfield's notion of language as "secondary response." The trouble was that this model worked only in carefully chosen cases: Jack getting thirsty and saying "Water" and Jill going up the hill to fetch it, or Malinowski's example of the Trobriand Island fisherman shouting "Mackerel here!" whereupon other fishermen respond by paddling over. But the theory didn't seem to work when, the fishing over, the feast eaten, the islanders were sitting around the fire spinning tales about long past or mythical events.

No less astonishing to the Martian is the more recent countervailing view that human language is utterly *unlike* animal communication (Chomsky), so much so that it was felt necessary to revive the old Rationalist notion of innate ideas to account for it (Chomsky). Maybe Hockett was right after all. Anyhow, what strikes the Martian most about the controversy is the extreme character of the alternatives. If he understands correctly, it appears as if, once the inadequacy of the behaviorist model is admitted, one has no choice but to chuck "empiricism," rummage in the philosophical attic, and dust off a somewhat decrepit mind-body dualism. Surely, thinks the Martian, empiricism as it applies to science is not a dogma about the nature of the mind—that it is a *tabula rasa* or whatever—but rather a proposition about the practice of the scientific method, namely, that the scientist relies on data which he obtains through his senses, to account for which he constructs theories and models, and to confirm the latter he must return to sense data.

In what follows, the Martian will revive another idea, not quite so dusty nor so far removed from the practice of science. This is Charles Peirce's theory of abduction, which is an analysis of scientific hypothesis formation, peculiarly apposite, as the Martian sees it, to linguistic theorizing, and which avoids such ideological extremes as mechanism and mentalism.

From an orbital perspective, it is possible to make other, more or less elementary observations.

It seems to the Martian, to begin with, that the transformationalists' assault on the learning-theory model was both long overdue and remarkably successful (Fodor and Katz, Chomsky) and that, as a consequence, the latter has been dismantled and can no longer be entertained as a serious explanation of language as phenomenon. The watershed was probably marked by the appearance of Chomsky's celebrated review of Skinner's *Verbal Behavior*. Linguistic theory would never thereafter be the same.

But, unless the Martian is very much mistaken—and it is here that he does resemble somewhat the boy who noticed something wrong with the king—it appears to him that while the prevailing behaviorist theory has been dismantled, no other theory has been advanced to take its place, this in spite of all the talk by transformationalists about "explanatory models."

It is somewhat as if the Ptolemaic geocentric universe had been dismantled but Copernicus had not yet come along with his heliocentric model.

Accordingly, the assumption will be made in what follows that linguistic theory has not yet reached the level of explanatory adequacy of, say, seventeenth-century biology. It was then that, following the work of Harvey and Malpighi, it became possible to construct crude but accurate models of cardiac and renal function; to suppose, for example, that the heart is like a unidirectional pump or the kidney is like a filter. One may not say as much at the present time about the unique human capacity for language. True, a schema of sorts has been suggested (Chomsky; Katz) to show what happens when a child exposed to fragments of a language acquires a competence in that language: primary linguistic data→LAD→ Grammar (where LAD is the Language Acquisition Device). What seems fairly obvious, however, is that despite claims to the contrary this schema is in no sense an explanatory model. It is no more than a statement of the problem under investigation. The "LAD" appears to be a black box whose contents are altogether unknown.

Finally, the Martian shall make bold to put forward a crude model not entirely of his own devising—Charles Peirce is its earthly progenitor.

1. Descriptive or structural linguistics cannot be regarded as a theory of language if the word *theory* is used as it is used in other sciences.

Structural or descriptive linguistics (Harris) deals with regularities in certain features of speech. These regularities are in the distributional relations among the features of speech in question, i.e., the occurrence of these features relative to each other within utterances. The procedure of structural linguistics is "to begin with the raw data of speech and with a statement of grammatical structure . . . essentially a twice-made application of two major steps: the setting up of elements, and the statement of the distribution of these elements relative to each other. First, the distinct phonological elements are determined and the relations among them investigated. Then the distinct morphological elements are determined and the relations among them investigated." (Harris)

Such a discipline is undoubtedly beyond reproach—as far as it goes. Indeed one might well agree with Lévi-Strauss in setting up the method of structural linguistics as a model for anthropologists, a distributional method which Lévi-Strauss in fact applies to other cultural phenomena such as art, myth, ritual, religion, even cooking (Lévi-Strauss).

Yet it must not be forgotten that this method, rigorous as it is, does not pretend to be other than descriptive. Thus if one were studying hematology, one could imagine a science called "structural hematology" which consisted of a description of the cellular and chemical components of the blood and of certain "distributional" relations between them, e.g., a high nonprotein nitrogen is regularly associated with a low hemoglobin. But such a discipline, however rigorous, could never serve as a theory of blood formation or as a theory of the function of hemoglobin. Accordingly, the method of structural linguistics has at its core a fundamental ambiguity. This ambiguity can be expressed by two questions which presently go not only unanswered but unasked: (1) Does structuralism make the assumption that both language and culture are by their very nature phenomena of such an order that the search for distributional regularities is a *terminus ad quem* for both linguists and anthropologists? (2) Or is it rather the case that the current status of both arts is so primitive that we are necessarily at a stage comparable to Linnaean taxonomy, and so it goes without saying that at some future time linguistics shall arrive at a general explanatory theory bearing roughly the same relation to descriptive linguistics that Darwinean theory bears to Linnaean taxonomy?

The answer to either question is not clear, because, for one reason, the questions are not asked. What is clear is that in any case descriptive or structural linguistics is not a theory of language in the ordinary use of the word *theory*.

2. Behaviorism, both in its early Pavlovian and Watsonian versions, and in the later refinements of modern learning theory, does indeed offer a plenary model of language as phenomenon, which meets all the specifications of explanatory theory except one: It is wrong.

S-R theory, however modified by little *s*'s and *r*'s, by "intervening variables," "dispositions to respond," "habit structures," "generalization and analogy," "stimulus control," "network of associative connections," and the like, fails to address itself to, let alone explain, those very features of language behavior which set it apart from other forms of animal communication, e.g., the phenomenon of symbolization or naming, the sentence as the basic unit of language behavior, the learning performance of a child, who, upon exposure to a fragmentary input of a language, is able to utter and understand any number of new sentences in the language—this after a relatively short period and without anyone taking much trouble about it.

3. Transformational generative grammar is not an explanatory theory of language, although it has been advertised as such

(Chomsky). That it fails to serve as such is not a consequence of its stated objective, which is in fact correct; namely, to specify the character of the device which mediates the processing of the input, the primary data, and the output, the grammar of the language. Nor does it fail as theory primarily because of the putative and unconfirmed status of so-called "deep structures," from which surface structures are derived by transformations (Hockett).

Transformational grammar is not an explanatory theory of language as phenomenon but rather a formal description, an algorithm, of the competence of a person who speaks a language. There is no evidence that this algorithm bears a necessary relation to what is happening inside the head of a person who speaks or understands a sentence. There is evidence in fact that it does not.

Transformational grammar also fails as theory because it violates a cardinal rule of scientific explanation, namely, that a theory cannot use as a component of its hypothesis the very phenomenon to be explained. That is to say, if one sets out to explain the appearance of an apple on an apple tree, it will not do to suppose that apple B, which we have in hand, derives from putative apple A, which we hypothesize as its progenitor. An adequate account of the origins of either apples or sentences must contain in the one case only nonapple elements, e.g., pollen, ovary, ovule, etc., and in the other case nonsentential elements. So it will not do for an explanatory theory of language which must presumably account for the utterance and understanding of a sentence or "surface structure" to hypothesize a "deep structure" as its source when deep structures are themselves described as "kernel sentences" (Chomsky) or "underlying propositions" (Chomsky), when in fact it is the phenomenon of sentence utterance itself in whatever form, kernel sentences or propositions, that is unique among species and therefore, one would think, the major goal of theorizing.

3.1. The main error of a generative grammar considered as a theory of language is that its main component is syntactical with semantic and phonological components considered as "interpretations" thereof (Chomsky). This awarding of the prime role to syntax rules out nonsyntactical elements, for example, semological and phonological components, as primitive generative components of deep structures and in effect posits syntax as an underivable and therefore unexplainable given.

Thus, the phrase-marker or general rule of sentence formation is given as the coupling of syntactical elements:

$$S \rightarrow NP\text{--}VP$$

In point of fact, the phrase-marker does not represent the class of all classes of sentences or even the class of all declarative sentences. Consider the one-word sentence in which a child points at a round red inflated object and looks questioningly at his father, whereupon the father says *Balloon*. Where are the *NP* and *VP* of this sentence? What have been coupled here are not two syntactical elements but a class of sounds and a class of experienced objects. The only way this one-word naming sentence can be captured under a syntactical rubric is to consider it as an elliptical version of the *NP--VP* form *That is a balloon,* and even this strategy does not give an account of the special semiotic status of the demonstrative *that.* To parse the one-word naming sentence syntactically is to tailor data to fit theory. It is rather for theory to accommodate data.

It is important to notice, as we shall presently see, that while this one-word sentence does not fit the syntactical phrase-marker *NP--VP,* it fits very well the more informal definition of a sentence given by the ordinary-language analysts as comprising (1) what one talks about and (2) what one says about it (Strawson). What the father and child are talking about is the experienced balloon itself considered as a member of a class of such objects. What the father says about it is that it is named by a class of sounds *balloon.*

3.2. The phrase-marker *NP--VP* describes a subclass of declarative sentences. A general rule of sentence formation must accommodate nonsyntactical as well as syntactical elements such as "noun phrases" and "verb phrases."

3.3. The central component of the LAD is not syntactical but rather semological-phonological (Chafe). The syntactical component is nothing more nor less than the formal properties which issue from the semological-phonological linkage and later from combinations of semological-phonological complexes or semantically contentive words (Brown's usage, see Brown and Bellugi).

Thus the formal properties of syntax are already present in two-word combinations of "contentives" in children's sentences. Later these formal properties are explicitly marked by the addition of "functors" (Brown and Bellugi).

3.4. Accordingly, a rule of sentence formation must be sufficiently general to accommodate both the purely syntactical NP–VP sentence and the naming sentence in which a class of experience (semology) is linked with a class of sounds (phonology) (Chafe).

Some such general rule may be formulated as follows:

$$(1)\ \text{Sentence} \rightarrow S\ (is)\ P$$

The "subject" and "predicate" form seems advisable for no other reason than that these terms are sufficiently general to accommodate both naming sentences and NP–VP sentences. Thus "subject" and "predicate" are used not to revive Aristotelian categories but as a shorthand description of a sentence as comprising (1) what one talks about and (2) what one says about it. "Subject" fairly describes both the balloon in the one-word naming sentence *Balloon* and the NP in *The boy hit the dog*.

The copula is indispensable because something is asserted in a sentence. The parenthesis is added because such assertion does not always require the presence of a verb phrase, e.g., *Balloon*.

Subclass (1a), the naming sentence, might be formulated by the semiotic rule

$$(1a)\ \text{Sentence} \rightarrow IE_c\ (is)\ S_c$$

where I is an index, either an item of behavior, a pointing at or looking at, or some such functor as *that* in *That is a balloon*; E is an experience, subscript c added to indicate that it is not such-and-such an experience which is pointed at or looked at as a singular but rather as one of a *class* of such experiences. Similarly, S_c is not such-and-such a sound but rather an utterance understood as a class of such sounds (phonology). To use Chafe's terminology, we are dealing not with substances but with forms (Chafe).

Note that it is preferable to use E_c to designate a semological class of experience rather than, say, O_c for a class of objects, e.g., ballons. For in fact a child not only names things (table, doggie, ball) but actions (play, see, drop) and qualities (blue, broke, bad) (Brown and Bellugi). What such words have in common is not a syntactical property but a semantic property. Thus they are not all nouns; some are verbs and adverbs. But they are all semantically contentive.

The second subclass is the standard "syntactical" declarative sentence form:

$$\text{(1b) Sentence} \rightarrow NP\text{–}VP$$

Sentences of this form, I shall suggest, appear first in children's speech as those two-word combinations in which contentive words are selected from an inventory of semophones stored up by naming sentences and are paired to form primitive versions of adult *NP–VP* sentences. Thus: *Bobby wet, Doggie fall, Mommy lunch* (Mommy had her lunch), etc.

3.5. Four immediate advantages accrue to a linguistic model which proposes a semological-phonological linkage as its genetically prime component:

(1) It is a transsyntactical theory; that is, it is founded on a general semiotic—the science of the relations between people and signs and things—which specifies syntax as but one dimension of sentential theory. Accordingly, it provides theoretical grounds for distinguishing between the two types of declarative sentences, the naming sentence and the *NP–VP* sentence.

(2) It accords with the data of language acquisition and provides a model for understanding the ontogenesis of speech in children, in particular the stages of word and "phrase" acquisition, a sequence which is presently accounted for by purely descriptive "generative rules of phrase formation."

(3) It allows the possibility, as we shall see, of looking for a neurophysiological correlate of such a model, a possibility which is disallowed in principle by a generative theory which postulates syntax as a central underived component.

(4) It permits the assimilation of linguistic theory to a more general theory of all symbolic transactions, a theory which must in turn accommodate such nonsyntactical "sentences" as metaphor, a painting, a sculpture, a piece of music. From this larger perspective it will be seen that the division of language into two kinds of sentences is not as arbitrary and unsatisfactory as it might at first appear. Rather is it the case that the standard syntactical sentence of language, the coupling of subject and predicate, is a special case of the more fundamental human capacity to couple any two things at all and through the mirror of the one see the other. Thus, the child's sudden inkling that the thing ball "is" the sound *ball* is the progenitor not only of all future sentences about balls but also of his grasp of metaphor, art, and music.

4. The two kinds of sentences formed by (1a) and (1b) can be regarded not only as representing the formal subclasses of constative sentences—anyone at any time can name things with one-word sentences or assert propositions about things and events and relations—but also as delineating major stages in the ontogenesis of language. In the initial naming stage of language acquisition, the first sentences children utter are the linking of semological elements (forms of experience) with phonological elements (forms of sound). As a consequence of this extraordinary naming activity, a repertoire of semological-phonological complexes or "contentive" words is formed. For the sake of convenience I propose to call these semological-phonological complexes "semophones." Once such a lexicon of semophones is available, it becomes possible by combining any two semophones to form a large number of primitive NP–VP sentences.

4.1. One test of a theory of language is its utility in accounting for the acquisition of language, in particular the ontogenesis of speech as it is observed in intensive studies of individual children.

Judged by the standard of adult syntax, the early manifestations of speech in children appear vagarious and fragmentary. In studies of individual children, such speech forms have been described variously as "single-word utterances," "phrases," "holophrases," "sentence fragments," "telegraphic sentences," and so on.

Such studies, however, generally agree in specifying certain stages of language development.

Some time around the end of the first year of life, most children go through a naming stage. As Brown and Bellugi put it, at this period "most children are saying many words and some children go about the house all day long naming things (*table, doggie, ball,* etc.) and actions (*play, see, drop,* etc.) and an occasional quality (*blue, broke, bad,* etc.).

It is interesting to note that the best-known studies of the acquisition of speech in children (Braine, Brown, Ervin, McNeill), while taking note of the naming stage and of "one-word utterances," skip over it and address themselves to "phrases" of two or more words. The assumption seems to be made both that there is assuredly such a thing as a naming stage and also that there is not much to be said about it. This may be true, but it nevertheless seems curious, considering the fact that no other species on earth ever names anything at all, much less goes about naming everything under the sun or asking its name, that investigators of the genesis of language in children should not have been more intrigued by this apparently unique activity. On the other hand, what is one to say about it? A child names something or hears it named, understands or misunderstands what is named, and that is that. One can only conclude either (1) that the phenomenon of naming is the most transparent of events and therefore there is little to be said about it, or (2) that it is the most mysterious of phenomena and therefore one can't say much about it. As Fodor said, nobody knows what a name is.

I wish to suggest that one reason for the indifference of these psycholinguistic studies to the naming stage of language acquisition is a necessary consequence of a commitment to structuralism as linguistic theory. That is to say, if one regards grammatical patterns and distributional relations as the primary goal of linguistics, one can't have much to say when confronted with a single word. For as soon as theory abstracts from behavior and the relation of words to things, and addresses itself only to the relation of words to words, the theorist can only watch the naming child with bemused interest and mark time until he begins to put two or more words together.

The second stage of language acquisition is characterized by two-word utterances, usually described as "pivot-open" constructions. The pivot class has fewer members than the open class. Thus, a child will say *my sock, my boat, my fan*, or *big plane, big shoe, big sock*, etc. (Braine); *that knee, that coffee, that Adam*, or *two coat, two stool, two Tinkertoy*, etc. (Brown and Bellugi); *this arm, this baby, this yellow*, or *the other, the pretty, the dolly's*, or *here baby, here yellow*, etc. (Ervin). The following rule therefore holds for both single-word utterances and pivot-open combinations (McNeill):

$$S \rightarrow (P) + O$$

which would account in a purely descriptive manner for such utterances as *ball* or *my ball* or *here ball* or *there yellow* or *there drop*, whatever syntactical or sentential differences may exist.

It has been noted that members of the pivot class are usually functors (*a, that, the, here*) but not always (*pretty, big*), while open-class words are nearly always contentives (*boy, coffee, sock, knee, wet, yellow*).

The third stage is characterized by two developments:

(1) Differentiation of the pivot class.

For example, *car*, through successive expansions *a car, that a car, that a big car*, eventually reaches its adult form *that is a big car* (see Brown and Bellugi; McNeill). Descriptive rules can be inferred:

$NP \rightarrow (P) + N$		*car, a car*
$NP_1 \rightarrow Dem + Art + M + N$		*that a my car*
$NP_2 \rightarrow Art + M + N$		*a big car*
$NP_3 \rightarrow Dem + M + N$		*that big car*
$NP_4 \rightarrow Art + N$		*the car*
$NP_5 \rightarrow M + N$		*my car*
$NP_6 \rightarrow Dem + N$		*that car*

These rules allow, for example, *that a big horsie* but not *a big that horsie*.

(2) The open-open construction.

Instead of saying *here man, here car, here coffee* or *a bridge, a man, a daddy,* the child begins to combine two words of the open class: *man car* (a man is in the car), *car bridge* (the car is under the bridge), *coffee Daddy* (here is coffee for Daddy), etc. (Braine).

These open-open constructions are often uttered in strong contextual situations, for example, where mother and child are looking at the same thing. The mother, in other words, is a reliable interpreter. Indeed, the mother actually repeats and expands the child's utterance, keeping the order of the contentives but adding functors and inflections, as much as to say, "Isn't this what you mean?" Some examples of open-open combinations with the mother's "interpretations" and expansion and, presumably, the child's approval (from Brown and Bellugi):

Child	Mother
Baby high chair	*Baby is in the high chair*
Mommy eggnog	*Mommy had her eggnog*
Eve lunch	*Eve is having her lunch*
Mommy sandwich	*Mommy'll have a sandwich*

Note one consequence of the transition from the pivot-open to the open-open construction. The child's discovery of the latter makes possible an almost exponential increase in the number even of two-word utterances—a fact of the highest significance in any attempt to account for that unique characteristic of the Language Acquisition Device: the ability to utter and understand any number of new sentences. The number of two-word combinations noted by Braine in one child observed at regular intervals went so: 14, 24, 54, 89, 350, 1400, 2500 +(Braine).

Such then is a too-brief and much-oversimplified summary of the highlights of language acquisition as it is actually observed to occur in children.

Judged by the criterion of adult *NP–VP* syntax, child's speech appears somewhat fragmentary and vagarious, an assortment of one-word utterances, phrases, fragments, "pivot-open" and "open-open" combinations, the whole odd lot accounted for by purely descriptive "generative phrase rules."

The real issue seems to be whether the utterances of children, or of anyone at all for that matter, can be understood by a textual analysis which abstracts from the behavior of people who utter sounds to each other about one thing or another. What if sentences have components other than lexical items? If this is so, then a theory of the ontogenesis of language deriving exclusively from the study of corpora of speech must necessarily issue in a purely descriptive structuralism or a formal deductive calculus which transforms one kind of sentence to another by "rules" which, as matters stand now, cannot even in principle be correlated with anything that happens inside people's heads.

One wonders therefore: How might the development of child's speech appear when viewed by a transsyntactical theory of sentences, which sees the conventional NP–VP construction as a subclass of the class of all sentences?

I think it can be shown that if the speech of children is viewed not merely as a corpus from which certain descriptive grammatical rules can be inferred but as a behavior which implicates both syntactical and "nonsyntactical" elements, it is possible to arrive at more general *semiotic* rules of sentence formation. The various descriptive rules of "phrase formation" will then be seen to be coherent stages in the emergence of sentence utterances.

(1) The "one-word utterance," so characteristic of the first stage of language acquisition, is nothing more or less than the earliest appearance of the naming sentence, a complete sentence in semiotic terms albeit lacking some later syntactical and functional elements.

The rule involved is not a phrase rule, such as

$$NP \rightarrow N$$
(Brown and Bellugi)

where NP is "noun phrase" and N a "noun," or a rule for "pivot-open" combinations

$$(P) + O$$

but rather the general behavioral rule of formation of the naming sentence

$$S \rightarrow (I) \, (E_c) \, \text{(is)} \, S_c$$

where I, the index, is in this case an item of behavior (e.g., a pointing at or looking at), E_c is the thing or quality or action experienced by the child and indicated as one of a class of such experiences, (is) is the copula dispensed with until the final adult form, S_c is the contentive word, usually a sound—e.g., noun *ball*, adjective *yellow*, verb *hop*—uttered as a member of a class of such words. (As Charles Peirce would say, a contentive word or symbol is not a single thing but a kind of thing [Peirce]).

(2) A descriptive rule for the formation of pivot-open constructions has been given as

$$S \rightarrow P + O \qquad \text{(e.g., } a \ knee, \ a \ man, \ a \ Mommy}$$
$$\text{[McNeill])}$$

A more general rule, which allows for the expansion and differentiation of the pivot class, is given by Brown as a rule for generating noun phrases:

$$NP \rightarrow (\text{Dem}) + (\text{Art}) + (M) + N$$

This rule accommodates not only one-word utterances, *car, boat, yellow*, and pivot-open constructions, *my car, my boat, my yellow*, but also such "phrases" as *that a car, that a my car*, etc.

What needs to be noted, however, is that *none of these expressions is a phrase*, save only in that sense decreed by a purely syntactical definition of sentences. Rather, all are complete semiotic sentences as provided by the general rule for naming sentences (1). Where this rule differs from Brown's descriptive phrase rule is in its specifying (a) that what is formed is not a phrase but a sentence, (b) that the index I is a general semiotic class of which Brown's demonstratives (*that, there*) belong to the syntactical subclass, (c) that the copula is added because the final adult form requires it.

Thus it is not a grammatical vagary, to be accounted for by a descriptive rule, that a child may say *that a blue flower* but never *a that blue flower* or *blue a that flower* (Brown and Bellugi). What Brown calls the "privileges peculiar to demonstrative pronouns" is in fact specified by the more general semiotic rule which requires the initial positioning of the index (*I*), whether it be a demonstrative (*there, that*) or a behavioral item (looking, pointing). You can't name something for someone without first pointing at it.

To summarize (1) and (2): Nearly the entire class of pivot-open constructions, plus the entire class of expanded utterances generated by the rules for "differentiation of the pivot class," are not "phrases" to be accounted for by lists of descriptive generative rules. Rather are all such utterances specified by a general semiotic rule of sentence formation, in this case the naming sentence, in which both behavioral and syntactical components are ordered by presiding semiotic considerations.

(3) The open-open construction, which appears somewhere around the second birthday and accounts for the exponential explosion of language, is semiotically different from the naming sentence. It is in fact nothing more nor less than the adult *NP–VP* sentence *without functors*. It always comprises the pairing of contentives, often "nouns," but also quality words and action words, e.g., *baby wet, car go, man car* (the man is in the car), etc.

Braine uses a juncture symbol (#) between the two words of an open-open construction to distinguish it from an otherwise similar utterance having a quite different meaning. Thus, again relying on the mother as the best of all interpreters:

> *baby#chair*   (The baby is in his chair)
>
> *baby chair*   (There is the baby's chair)

The juncture symbol # is thus a semiotic mark which might be inserted between the "subject" *S* and "predicate" *P* of all sentences, whether naming sentences or *NP–VP* syntactical sentences. It marks a behavioral pause between what I am talking about and what I say about it.

Accordingly, it will be seen that the conventional syntactical "phrase marker" is in fact a special instance of a more general semiotic structure. Everyone is familiar with the *NP–VP* phrase-marker for a sentence like *The baby is in his chair*. A quite different but equally justifiable semiotic phrase-marker could be designed for the naming sentence *baby chair*, as diagrammed in Figure 10.

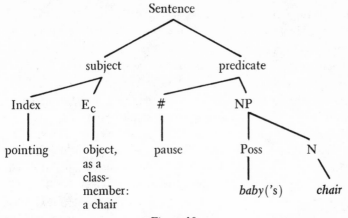

Figure 10

There is only one lexical-syntactical item in this sentence, the NP *baby chair*. The other elements are behavioral (pointing, pause) or environmental (chair experienced as a class member).

Contrast the semiotic phrase-marker of the naming sentence *baby chair* with the conventional phrase-marker of the open-open construction *baby #chair* (the baby is in his chair), as in Figure 11.

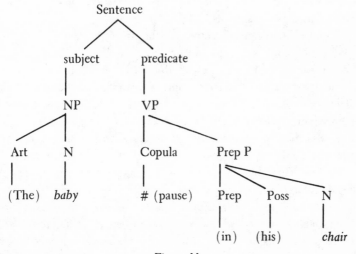

Figure 11

To summarize 4.1: There are, semiotically speaking, two basic classes of linguistic sentences (we will say nothing here about non-linguistic "sentences," e.g., van Gogh's painting "The Chair," which assuredly uses a symbol to assert something about something else): the naming sentence and the NP–VP sentence.

Both kinds of sentence are acquired, understood, and uttered without the use of functors and other syntactical forms.

The addition of functors to child speech can be understood as the behaviorally necessary substitutes for a diminishing context. Thus a two-year-old child, sitting on his mother's lap and looking with her out the window and saying *boy lawnmower* can be reliably understood to mean: The boy is pushing the lawnmower. But as context drops away, until at length the child is twelve and is reporting over the telephone to his mother about the performance of the gardener, the speaker needs his functors and must say *Yes, the boy is still pushing the lawnmower.*

5. As a genetic theory of language acquisition, we may hypothesize two basic stages, at each of which occurs a coupling of elements and in neither does it seem necessary to postulate a "deep syntactical structure" from which uttered sentences are derived by a series of transformations.

(1) The formation of semophones by the coupling of semological and phonological elements.

Much of the linguistic activity of the first two years of life goes toward the building up of an inventory, or lexicon, of semantically contentive words through which the world of experience is segmented, perceived, abstracted from, and named. So enduring and stable are these semological-phonological combinations that it seems appropriate to regard them as sound-meaning units, perhaps to be designated by some such term as *semophone*—the "phone" in this case signifying not a phone in the technical linguistic sense but rather the hierarchy of sound units: sound, phoneme, morpheme, word (Chafe).

As the neurophysiological correlate of such a coupling, one can only suppose that there come to be established stable functional interconnections between the visual and auditory cortexes. May we not at this point make bold to reach for the explanatory level of seventeenth-century physiology with its crude but accurate models of body functions—the heart is like a pump, the kidney is like a filter? Accordingly, may we not suggest that the LAD is like a coupler?

The semological and phonological components of the semophone are thoroughly interpenetrated. The resulting configuration is a much more stable and enduring entity than can be expressed by association psychology. Thus it is not so much the case that words like *yellow, wet, glass, hop, Elmer, quick* "call up" such and such an association or have such and such a "connotation." Rather is it the case that these sounds are interpenetrated and transformed by the classes of experience to which they refer. The contentive word in a sense contains the thing. *Yellow* becomes yellow.

(2) The formation of *NP–VP* sentences by the coupling of semophones.

Semophones are paired in the child's open-open constructions to form the basic or contentive elements of the adult *NP–VP* sentence. One of the major tasks of an explanatory linguistic theory is to account for the practically unlimited number of new sentences which can be uttered and understood by a three- or four-year-old child, following the input of limited and fragmentary data. If the basic component of the LAD is a coupler, it will be seen that this extraordinary generative capacity can be accounted for in two ways: (1) The exponential increase in the number of open-open constructions which can be formed once an inventory of semophones is established. Thus, an inventory of n semophones (*car, wet, Daddy, sock* . . .) will yield an $n^2 - n$ number of open-open sentences (*car wet, car Daddy, Daddy wet, Daddy sock* . . .). An inventory of 100 semophones will yield a possible 9,900 open-open sentences. (2) A single open-open sentence is susceptible to as many sentential interpretations as context allows. Thus a child, sitting on his mother's lap and looking out the window, who utters the sentence *car Daddy*, can be reliably understood by his mother to be saying *Daddy is getting in the car, Daddy is washing the car, Daddy is kicking the car*, depending on whether in fact Daddy is getting in the car, washing the car, kicking the car.

Indeed, the number of sentences made possible by (1) the exponential increase of the number of open-open combinations and (2) the contextual application of any one such combination to any number of mutually perceived situations becomes, for all practical purposes, unlimited.

5.1. Two characteristic transformations occur in the two types of coupling or sentence formation.

In (1), the naming sentence, the phonological element is transformed by the semological element. *Yellow* becomes yellow, *wet* becomes wet, *hollow* becomes hollow.

In (2), the open-open coupling, it is the *linkage* itself which is transformed. Thus the linkage between *Daddy* and *car* in *Daddy#car* becomes is getting into, is washing, is kicking, as the case may be.

Functors or grammatical markers are added to open-open combinations not as a result of overt imitation of adult sentences (Ervin) but the other way around, through the parent's imitation and expansion of the child's sentence (Brown and Bellugi).

Presumably the exigencies of communication require that, as context is withdrawn, functors be added. With the child's increasing mobility and his increasing number of reports of what has happened out of the hearer's sight, functors come into play. The following conversation occurred between my two-year-old grandson, arriving in some excitement to make a report, and his mother:

Child: *Daddy tractor!*
Mother: *Daddy is driving the tractor?*
Child: (Silence)
Mother: *Daddy is fixing the tractor?*
Child: (Silence with a half nod)
Mother: *Daddy is under tractor?*
Child: *Daddy under tractor!*

5.11. The question must be raised about grammatical transformations: Is there any evidence to support the theory that the so-called grammatical transformation, whatever its usefulness to the linguist as an analytical tool, actually operates in the acquisition of language?

Thus, it may be unexceptionable to say with Chomsky that:

If S_1 is a grammatical sentence of the form
$$NP_1–Aux–V–NP_2$$
then the corresponding string of the form
$$NP_2–Aux + be + en–V–by + NP_1$$
is also a grammatical sentence.

Using this transformation rule, one can obtain *Lunch is being eaten by John* from *John is eating lunch*.

But it does not necessarily follow that because a linguist analyzing the corpus of a language can derive one kind of sentence from another kind of sentence by a rule, a formal operation, or because he hypothesizes putative "deep structures" from which "surface structures" are generated by "transformations," this is what happens when a child learns a language. Indeed, if one follows the principle of parsimony in theorizing, one wonders why such a formal schematism cannot be dispensed with altogether.

For is not the adult passive sentence already implicit in the early open-open construction, later to be filled out by the required functors which the child learns through adult imitation and expansion?

For example, keeping in mind the general *S–P* form of the sentence, that is, its division into what one is talking about and what one says about it, one can easily imagine some such sequence as follows: Mother and child are watching a dog from the window. Various events occur in which the dog is both subject of attention and subject of sentences about these events. Whether the dog does things or whether things happen to the dog, the dog is what we are talking about.

Child	Mother
Dog run	*Yes, the dog is running.*
Dog man	*Yes, the dog is barking at the man.*
Dog car	*Yes, the dog is chasing the car.*
Dog car!	*Yes, the dog was run over by the car!*

Conceivably, then, the child might "verify" the mother's interpretation of the last sentence by adding one of her passive functors: *Dog run by car!* (Such, in fact, was my grandson's first attempt at the passive: his imitation of an adult's expansion of his original open-open construction.)

The question of course can only be answered by systematic behavioral studies. The point is that it is open to confirmation, or nonconfirmation, by such studies.

6. Is an explanatory theory of language possible?

In this connection, I would like to mention Charles Peirce's theory of abduction, or explanatory hypothesis, as a valid and possibly useful strategy in approaching language as a phenomenon. My reasons for doing so are two: (1) The present state of theoretical linguistics, considered as a natural science, is so confused, comprising as it does incoherent elements of structuralism and "learning theory" and even Cartesian mentalism, that it might be worthwhile to take a step back, so to speak, in order to view the phenomenon of language from the perspective of perhaps the best-known American theorist of the scientific method. If one should object that Peirce's theory is almost a hundred years old, I can only reply that since theoretical linguistics is at least three hundred years behind theoretical physics, Peirce can be regarded as being, linguistically at least, ahead of his time. (2) Peirce's theory of abduction has been revived recently (Chomsky) but in such an odd and what I consider a wrongheaded fashion that there is some danger that its usefulness to linguistics might be permanently impaired.

The assumption will be made then that an explanatory theory of language does not presently exist: that behaviorism does indeed provide an explanatory model but that it is wrong; that structural linguistics and transformational grammar are not explanatory theories (v.s.).

Further, we will accept the following description of both the problem at hand and our ignorance: that every normal human being, and no doubt most abnormal ones as well, are uniquely equipped with what can be characterized abstractly as a Language Acquisition Device (LAD) whose structure and function are unknown but which receives as input primary linguistic data, speech from fluent speakers within hearing range, and has as its output a competence in the language, that is, the ability to utter and understand any number of new sentences (Katz; Chomsky).

Now how does Peirce's theory of abduction relate to the problem at hand, namely, approaching the black box, LAD, toward the end of discovering its workings? Let us reassure ourselves at the outset. Surely the enterprise is worth undertaking, if for no other reason than the depth of our ignorance and the wide divergence of the guesses on the subject. In view of the uniqueness of the human capacity for speech, how different are these workings from the workings of other brains? Are they qualitatively different or quantitatively different? Does the black box hold Cartesian mind-stuff or S-s-r-R neuron circuitry? or both? Certainly it would be a start in the right direction if we had some notion of what to look for, what *kind* of thing. It is here that abduction or Peirce's explanatory hypothesis might be of some help.

Let us be clear, first, how Peirce distinguished abduction from induction and deduction, the other two logical components of the scientific method. He believed that neither deduction nor induction could arrive at explanatory theory but only abduction. No new truth can come from deduction or induction. Deduction explores the logical consequences of statements. Induction seeks to establish facts. Abduction starts from facts and seeks an explanatory theory (Peirce). As a classical example of abduction, Peirce cited Kepler's theory of the elliptical form of Mars's orbit. Though Kepler had made a large number of observations of the longitudes and latitudes of Mars, and even if he had made a million more, no induction or generalization from these facts could have arrived at the nature of Mars's orbit. At some stage or other, Kepler had to make a guess, construct a model, then see if the model would (1) fit all the facts at hand and (2) predict new facts which could be verified by observation.

Peirce listed three kinds of abductions or explanatory hypotheses: (1) those which account for observed facts through "natural chance" or statistical methods, e.g., the kinetic theory of gases; (2) those which render the facts necessary through a mathematical demonstration of their truth, e.g., Kepler's elliptical theory of planetary orbits; and (3) those which account for facts by virtue of the very economy and simplicity of the explanatory model (Peirce).

Presumably we are looking here for 3, at least for the present.

Certainly no statistical method or mathematical model known to me has any relevance to what goes on inside a child's head when he acquires language in the second and third year of life.

Peirce also makes much of the fact, and Chomsky echoes it, that "man's mind has a natural adaptation to imagining correct theories" (Chomsky). A physicist comes across some new phenomenon in the laboratory. According to Peirce, there are "trillions of trillions of hypotheses" which might be made to account for it, "of which only one is true" (Peirce). Yet as matters usually turn out, the physicist usually hits on the correct hypothesis "after two or three or at the very most a dozen guesses." This successful guessing or hypothesizing of scientists is not, according to Peirce, a matter of luck. Peirce's own explanation of the extraordinary success (in the face of such odds) of scientific theorizing is founded in his own allegiance to philosophical realism, the belief that general principles actually operate in nature apart from men's minds and that men's minds are nevertheless capable of knowing these principles. But how is this possible? Peirce hazards the guess that, since "the reasoning mind is a product of the universe," it is natural to suppose that the laws and uniformities that prevail throughout the universe should also be "incorporated in his own being" (Peirce).

Maybe so. This is only speculation, however interesting, about why abduction works. What concerns us here, entirely apart from Peirce's philosophical realism and his explanation of it, is his theory of abduction itself, which I take to be nothing more nor less than the method of hypothesis formation as it is used in practice by scientists in general, whether one is theorizing about why volcanoes erupt or why people speak and animals don't. Peirce's theory of abduction, particularly of the third type, is both sufficiently rigorous that it achieves the level of explanatory adequacy and sufficiently nonspecific that it does not require a commitment to ideology and hence does not fall into the deterministic trap of behaviorism and learning theory. Explanatory theory at the level of the human acquisition of language, it seems fair to paraphrase Peirce, does not require a mechanism, or, in Peircean terms, a "dyadic" model.

I have taken the trouble to review Peirce's theory of abduction both because of its possible value to linguistic theory and to call attention to the odd use to which Chomsky has put it.

Chomsky has revived Peirce's theory of abduction, not in order to arrive at an explanatory theory of language, but rather to attribute the capacity for abduction to the child who acquires language. In the same way that, as Peirce speculated, man is somehow attuned to the rest of the universe so that he is able to theorize successfully about it, so it is that "knowledge of a language—a grammar—can be acquired only by an organism that is 'preset' with a severe restriction on the form of grammar."

> This innate restriction is a precondition, in the Kantian sense, for linguistic experience, and it appears to be the critical factor in determining the course and result of language learning. The child cannot know at birth which language he is to learn, but he must know that its grammar must be of a predetermined form that excludes many imaginable languages. Having selected a permissible hypothesis, he can use inductive evidence for corrective action, confirming or disconfirming his choice. (Chomsky)

What is odd of course is not Chomsky's idea that language can only be learned by an organism "preset" with a severe restriction on the form of grammar—this squares very well with the suggestion made in this paper that all sentences in any language must take the form of a coupling made by a coupler—but rather Chomsky's proposal to shift the burden of explanation from the linguist, the theorist of language as a phenomenon, to the child, the subject under study. Chomsky's theory of language is that the child is capable of forming a theory of language.

Now Chomsky's abdication may or may not be justified. Perhaps in the long run it will turn out that it is not possible to arrive at an explanatory theory of language in any ordinary sense of the word and that the only "explanation" available is that the child somehow hits on the grammar of a language after a fragmentary input. If this is so, we must face up to the fact that we have reverted to homunculus biology, explaining human potentialities both in spermatozoa and in children by supposing that each somehow has a little man locked inside. I believe, however, that by the serious use of abduction, hypothesis, not the attributing of it to the child but the figuring out of what goes on inside the head of a child, the theorist can hope to make a start toward the construction of a relatively simple and parsimonious model along Peircean lines.

It is curious to note in passing that if one is seeking philosophical progenitors for Peirce's theory of abduction and the realism underlying his analysis of the scientific method, one is inevitably led not to Descartes and a mind-body dualism but, according to Peirce, to Duns Scotus!

7. Suppose one were to advance the following tentative hypothesis:

The basic and genetically prime component of the LAD is a semological-phonological device through which semological elements are coupled with phonological elements. Such linkages form a finite inventory of semological-phonological configurations or "semophones," stable functional entities which correspond to semantically contentive words, e.g., *wet, yellow, sock, knee*. These semophones in turn become available for couplings to form a large number of "open-open" combinations, which are nothing less than primitive forms of the adult NP–VP sentence.

If this is the case, two questions arise: (1) Does such a model allow the possibility of looking for a neurophysiological correlate of the LAD—a possibility apparently disallowed by a basically syntactical model—and (2) if so, is there presently any evidence of such a correlate?

For some time I had supposed that the basic event which occurs when one utters or understands a sentence must be triadic in nature (Percy). That is to say, sentences comprise two elements which must be coupled by a coupler. This occurs in both the naming sentence, when semological and phonological elements are coupled, and in the standard declarative NP–VP sentence which comprises what one talks about and what one says about it.

Thus, when the father in Peirce's example points out an object and utters the sound *balloon* and the son looks and nods, an event of the order of that shown in Figure 12 must occur somewhere inside both father and son.

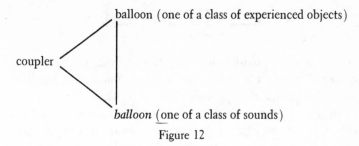

Figure 12

Later, when the son is older and utters some such sentence as *That balloon is loose,* a coupling of another sort occurs, as in Figure 13, also a triadic event.

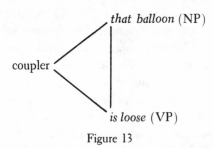

Figure 13

Let us say nothing about the physiological or ontological status of the "coupler." Suffice it for the present to say that if two elements of a sentence are coupled, we may speak of a coupler. Indeed, the behavioral equivalent of Descartes's *cogito ergo sum* may be: If the two elements of a sentence are coupled, there must be a coupler. The latter dictum would seem to be more useful to the behavioral scientist, including transformational linguists, than Descartes's, because Descartes's thinking is not observable but his speech is.

Accordingly, I had supposed that what the neurophysiologist and anatomist should look for in the brain is not a neuron circuitry transmitting S-R arcs with little *s*'s and *r*'s interposed (what Peirce would call a series of dyads) of the following order:

$$S \longrightarrow \boxed{s \longrightarrow r} \longrightarrow R$$

but rather a structural-functional entity with the following minimal specifications: (1) It must be, considering the unique and highly developed language trait in man, something which is present and recently evolved in the human brain and either absent or rudimentary in the brains of even the highest nonhuman primates. (2) It should be structurally and functionally triadic in character, with the "base" of the triad comprising what must surely be massive interconnections between the auditory and visual cortexes. What else indeed is the child up to for months at a time when it goes around naming everything in sight—or asking its name—than establishing these functional intercortical connections?

It was with no little interest, therefore, that I came across the work of Norman Geschwind, who believes he has identified just such a recently evolved structure, "the human inferior parietal lobule, which includes the angular and supramarginal gyri, to a rough approximation areas 39 and 40 of Brodmann. In keeping with the views of many anatomists, Crosby *et al.* comment that these areas have not been recognized in the macaque. Critchley, in his review of the anatomy of this region, says that even in the higher apes these areas are present in only rudimentary form" (Geschwind). And further:

> In man, with the introduction of the angular gyrus region, intermodal associations become powerful. In a sense the parietal association area frees man to some extent from the limbic system . . .
>
> The development of language is probably heavily dependent on the emergence of the parietal association areas since at least in what is perhaps its simplest aspect (object naming) language depends on associations between other modalities and audition. Early language experience, at least, most likely depends heavily on the forming of somesthetic-auditory and visual-auditory associations, as well as auditory-auditory associations. (Geschwind)

Such findings are adduced here as a matter of interest only and to show that at least the model here adumbrated gives a hint what to look for. Being fully aware of the strong feelings of many psychologists and psycholinguists against such localization of cognitive functions (e.g., Lenneberg and Premack), and being myself altogether incompetent to evaluate Geschwind's findings, I suggest only that if a triadic theory of language acquisition is correct, one might expect to find some such structure. If Geschwind is right, what he has uncovered is the cortical "base" of the triadic structure of the typical semological-phonological naming sentence (Figure 14).

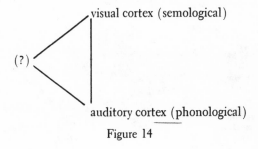

Figure 14

The apex of the triangle, the coupler, is a complete mystery. What it is, an "I," a "self," or some neurophysiological correlate thereof, I could not begin to say.

BIBLIOGRAPHY

BIBLIOGRAPHY

Anderson, James F. *The Bond of Being.* St. Louis: Herder, 1954.

Bernard, L. L. "Social Psychology." In *Encyclopedia of the Social Sciences.* New York: Macmillan, 1934.

Bidney, David. *Theoretical Anthropology.* New York: Schocken, 1967.

Binswanger, Ludwig. "The Existential Analysis School of Thought." In *Existence,* edited by Rollo May, Ernest Angel, and Henri F. Ellenberger. New York: Basic Books, 1958.

Bloomfield, Leonard. "Linguistic Aspects of Science." In *International Encyclopedia of Unified Science.* Chicago: University of Chicago Press, 1935.

Boas, Franz. *Race, Language and Culture.* New York: Free Press, 1966.

Bowlby, John. "Critical Phases in the Development of Social Responses in Man." *New Biology,* vol. 14, Baltimore: Penguin Books, 1953.

Braine, Martin. "The Ontogeny of English Phrase Structure." *Language,* vol. 39, 1963.

Braithwaite, Richard B. *Scientific Explanation.* Cambridge: Cambridge University Press, 1953.

Bridgman, P. W. *The Nature of Physical Knowledge.* New York: Marquette, 1936.

Brown, Roger, and Bellugi, Urdula. "Three Processes in the Child's Acquisition of Syntax." In *New Directions in the Study of Language,* edited by Eric H. Lenneberg. Cambridge, Mass.: MIT Press, 1964.

Brunswik, Egon. "The Conceptual Framework of Psychology." *International Encyclopedia of Unified Science.*

Buber, Martin. "Distance and Relation." William Alanson White Memorial Lectures, 4th series. *Psychiatry,* vol. 20, 1957.

Carnap, Rudolf. "Formal and Factual Science." In *Readings in the Philosophy of Science.* New York: Appleton-Century-Crofts, 1953.

——. *Introduction to Semantics.* Cambridge, Mass.: Harvard University Press, 1948.

——. *Logical Syntax of Language*. New York: Humanities Press, 1964.

Carroll, John B. *The Study of Language*. Cambridge, Mass.: Harvard University Press, 1955.

——, ed. *Language, Thought, and Reality*. New York: John Wiley, 1956.

Cassirer, Ernst. *Essay on Man*. New Haven: Yale University Press, 1944.

——. *The Philosophy of Symbolic Forms*. New Haven: Yale University Press, 1955.

——. *Substance and Function*. New York: Dover, 1953.

Chafe, Wallace L. "Language as Symbolization." *Language*, vol. 43, 1967.

Chase, Stuart. *The Tyranny of Words*. New York: Harcourt Brace.

Cherry, Colin. *On Human Communication*. New York: John Wiley, 1957.

Chomsky, Noam. *Aspects in the Theory of Syntax*. Cambridge, Mass.: MIT Press, 1965.

——. *Cartesian Linguistics*. New York: Harper and Row, 1966.

——. "Current Issues in Linguistic Theory." *The Structure of Language*, edited by Ferry A. Fodor and Jerrold J. Katz. Englewood Cliffs, N.J.: Prentice-Hall, 1964.

——. "Explanatory Models in Linguistics." *Logic, Methodology and Philosophy of Science*, edited by E. Nagel, P. Suppes, and A. Tarski. Stanford, Calif.: Stanford University Press, 1962.

——. *Language and Mind*. New York: Harcourt Brace, 1968.

——. "Review of B. F. Skinner's *Verbal Behavior*." *Language*, vol. 35, 1959.

Collins, James. *The Existentialists*. Chicago: Henry Regnery, 1952.

Cornforth, Maurice. "Logical Empiricism." In *Philosophy for the Future*. New York: Macmillan, 1949.

Crockett, Campbell. "The Short and Puzzling Life of Logical Positivism." *The Modern Schoolman*, vol. 31, January 1954.

Dawson, Christopher. "Sociology as a Science." *Cross Currents*, vol. 4, 1954.

Dewey, John. *Quest for Certainty*. New York: Putnam, 1960.

——. *Reconstruction in Philosophy*. New York: Beacon Press, 1920.

Einstein, Albert. *Essays in Science*. New York: Philosophical Library, 1934.

Ervin, Susan M. "Imitation and Structural Change in Children's Language." *New Directions in the Study of Language*.

Farber, Leslie H. "Martin Buber and Psychiatry." *Psychiatry*, vol. 19, 1956.

Feigl, Herbert, and Brodbeck, May, eds. *Readings in the Philosophy of Science*. New York: Appleton-Century-Crofts, 1953.

Friend, J. W., and Feibleman, J. *What Science Really Means.* London: Allen and Unwin, 1937.

Geschwind, Norman. "Disconnection Syndromes in Animals and Man." *Brain,* vol. 88, 1965.

Grinker, Roy R., ed. *Toward a Unified Theory of Human Behavior.* New York: Basic Books, 1959.

Harris, Zellig S. "Discourse Analysis." *Language,* vol. 28, 1952.

———. *Structural Linguistics.* Chicago: University of Chicago Press, 1951.

Herskovits, Melville. *Man and His Works.* New York: Knopf, 1948.

Hocking, William E. "Marcel and the Ground Issues of Metaphysics." *Philosophy and Phenomenological Research,* June 1954.

Hoijer, Harry, ed. *Language in Culture.* Chicago: University of Chicago, 1954.

Jaffe, Joseph. "Language of the Dyad." *Psychiatry,* vol. 21, 1958.

Jung, Carl G. *Psychology and Religion.* New Haven: Yale University Press, 1938.

Kant, Immanuel. *Critique of Pure Reason.* New York: Dutton, 1934.

Katz, Jerrold J. *The Philosophy of Language.* New York: Harper, 1966.

Keller, Helen. *The Story of My Life.* New York: Doubleday, 1954.

Kierkegaard, Søren. *Philosophical Fragments.* Princeton, N.J.: Princeton University Press, 1952.

———. *The Present Age.* Princeton, N.J.: Princeton University Press, 1949.

Klubertanz, G. P. "The Psychologists and the Nature of Man." *The Nature of Man.* American Catholic Philosophical Association, 1951.

Korzybski, Alfred. *Science and Sanity.* New York: Country Life Press, 1950.

Kroeber, A. L. *Anthropology.* New York: Harcourt Brace, 1948.

Langer, Susanne. *Feeling and Form.* New York: Scribner's, 1953.

———. *Introduction to Symbolic Logic,* 3rd ed. New York: Dover, 1953.

———. *Philosophy in a New Key,* 3rd ed. Cambridge, Mass.: Harvard University Press, 1957.

Lévi-Strauss, Claude. *Structural Anthropology.* Garden City, N.Y.: Doubleday, 1967.

Lévy-Bruhl, L. *How Natives Think.* New York: Knopf, 1926.

Linski, L., ed. *Semantics and the Philosophy of Language.* Urbana: University of Illinois Press, 1952.

Linton, Ralph. *The Tree of Culture.* New York: Knopf, 1955.

Mainx, F. "Ways of Work in Biology." *International Encyclopedia of Unified Science.*

Malinowski, Bronislaw. *The Dynamics of Culture Change.* New Haven: Yale University Press, 1945.

Mandelbaum, David G., ed. "Selected Writings of Edward Sapir." In

Language, Culture and Personality. Berkeley: University of California Press, 1951.

Marcel, Gabriel. *Being and Having.* Boston: Beacon Press, 1951.

———. *The Mystery of Being.* Chicago: Henry Regnery, 1951.

Maritain, Jacques. *Art and Scholasticism.* New York: Scribner's, 1947.

———. *Creative Intuition in Art and Poetry.* New York: Pantheon, 1953.

———. *Ransoming the Time.* New York: Scribner's, 1948.

May, Rollo; Angel, Ernest; and Ellenberger, Henri F., eds. *Existence.* New York: Basic Books, 1958.

McQuown, Norman A. "The Cultural Content of Language Materials." In *Language in Culture.*

Mead, George. *Mind, Self and Society.* Chicago: University of Chicago Press, 1952.

Mehta, Ved. *John Is Easy to Please.* New York: Farrar, Straus and Giroux, 1971.

Morris, Charles. "Foundations of the Theory of Signs." *International Encyclopedia of Unified Science.*

———. *Signs, Language and Behavior.* Englewood Cliffs, N.J.: Prentice-Hall, 1950.

Mullahy, Patrick. "Philosophical Anthropology versus Empirical Science." *Psychiatry,* vol. 18, 1955.

Murray, Henry A. "A Mythology for Grownups." *Saturday Review,* January 1960.

Nagel, Ernest. "The Causal Character of Modern Physical Theory." *Readings in the Philosophy of Science.*

———. *Sovereign Reason.* Urbana, Ill.: University of Illinois Press, 1954.

Ogden, C. K., and Richards, I. A. *The Meaning of Meaning.* New York: Harcourt Brace, 1953.

Pap, A. "Does Science Have Metaphysical Presuppositions?" In *Readings in the Philosophy of Science.*

Peirce, Charles S. *Collected Papers.* Cambridge, Mass.: Harvard University Press.

———. *Philosophical Writings.* New York: Dover, 1955.

Reichenbach, Hans. *The Rise of Scientific Philosophy.* Los Angeles: University of California Press, 1951.

Richards, Ivor A. *The Philosophy of Rhetoric.* Oxford: Oxford University Press, 1965.

Rioch, David McK. "Psychiatry as a Biological Science." *Psychiatry,* vol. 18, 1955.

Ruesch, Jurgen. "Psychiatry and the Challenge of Communication." *Psychiatry,* vol. 17, 1954.

Russell, Bertrand. *An Inquiry into Meaning and Truth.* New York: Humanities Press, 1940.

——. *Our Knowledge of the External World.* New York: Humanities Press, 1961.

Sapir, Edward. "Language." *Encyclopedia of the Social Sciences.*

Sartre, Jean-Paul. *Being and Nothingness.* New York: Citadel Press, 1965.

Schachtel, Ernest G. "The Development of Focal Attention and the Emergence of Reality." *Psychiatry,* vol. 17, 1954.

——. "On Memory and Childhood Amnesia." *Psychiatry,* vol. 10, 1947.

Schutz, Alfred. "Concept and Theory Formation in the Social Sciences." *Journal of Philosophy,* vol. 51, 1954.

Sellars, Roy Wood. "Materialism and Human Knowing." In *Philosophy for the Future.*

Shannon, Claude E., and Weaver, Warren. *The Mathematical Theory of Communication.* Urbana, Ill.: University of Illinois Press, 1949.

Smith, Frank, and Miller, George A. *The Genesis of Language.* Cambridge, Mass.: Harvard University Press, 1966.

Steiner, George. *Extraterritorial.* New York: Atheneum, 1971.

Strawson, P. F. "On Referring." In *Philosophy and Ordinary Language,* edited by Charles E. Caton. Urbana, Ill.: University of Illinois Press, 1963.

Sullivan, Harry Stack. *The Interpersonal Theory of Psychiatry.* New York: Norton, 1968.

Tarski, Alfred. "The Semantic Conception of Truth." *Philosophy and Phenomenological Research,* vol. 4, 1944.

Veatch, Henry Babcock. *Intentional Logic.* New Haven: Yale University Press, 1952.

Whitehead, Alfred North. *Science in the Modern World.* New York: Macmillan, 1950.

Whorf, Benjamin Lee. "Language and Logic." In *Language, Thought, and Reality.*

Wilhelmsen, Frederick D. "The Philosopher and the Myth." *The Modern Schoolman,* vol. 32, November 1954.

Will, Otto A., and Cohen, Robert A. "Linguistic Transcription and Specification of Psychiatric Interview Materials." *Psychiatry,* vol. 20, 1957.

Wilson, R. A. *The Miraculous Birth of Language.* New York: Philosophical Library, 1948.

Zilsel, E. "Physics and the Problem of Historico-Sociological Laws." In *Readings in the Philosophy of Science.*